LANGUAGE, DISCOURSE, SOCIETY
General Editors: Stephen Heath, Colin MacCabe and Denise Riley

published titles

Stanley Aronowitz
SCIENCE AS POWER: Discourse and Ideology in Modern Society

Mikkel Borch-Jacobsen
THE FREUDIAN SUBJECT

Norman Bryson
VISION AND PAINTING: The Logic of the Gaze

Teresa de Lauretis
ALICE DOESN'T: Feminism, Semiotics, Cinema
FEMINIST STUDIES/CRITICAL STUDIES (*editor*)
TECHNOLOGIES OF GENDER: Essays on Theory, Film, and Fiction

Mary Ann Doane
THE DESIRE TO DESIRE: The Woman's Film of the the 1940s

Alan Durant
CONDITIONS OF MUSIC

Jane Gallop
FEMINISM AND PSYCHOANALYSIS: The Daughter's Seduction

Peter Gidal
UNDERSTANDING BECKETT: A Study of Monologue and Gesture in the Works of Samuel Beckett

Peter Goodrich
LEGAL DISCOURSE: Studies in Linguistics, Rhetoric and Legal Analysis

Paul Hirst
ON LAW AND IDEOLOGY

Ian Hunter
CULTURE AND GOVERNMENT: The Emergence of Literary Education

Andreas Huyssen
AFTER THE GREAT DIVIDE: Modernism, Mass Culture and Postmodernism

Nigel Leask
THE POLITICS OF IMAGINATION IN COLERIDGE'S CRITICAL THOUGHT

Michael Lynn-George
EPOS: WORD, NARRATIVE AND THE *ILIAD*

Colin MacCabe
JAMES JOYCE AND THE REVOLUTION OF THE WORD
THE TALKING CURE: Essays in Psychoanalysis and Language (*editor*)

Louis Marin
PORTRAIT OF THE KING

Christian Metz
PSYCHOANALYSIS AND CINEMA: The Imaginary Signifier

Jeffrey Minson
GENEALOGIES OF MORALS: Nietzsche, Foucault, Donzelot and the Eccentricity of Ethics

Laura Mulvey
VISUAL AND OTHER PLEASURES

Douglas Oliver
POETRY AND NARRATIVE IN PERFORMANCE

Michel Pêcheux
LANGUAGE, SEMANTICS AND IDEOLOGY

Jean-Michel Rabaté
LANGUAGE, SEXUALITY AND IDEOLOGY IN EZRA POUND'S *CANTOS*

Denise Riley
'AM I THAT NAME?': Feminism and the Category of 'Women' in History

Jacqueline Rose
THE CASE OF PETER PAN OR THE IMPOSSIBILITY OF CHILDREN'S FICTION

Brian Rotman
SIGNIFYING NOTHING: The Semiotics of Zero

Raymond Tallis
NOT SAUSSURE: A Critique of Post-Saussurean Literary Theory

David Trotter
CIRCULATION: Defoe, Dickens and the Economies of the Novel
THE MAKING OF THE READER: Language and Subjectivity in Modern American, English and Irish Poetry

Peter Womack
IMPROVEMENT AND ROMANCE: Constructing the Myth of the Highlands

forthcoming titles

John Barrell
ESSAYS

James Donald
A SENTIMENTAL EDUCATION: Essays on Schooling and Popular Culture

Alan Durant
SOUNDTRACK AND TALKBACK

Piers Gray
MODERNISM AND THE MODERN

Ian Hunter, David Saunders and Dugald Williamson
ON PORNOGRAPHY

Rod Mengham
CONTEMPORARY BRITISH POETICS

Jean-Claude Milner
FOR THE LOVE OF LANGUAGE

Jeffrey Minson
GENESIS AND AUTHORSHIP
PERSONAL POLITICS AND ETHICAL STYLE

Denise Riley
POETS ON POETICS

Michael Ryan
POLITICS AND CULTURE

James A. Snead and Cornel West
SEEING BLACK: A Semiotics of Black Culture in America

Series Standing Order

If you would like to receive future titles in this series as they are published, you can make use of our standing order facility. To place a standing order please contact your bookseller or, in case of difficulty, write to us at the address below with your name and address and the name of the series. Please state with which title you wish to begin your standing order. (If you live outside the United Kingdom we may not have the rights for your area, in which case we will forward your order to the publisher concerned.)

Customer Services Department, Macmillan Distribution Ltd
Houndmills, Basingstoke, Hampshire, RG21 2XS, England.

Technologies of Gender

Essays on Theory, Film, and Fiction

Teresa de Lauretis
Professor of the History of Consciousness
University of California, Santa Cruz

**MACMILLAN
PRESS**

First published in the USA by Indiana University Press 1987
First published in the UK by Macmillan 1989

Published by
THE MACMILLAN PRESS LTD
Houndmills, Basingstoke, Hampshire RG21 2XS
and London
Companies and representatives
throughout the world

Printed in Hong Kong

British Library Cataloguing in Publication Data
De Lauretis, Teresa
Technologies of gender: essays on theory
film and fiction.—(Language, discourse,
society series).
1. Cinema films. Special subjects: Women
2. Literature. Special themes: Women–
Critical studies
I. Title   II. Series
791.43′09′09352042
ISBN 0–333–48687–0 (hardcover)
ISBN 0–333–48688–9 (paperback)

For her who rides the chariot of the sun

CONTENTS

PREFACE

The essays here collected, except one, were written between 1983 and 1986. Like the book I wrote immediately before them, *Alice Doesn't: Feminism, Semiotics, Cinema* (1984), and which to a large extent constitutes their theoretical framework, these essays also carry on an argument by means of textual readings. In some, a novel or a film is read through theory, that is, by taking a particular issue or assumption in theoretical discourse as magnifying glass in order to refocus the reading around questions of gender representation. In other essays, the reading of a fictional, filmic, or critical text provides the occasion to articulate a theoretical problem or to engage with a current critical debate. All but the first essay were originally written as lectures, conference papers, or special-issue contributions, and because the context of address is a very important aspect of any piece of critical writing, a short note at the head of each essay will identify the occasion of its writing.

While all of the essays are centrally concerned with gender, the first one, "The Technology of Gender," specifically poses the question of how to theorize gender beyond the limits of "sexual difference" and the constraints that such a notion has come to impose on feminist critical thought. The essay takes its title and its conceptual premise from Foucault's theory of sexuality as a "technology of sex" and proposes that gender, too, both as representation and as self-representation, is the product of various social technologies, such as cinema, as well as institutional discourses, epistemologies, and critical practices; by that I mean not only academic criticism, but more broadly social and cultural practices. Going past Foucault, whose critique of the technology of sex does not take into account its differential solicitation of male and female subjects, or the conflicting investments of men and women in the discourses and practices of sexuality, the essay then considers the potential of Althusser's theory of ideological interpellation with regard to an understanding of gender as (self-)representation. It then argues that contemporary work in feminist theory goes further in defining the female-gendered subject as one that is at once inside and outside the ideology of gender: the female subject of feminism is one constructed across a multiplicity of discourses, positions, and meanings, which are often in conflict with one another and inherently (historically) contradictory. A feminist theory of gender, in other words, points to a conception of the subject as multiple, rather than divided or unified, and as excessive or heteronomous vis-à-vis the state ideological apparati and the sociocultural technologies of gender.

As the slight variance between its title and the volume's title is intended to suggest, the first essay is not meant to be an introduction to the volume as such, although it was written after the others and thus is chronologically the last, or the most recent; but it does not attempt to bring together the diverse concerns of the essays that follow it into a single critical argument. The volume is a collection of distinct, if related, essays. I feel, however, that "The Technology of Gender" is properly placed as the lead essay of the volume because it does lay out the inclusive parameters and the critical frame of reference for the exploration of gender-related questions throughout the book. The inclusion of one essay written several years earlier than the others is motivated by its compatibility with that critical frame of reference, as well as by its direct relevance to the topic of the volume.

A few words on the sequential ordering of the essays may be useful, since it is neither chronological nor strictly adherent to the three generic areas listed in the subtitle. The second essay, like the first, engages and rewrites "theory": "The Violence of Rhetoric" confronts structuralist and poststructuralist theory (Lévi-Strauss to Foucault and Derrida) with feminist readings of it (e.g., Spivak on Derrida on Nietzsche), as well as feminist work in social science (e.g., Breines and Gordon on family violence) and rhetorical analyses of scientific discourse (e.g., Keller's critique of the "genderization of science"). Essays 3 and 4 offer close textual readings of two contemporary novels, Umberto Eco's best-seller *The Name of the Rose* and Italo Calvino's *If on a winter's night a traveler*, readings which engage the texts to test the intriguing allegations of a possible love affair between feminism and postmodernism.

The essay that follows is anomalous in both topical and tropical location. First published in 1978 by a feminist collective's non-scholarly publication on art and politics, "Gramsci Notwithstanding, or, The Left Hand of History" is about neither theory or fiction, nor film. It is, and was written as, a presentation, or a record, of a specific textual practice in the Italian women's movement (a book based on unpublished women's letters, an experimental theatre performance based on the book, and the documentation of the theatrical production itself, also published in the book), and an instance of textual practice as feminist intervention in/against cultural hegemony. For this reason I have placed the essay after "Calvino and the

Amazons," almost as a response to Calvino's text—as another feminist rereading next to my own, or, better, as a feminist rewriting of cultural history—and before the last two essays, which are also about feminist interventions in cultural hegemony through the practice, this time, of women's cinema. Moreover, because of its somewhat heterogeneous or liminal character in this collection, the fifth essay serves well as a divider between the previous four, which engage theory and fiction, and the last three, which deal primarily with film.

"Fellini's 9½" is a reading of *Juliet of the Spirits*, the film Fellini made immediately after finishing his self-reflexive "masterpiece" *8½*, and where the representation of gender is so transparent as to reveal, in the very image of woman, the massive narrative shadow of a Fellini in drag. "Strategies of Coherence," on the uses and abuses of narrative in feminist avant-garde filmmaking, and particularly in the work of Yvonne Rainer, and the last essay in the volume are concerned with rethinking or reformulating the notion of "women's cinema" in light of current developments in feminist theory. Written almost concurrently with or just before "The Technology of Gender," the last two essays address questions of spectatorship, aesthetic response, and (self-)representation in the effort to specify the modes of consciousness of a feminist subjectivity and its inscription in certain critical textual practices.

Finally, then, while all the essays in the volume imply the feminist perspective articulated in *Alice Doesn't*, a development may be seen to have taken place (especially in essays 1, 7, and 8) with regard to the understanding of feminism as a radical *rewriting*, as well as a rereading, of the dominant forms of Western culture; a rewriting which effectively inscribes the presence of a different, and gendered, social subject. But even so, what these essays propose and argue for is a continued testing of the boundaries, an essaying of the no-man's land inhabited by "Alice," rather than a fully constructed view from "elsewhere." That must remain the project for another book.

TECHNOLOGIES
OF GENDER

1

THE TECHNOLOGY OF GENDER

In the feminist writings and cultural practices of the 1960s and 1970s, the notion of gender as sexual difference was central to the critique of representation, the rereading of cultural images and narratives, the questioning of theories of subjectivity and textuality, of reading, writing, and spectatorship. The notion of gender *as* sexual difference has grounded and sustained feminist interventions in the arena of formal and abstract knowledge, in the epistemologies and cognitive fields defined by the social and physical sciences as well as the human sciences or humanities. Concurrent and interdependent with those interventions were the elaboration of specific practices and discourses, and the creation of social spaces (gendered spaces, in the sense of the "women's room," such as CR groups, women's caucuses within the disciplines, Women's Studies, feminist journal or media collectives, and so on) in which sexual difference itself could be affirmed, addressed, analyzed, specified, or verified. But that notion of gender as sexual difference and its derivative notions—women's culture, mothering, feminine writing, femininity, etc.—have now become a limitation, something of a liability to feminist thought.

With its emphasis on the sexual, "sexual difference" is in the first and last instance a difference of women from men, female from male; and even the more abstract notion of "sexual differences" resulting not from biology or socialization but from signification and discursive effects (the emphasis here being less on the sexual than on differences as *différance*), ends up being in the last instance a difference (of woman) from man—or better, the very instance of difference *in* man. To continue to pose the question of gender in either of these terms, once the critique of patriarchy has been fully outlined, keeps feminist thinking bound to the terms of Western patriarchy itself, contained within the frame of a conceptual opposition that is "always already" inscribed in what Fredric Jameson would call "the political unconscious" of dominant cultural discourses and their underlying "master narratives"—be they biological, medical, legal, philosophical, or

1

literary—and so will tend to reproduce itself, to retextualize itself, as we shall see, even in feminist rewritings of cultural narratives.

The first limit of "sexual difference(s)," then, is that it constrains feminist critical thought within the conceptual frame of a universal sex opposition (woman as the difference from man, both universalized; or woman as difference *tout court,* and hence equally universalized), which makes it very difficult, if not impossible, to articulate the differences of women from Woman, that is to say, the differences among women or, perhaps more exactly, the differences *within women.* For example, the differences among women who wear the veil, women who "wear the mask" (in the words of Paul Laurence Dunbar often quoted by black American women writers), and women who "masquerade" (the word is Joan Riviere's) cannot be understood as sexual differences.[1] From that point of view, they would not be differences at all, and all women would but render either different embodiments of some archetypal essence of woman, or more or less sophisticated impersonations of a metaphysical-discursive femininity.

A second limitation of the notion of sexual difference(s) is that it tends to recontain or recuperate the radical epistemological potential of feminist thought inside the walls of the master's house, to borrow Audre Lorde's metaphor rather than Nietzsche's "prison-house of language," for reasons that will presently become apparent. By radical epistemological potential I mean the possibility, already emergent in feminist writings of the 1980s, to conceive of the social subject and of the relations of subjectivity to sociality in another way: a subject constituted in gender, to be sure, though not by sexual difference alone, but rather across languages and cultural representations; a subject en-gendered in the experiencing of race and class, as well as sexual, relations; a subject, therefore, not unified but rather multiple, and not so much divided as contradicted.

In order to begin to specify this other kind of subject and to articulate its relations to a heterogeneous social field, we need a notion of gender that is not so bound up with sexual difference as to be virtually coterminous with it and such that, on the one hand, gender is assumed to derive unproblematically from sexual difference while, on the other, gender can be subsumed in sexual differences as an effect of language, or as pure imaginary—nothing to do with the real. This bind, this mutual containment of gender and sexual difference(s), needs to be unraveled and deconstructed. A starting point may be to think of gender along the lines of Michel Foucault's theory of sexuality as a "technology of sex" and to propose that gender, too, both as representation and as self-representation, is the product of various social technologies, such as cinema, and of institutionalized discourses, epistemologies, and critical practices, as well as practices of daily life.

Like sexuality, we might then say, gender is not a property of bodies or something originally existent in human beings, but "the set of effects produced in bodies, behaviors, and social relations," in Foucault's words, by the deployment of "a complex political technology."[2] But it must be said first off, and hence the title of this essay, that to think of gender as the product and the process of a number of social technologies, of techno-social or bio-medical apparati, is to have already gone beyond Foucault, for his critical understanding of the technology of sex did not take into account its differential solicitation of male and female subjects, and by ignoring the conflicting investments of men and women in the discourses and practices of sexuality, Foucault's theory, in fact, excludes, though it does not preclude, the consideration of gender.

I will proceed by stating a series of four propositions in decreasing order of self-evidence and subsequently will go back to elaborate on each in more detail.

(1) Gender is (a) representation—which is not to say that it does not have concrete or real implications, both social and subjective, for the material life of individuals. On the contrary,

(2) The representation of gender *is* its construction—and in the simplest sense it can be said that all of Western Art and high culture is the engraving of the history of that construction.

(3) The construction of gender goes on as busily today as it did in earlier times, say the Victorian era. And it goes on not only where one might expect it to—in the media, the private and public schools, the courts, the family, nuclear or extended or single-parented—in short, in what Louis Althusser has called the "ideological state apparati." The construction of gender also goes on, if less obviously, in the academy, in the intellectual community, in avant-garde artistic practices and radical theories, even, and indeed especially, in feminism.

(4) Paradoxically, therefore, the construction of gender is also effected by its deconstruction; that is to say, by any discourse, feminist or otherwise, that would discard it as ideological misrepresentation. For gender, like the real, is not only the effect of representation but also its excess, what remains outside discourse as a potential trauma which can rupture or destabilize, if not contained, any representation.

1.

We look up *gender* in the *American Heritage Dictionary of the English Language* and find that it is primarily a classificatory term. In grammar, it is a category by which words and grammatical forms are classified according to not only sex or the absence of sex (which is one particular category, called "natural gender" and typical of the English language, for example) but also other characteristics, such as morphological characteristics in what is called "grammatical gender," found in Romance languages, for example. (I recall a paper by Roman Jakobson entitled "The Sex of the Heavenly Bodies" which, after analyzing the gender of the words for sun and moon in a great variety of languages, came to the refreshing conclusion that no pattern could be detected to support the idea of a universal law determining the masculinity or the femininity of either the sun or the moon. Thank heaven for that!)

The second meaning of *gender* given in the dictionary is "classification of sex; sex." This proximity of grammar and sex, interestingly enough, is not there in Romance languages (which, it is commonly believed, are spoken by people rather more romantic than Anglo-Saxons). The Spanish *género*, the Italian *genere*, and the French *genre* do not carry even the connotation of a person's gender; that is conveyed instead by the word for sex. And for this reason, it would seem, the word *genre*, adopted from French to refer to the specific classification of artistic and literary forms (in the first place, painting), is also devoid of any sexual denotation, as is the word *genus*, the Latin etymology of gender, used in English as a classificatory term in biology and logic. An interesting corollary of this linguistic peculiarity of English, i.e., the acceptation of gender which refers to sex, is that the notion of gender I am discussing, and thus the whole tangled question of the relationship of human gender to representation, are totally untranslatable in any Romance language, a sobering thought for anyone who might be still tempted to espouse an internationalist, not to say universal, view of the project of theorizing gender.

Going back to the dictionary, then, we find that the term *gender is a representation;* and not only a representation in the sense in which every word, every sign, refers to (represents) its referent, be that an object, a thing, or an animate being. The term *gender* is, actually, the representation of a relation, that of belonging to a class, a group, a category. Gender is the representation of a relation, or, if I may trespass for a moment into my second proposition, gender constructs a relation between one entity and other entities, which are previously constituted as a class, and that relation is one of belonging; thus, gender assigns to one entity, say an individual, a position within a class, and therefore also a position vis-à-vis other pre-constituted classes. (I am using the term *class* advisedly, although here I do not mean *social* class(es), because I want to retain Marx's understanding of class as a group of individuals bound together by social determinants and interests—including, very pointedly, ideology—which are neither freely chosen nor arbitrarily set.) So gender represents not an individual but a relation, and a social relation; in other words, it represents an individual for a class.

The neuter gender in English, a language that relies on natural gender (we note, in passing, that "nature" is ever-present in our culture, from the very beginning, which is, precisely, language), is assigned to words referring to sexless or asexual entities, objects or individuals marked by the absence of sex. The exceptions to this rule show the popular wisdom of usage: a child is neuter in gender, and its correct possessive modifier is *its*, as I was taught in learning English many years ago, though most people use *his*, and some, quite recently and rarely, and even then inconsistently, use *his or her*. Although a child does have a sex from "nature," it isn't until it becomes (i.e., until it is signified as) a boy or a girl that it acquires a gender.[3] What the popular wisdom knows, then, is that gender is not sex, a state of nature, but the representation of each individual in terms of a particular social relation which pre-exists the individual and is predicated on the *conceptual* and rigid (structural) opposition of two biological sexes. This conceptual structure is what feminist social scientists have designated "the sex-gender system."

The cultural conceptions of male and female as two complementary yet mutually exclusive categories into which all human beings are placed constitute within each culture a gender system, a symbolic system or system of meanings, that correlates sex to cultural contents according to social values and hierarchies. Although the meanings vary with each culture, a sex-gender system is always intimately interconnected with political and economic factors in each society.[4] In this light, the cultural construction of sex into gender and the asymmetry that characterizes all gender systems cross-culturally (though each in its particular ways) are understood as "systematically linked to the organization of social inequality."[5]

The sex-gender system, in short, is both a sociocultural construct and a semiotic apparatus, a system of representation which assigns meaning (identity, value, prestige, location in kinship, status in the social hierarchy, etc.) to individuals within the society. If gender representations are social positions which carry differential meanings, then for someone to be represented and to represent oneself as male or as female implies the assumption of the whole of those meaning effects. Thus, the proposition that the representation of gender is its construction, each term being at once the product and the process of the other, can be restated more accurately: *The construction of gender is both the product and the process of its representation.*

2.

When Althusser wrote that ideology represents "not the system of the real relations which govern the existence of individuals, but the imaginary relation of those individuals to the real relations in which they 'live" and which govern their existence, he was also describing, to my mind exactly, the functioning of gender.[6] But, it will be objected, it is reductive or overly simplistic to equate gender with ideology. Certainly Althusser does not do that, nor does traditional Marxist thought, where gender is a somewhat marginal issue, one limited to "the woman question."[7] For, like sexuality and subjectivity, gender is located in the private sphere of reproduction, procreation, and the family, rather than in the public, properly social, sphere of the superstructural, where ideology belongs and is determined by the economic forces and relations of production.

And yet, reading on in Althusser, one finds the emphatic statement *"All ideology has the function (which defines it) of 'constituting' concrete individuals as subjects"* (p. 171). If I substitute *gender* for *ideology*, the statement still works, but with a slight shift of the terms: Gender has the function (which defines it) of constituting concrete individuals as men and women. That shift is precisely where the relation of gender to ideology can be seen, and seen to be an effect of the ideology of gender. The shift from "subjects" to "men and women" marks the conceptual distance between two orders of discourse, the discourse of philosophy or political theory and the discourse of "reality." Gender is granted (and taken for granted) in the latter but excluded from the former.

Although the Althusserian subject of ideology derives more from Lacan's subject (which is an effect of signification, founded on misrecognition) than from the unified class subject of Marxist humanism, it too is ungendered, as neither of these systems considers the possibility—let alone the process of constitution—of a female subject.[8] Thus, by Althusser's own definition, we are entitled to ask, If gender exists in "reality," if it exists in "the real relations which govern the existence of individuals," but not in philosophy or political theory, what do the latter in fact represent if not "the imaginary relation of individuals to the real relations in which they live"? In other words, Althusser's theory of ideology is itself caught and blind to its own complicity in the ideology of gender. But that is not all: more important, and more to the immediate point of my argument, Althusser's theory, to the extent that a theory can be validated by institutional discourses and acquire power or control over the field of social meaning, can itself function as a techno-logy of gender.

The novelty of Althusser's theses was in his perception that ideology operates not only semi-autonomously from the economic level but also, fundamentally, by means of its engagement of subjectivity ("The category of the subject is constitutive of all ideology," he writes on p. 171). It is, thus, paradoxical and yet quite evident that the connection between gender and ideology—or the understanding of gender as an instance of ideology—could not be made by him. But the connection has been explored by other Marxist thinkers who are feminists, and better still the other way around, by some feminist thinkers who are also Marxists. Michèle Barrett, for one, argues that not only is ideology a primary site of the construction of gender, but "the ideology of gender . . . has played an important part in the historical construction of the capitalist division of labour and in the reproduction of labour power," and therefore is an accurate demonstration of "the integral connection between ideology and the relations of production."[9]

The context of Barrett's argument (originally made in her 1980 book *Women's Oppression Today*) is the debate elicited in England by "discourse theory" and other post-Althusserian developments in the theory of ideology, and more specifically the critique of ideology promoted by the British feminist journal *m/f* on the basis of notions of representation and difference drawn from Lacan and Derrida. She quotes Parveen Adams's "A Note on the Distinction between Sexual Division and Sexual Difference," where sexual division refers to the two mutually exclusive categories of men and women as given in reality: "In terms of sexual *differences,* on the other hand, what has to be grasped is, precisely, the *production* of differences through systems of representation; the work of representation produces differences that cannot be known in advance."[10]

Adams's critique of a feminist (Marxist) theory of ideology that relies on the notion of patriarchy as a given in social reality (in other words, a theory based on the fact of women's oppression by men) is that such a theory is based on an essentialism, whether biological or sociological, which crops up again even in the work of those, such as Juliet Mitchell, who would insist that gender is an effect of representation. "In feminist analyses," Adams maintains, the concept of a feminine subject "relies on a homogeneous oppression of women in a state, reality, given prior to representational practices" (p. 56). By stressing that gender construction is nothing but the effect of a variety of representations and discursive practices which produce sexual differences "not known in advance" (or, in my own paraphrase, gender is nothing but the variable configuration of sexual-discursive positionalities), Adams believes she can avoid "the simplicities of an always already antagonistic relation" between the sexes, which is an obstacle, in her eyes, to both feminist analysis and feminist political practice (p. 57). Barrett's response to this point is one I concur with, especially as regards its implications for feminist politics: "We do not need to talk of sexual division as 'always already' there; we can explore the historical construction of the categories of masculinity and femininity without being obliged to deny that, historically specific as they are, they nevertheless exist today in systematic and even predictable terms" (Barrett, pp. 70–71).

However, Barrett's conceptual framework does not permit an understanding of the ideology of gender in specifically feminist theoretical terms. In a note added to the 1985 reprinting of her essay, from which I have been quoting, she reiterates her conviction that "ideology is an extremely important site of the construction of gender but that it should be understood as part of a social totality rather than as an autonomous practice or discourse" (p. 83). This notion of "social totality" and the thorny problem of the "relative" autonomy of ideology (in general, and presumably of the ideology of gender in particular) from "the means and forces of production" and/or "the social relations of production" remain quite vague and unresolved in Barrett's argument, which becomes less focused and less engaging as she goes on to discuss the ways in which the ideology of gender is (re)produced in cultural (literary) practice.

Another and potentially more useful way to pose the question of gender ideology is suggested, though not followed through, in Joan Kelly's 1979 essay "The Doubled Vision of Feminist Theory." Once we accept the fundamental feminist notion that the personal is political, Kelly argues, it is no longer possible to maintain that there are two spheres of social reality: the private, domestic sphere of the family, sexuality, and affectivity, and the public sphere of work and productivity (which would include all of the forces and most of the relations of production in Barrett's terms). Instead we can envision several interconnected sets of social relations—relations of work, of class, of race, and of sex/gender: "What we see are not two spheres of social reality, but two (or three) sets of social relations. For now, I would call them relations of work and sex (or class and race, and sex/gender)."[11] Not only are men and women positioned differently in these relations, but—this is an important point—women are affected differently in different sets.

The "doubled" perspective of contemporary feminist analysis, Kelly continues, is one in which we can see the two orders, the sexual and the economic, operate together: "in any of the historical forms that patriarchal society takes (feudal, capitalist, socialist, etc.), a sex-gender system and a system of productive relations operate simultaneously . . . to reproduce the socioeconomic and male-dominant structures of that particular social order" (p. 61). Within that "doubled" perspective, therefore, it is possible to see quite clearly the working of the ideology of gender: *"woman's place,"* i.e., the position assigned to women by our sex/gender system, as she emphasizes, *"is not a separate sphere or domain of existence but a position within social existence generally"* (p. 57). That is another very important point.

For if the sex-gender system (which I prefer to call gender *tout court* in order to retain the ambiguity of the term, which makes it eminently susceptible to the grasp of ideology, as well as deconstruction) is a set of social relations obtaining throughout social existence, then gender is indeed a primary instance of ideology, and obviously not only for women. Furthermore, that is so regardless of whether particular individuals see themselves primarily defined (and oppressed) by gender, as white cultural feminists do, or primarily defined (and oppressed) by race and class relations, as women of color do.[12] The importance of Althusser's formulation of the subjective working of ideology—again, briefly, that ideology needs a subject, a concrete individual or person to work on—appears more clearly now, and more central to the feminist project of theorizing gender as a personal-political force both negative and positive, as I will propose.

To assert that the social representation of gender affects its subjective construction and that, vice versa, the subjective representation of gender— or self-representation—affects its social construction, leaves open a possibility of agency and self-determination at the subjective and even individual level of micropolitical and everyday practices which Althusser himself would clearly disclaim. I, nevertheless, will claim that possibility and postpone discussing it until sections 3 and 4 of this essay. For the moment, going back to proposition 2, which was revised as "The construction of gender is both the product and the process of its representation," I can rewrite it: *The construction of gender is the product and the process of both representation and self-representation.*

But now I must discuss a further problem with Althusser, insofar as a theory of gender is concerned, and that is that in his view, "ideology has no outside." It is a foolproof system whose effect is to erase its own traces completely, so that anyone who is "in ideology," caught in its web, believes "himself" to be outside and free of it. Nevertheless, there is an outside, a place from where ideology can be seen for what it is—mystification, imaginary relation, wool over one's eyes; and that place is, for Althusser, science, or scientific knowledge. Such is simply not the case for feminism and for what I propose to call, avoiding further equivocations, the subject of feminism.

By the phrase "the subject of feminism" I mean a conception or an understanding of the (female) subject as not only distinct from Woman with the capital letter, the *representation* of an essence inherent in all women (which has been seen as Nature, Mother, Mystery, Evil Incarnate, Object of [Masculine] Desire and Knowledge, Proper Womanhood, Femininity, et cetera), but also distinct from women, the real, historical beings and social subjects who are defined by the technology of gender and actually engendered in social relations. The subject of feminism I have in mind is one *not* so defined, one whose definition or conception is in progress, in this and other feminist critical texts; and, to insist on this point one more time, the subject of feminism, much like Althusser's subject, is a theoretical construct (a way of conceptualizing, of understanding, of accounting for certain *processes*, not women). However, unlike Althusser's subject, who, being completely "in" ideology, believes himself to be outside and free of it, the subject that I see emerging from current writings and debates within feminism is one that is at the same time inside *and* outside the ideology of gender, and conscious of being so, conscious of that twofold pull, of that division, that doubled vision.

My own argument in *Alice Doesn't* was to that effect: the discrepancy, the tension, and the constant slippage between Woman as representation, as the object and the very condition of representation, and, on the other hand, women as historical beings, subjects of "real relations," are motivated and sustained by a logical contradiction in our culture and an irreconcilable one: women are both inside and outside gender, at once within and without representation.[13] That women continue to become Woman, continue to be caught in gender as Althusser's subject is in ideology, and that we persist in that imaginary relation even as we know, as feminists, that we are not *that*, but we are historical subjects governed by real social relations, which centrally include gender—such is the contradiction that feminist theory must be built on, and its very condition of possibility. Obviously, then, feminism cannot cast itself as science, as a discourse or a reality that is outside of ideology, or outside of gender as an instance of ideology.[14]

In fact, the shift in feminist consciousness that has been taking place during this decade may be said to have begun (if a convenient date is needed) with 1981, the year of publication of *This Bridge Called My Back*, the collection of writings by radical women of color edited by Cherríe Moraga and Gloria Anzaldúa, which was followed in 1982 by the Feminist Press anthology edited by Gloria Hull, Patricia Bell Scott, and Barbara Smith with the title *All the Women Are White, All the Blacks Are Men, but Some of Us Are Brave*.[15] It was these books that first made available to all feminists the feelings, the analyses, and the political positions of feminists of color, and their critiques of white or mainstream feminism. The shift in feminist consciousness that was initially prompted by works such as these is best characterized by the awareness and the effort to work through feminism's complicity with ideology, both ideology in general (including classism or bourgeois liberalism, racism, colonialism, imperialism, and, I would also add, with some qualifications, humanism) and the ideology of gender in particular—that is to say, heterosexism.

I said complicity, not full adherence, for it is obvious that feminism and a full adherence to the ideology of gender, in male-centered societies, are mutually exclusive. And I would add, further, that the consciousness of our complicity with gender ideology, and the divisions and contradictions attendant upon that, are what must characterize all feminisms today in the United States, no longer just white and middle-class women, who were the first to be forced to examine our relation to institutions, political practice, cultural apparati, and then to racism, anti-Semitism, hetero-sexism, classism, and so forth; for the consciousness of complicity with the gender ideologies of their particular cultures and subcultures is also emerging in the more recent writings of black women and Latinas, and of those lesbians, of whatever color, who identify themselves as feminists.[16] To what extent this newer or emerging consciousness of complicity acts with or against the consciousness of oppression, is a question central to the understanding of ideology in these postmodern and postcolonial times.

That is why, in spite of the divergences, the political and personal differences, and the pain that surround feminist debates within and across racial, ethnic, and sexual lines, we may be encouraged in the hope that feminism will continue to develop a radical theory and a practice of sociocultural transformation. For that to be, however, the ambiguity of gender must be retained—and that is only seemingly a paradox. We cannot resolve or dispel the uncomfortable condition of being at once inside and outside gender either by desexualizing it (making gender merely a metaphor, a question of *différance,* of purely discursive effects) or by androgynizing it (claiming the same experience of material conditions for both genders in a given class, race, or culture). But I have already anticipated what I shall discuss further on. I have trespassed again, for I have not yet worked through the third proposition, which stated that the construction of gender through its representation goes on today as much as or more than in any other times. I will begin with a very simple, everyday example and then go on to more lofty proofs.

3.

Most of us—those of us who are women; to those who are men this will not apply—probably check the *F* box rather than the *M* box when filling out an application form. It would hardly occur to us to mark *M*. It would be like cheating or, worse, not existing, like erasing ourselves from the world.

(For men to check the *F* box, were they ever tempted to do so, would have quite another set of implications.) For since the very first time we put a check mark on the little square next to the *F* on the form, we have officially entered the sex-gender system, the social relations of gender, and have become en-gendered as women; that is to say, not only do other people consider us females, but from that moment on *we* have been representing ourselves as women. Now, I ask, isn't that the same as saying that the *F* next to the little box, which we marked in filling out the form, has stuck to us like a wet silk dress? Or that while we thought that we were marking the *F* on the form, in fact the *F* was marking itself on us?

This is, of course, the process described by Althusser with the word *interpellation,* the process whereby a social representation is accepted and absorbed by an individual as her (or his) own representation, and so becomes, for that individual, real, even though it is in fact imaginary. However, my example is all too simple. It does not explain how the representation is constructed and how it is then accepted and absorbed. For that purpose we turn, first, to Michel Foucault.

The first volume of Foucault's *History of Sexuality* has become highly influential, especially his bold thesis that sexuality, commonly thought to be a natural as well as a private, intimate matter, is in fact completely constructed in culture according to the political aims of the society's dominant class. Foucault's analysis begins from a paradox: the prohibitions and regulations pertaining to sexual behaviors, whether spoken by religious, legal, or scientific authorities, far from constraining or repressing sexuality, have on the contrary produced it, and continue to produce it, in the sense in which industrial machinery produces goods or commodities, and in so doing also produces social relations.

Hence the notion of a "technology of sex," which he defines as "a set of techniques for maximizing life" that have been developed and deployed by the bourgeoisie since the end of the eighteenth century in order to ensure its class survival and continued hegemony. Those techniques involved the elaboration of discourses (classification, measurements, evaluation, etc.) about four privileged "figures" or objects of knowledge: the sexualization of children and of the female body, the control of procreation, and the psychiatrization of anomalous sexual behavior as perversion. These discourses, which were implemented through pedagogy, medicine, demography, and economics, were anchored or supported by the institutions of the state, and became especially focused on the family; they served to disseminate and to "implant," in Foucault's suggestive term, those figures and modes of knowledge into each individual, family, and institution. This technology, he remarked, "made sex not only a secular concern but a concern of the state as well; to be more exact, sex became a matter that required the social body as a whole, and virtually all of its individuals, to place themselves under surveillance."[17]

The sexualization of the female body has indeed been a favorite figure or object of knowledge in the discourses of medical science, religion, art, literature, popular culture, and so on. Since Foucault, several studies have appeared that address the topic, more or less explicitly, in his historical methodological framework;[18] but the connection between woman and sexuality, and the identification of the sexual with the female body, so pervasive in Western culture, had long been a major concern of feminist criticism and of the women's movement quite independently of Foucault, of course. In particular, feminist film criticism had been addressing itself to that issue in a conceptual framework which, though not derived from Foucault, yet was not altogether dissimilar.

For some time before the publication of volume I of *The History of Sexuality* in France (*La volonté de savoir,* 1976), feminist film theorists had been writing on the sexualization of the female star in narrative cinema and analyzing the cinematic techniques (lighting, framing, editing, etc.) and the specific cinematic codes (e.g., the system of the look) that construct woman as image, as the object of the spectator's voyeurist gaze; and they had been developing both an account and a critique of the psycho-social, aesthetic, and philosophical discourses that underlie the representation of the female body as the primary site of sexuality and visual pleasure.[19] The understanding of cinema as a social technology, as a "cinematic apparatus," was developed in film theory contemporaneously with Foucault's work but independently of it; rather, as the word *apparatus* suggests, it was directly influenced by the work of Althusser and Lacan.[20] There is little doubt, at any rate, that cinema—the cinematic apparatus—is a technology of gender, as I have argued throughout *Alice Doesn't,* if not in these very words, I hope convincingly.

The theory of the cinematic apparatus is more concerned than Foucault's with answering both parts of the question I started from: not only how the representation of gender is constructed by the given technology, but also how it becomes absorbed subjectively by each individual whom that technology addresses. For the second part of the question, the crucial notion is the concept of spectatorship, which feminist film theory has established as a gendered concept; that is to say, the ways in which each individual spectator is addressed by the film, the ways in which his/her identification is solicited and structured in the single film,[21] are intimately and intentionally, if not usually explicitly, connected to the spectators' gender. Both in the critical writings and in the practices of women's cinema, the exploration of female spectatorship is giving us a more subtly articulated analysis of the modalities of film viewing for women and increasingly sophisticated forms of address in filmmaking (as discussed in chapters 7 and 8).

This critical work is producing a knowledge of cinema *and* of the technology of sex which Foucault's theory could not lead to, on its own terms; for there, sexuality is not understood as gendered, as having a male form and a female form, but is taken to be one and the same for all—and consequently male (further discussion of this point is to be found in chapter 2). I am not speaking of the libido, which Freud said to be only one, and I think he may have been right about that. I am speaking here of sexuality as a construct and a (self-) representation; and that does have both a male form and a female form, although in the patriarchal or male-centered frame of mind, the female form is a projection of the male's, its complementary opposite, its extrapolation—Adam's rib, so to speak. So that, even when it is located *in* the woman's body (seen, Foucault wrote, "as being thoroughly saturated with sexuality," p. 104), sexuality is perceived as an attribute or a property of the male.

As Lucy Bland states in response to an article on the historical construction of sexuality along Foucauldian lines—an article which not surprisingly omits what she considers "one of the *central* aspects of the historical construction of sexuality, namely its construction as gender specific"—the various conceptions of sexuality throughout Western history, however diverse among themselves, have been based on "the perennial contrast of 'male' to 'female' sexuality."[22] In other words, female sexuality has been invariably defined both in contrast and in relation to the male. The conception of sexuality held by feminists of the first wave, at the turn of the century, was no exception: whether they called for "purity" and opposed all sexual activity for degrading women to the level of men, or whether they called for a free expression of the "natural" function and "spiritual" quality of sex on the part of women, sex meant heterosexual intercourse and primarily penetration. It is only in contemporary feminism that the notions of a different or autonomous sexuality of women and of non-male-related sexual identities for women have emerged. But even so, Bland observes, "the displacement of the sexual act as penetration from the centre of the sexual stage remains a task still facing us today" (p. 67).

> The polarity 'male'/'female' has been and remains a central theme in nearly all representations of sexuality. Within 'common-sense', male and female sexuality stand as distinct: male sexuality is understood as active, spontaneous, genital, easily aroused by 'objects' and fantasy, while female sexuality is thought of in terms of its *relation to* male sexuality, as basically expressive and responsive to the male. (p. 57)

Hence the paradox that mars Foucault's theory, as it does other contemporary, radical but male-centered, theories: in order to combat the social technology that produces sexuality and sexual oppression, these theories (and their respective politics) will deny gender. But to deny gender, first of all, is to deny the social relations of gender that constitute and validate the sexual oppression of women; and second, to deny gender is to remain "in ideology," an ideology which (not coincidentally if, of course, not intentionally) is manifestly self-serving to the male-gendered subject.

In their collective book, the authors of *Changing the Subject* discuss the importance and the limits of discourse theory, and develop their own theoretical proposals from a critique as well as an acceptance of the basic premises of poststructuralism and deconstruction.[23] For example, they accept "the post-structuralist displacement of the unitary subject, and the revelation of its constituted and not constitutive character" (p. 204), but maintain that the deconstruction of the unified subject, the bourgeois individual ("the subject-as-agent"), is not sufficient for an accurate understanding of subjectivity. In particular, Wendy Hollway's chapter "Gender difference and the production of subjectivity" postulates that what accounts for the content of gender difference is gender-differentiated meanings and the positions differentially made available to men and women in discourse. Thus, for example, since all discourses on sexuality are gender-differentiated and therefore multiple (there are at the very least two in each specific instance or historical moment), the same practices of (hetero)sexuality are likely to "signify differently for women and men, because they are being read through different discourses" (p. 237).

Hollway's work concerns the study of heterosexual relations as "the primary site where gender difference is re-produced" (p. 228), and is based on the analysis of empirical materials drawn from individual people's accounts of their own heterosexual relationships. Her theoretical project is, "How can we understand gender difference in a way which can account for changes?"

> If we do not ask this question the change of paradigm from a biologistic to a discourse theory of gender difference does not constitute much of an advance. If the concept of discourses is just a replacement for the notion of ideology, then we are left with one of two possibilities. Either the account sees discourses as mechanically repeating themselves, or—and this is the tendency of materialist theory of ideology—changes in ideology follow from changes in material conditions. According to such a use of discourse theory people are the victims of certain systems of ideas which are outside of them. Discourse determinism comes up against the old problem of agency typical of all sorts of social determinisms. (p. 237)

The "gap" in Foucault's theory, as she sees it, consists in his account of historical changes in discourses. "He stresses the mutually constitutive relation between power and knowledge: how each constitutes the other to produce the truths of a particular epoch." Rather than equating power with oppression, Foucault sees it as productive of meanings, values, knowledges, and practices, but inherently neither positive nor negative. However, Hollway remarks, "he still does not account for how people are constituted as a result of certain truths being current rather than others" (p. 237). She then reformulates, and redistributes, Foucault's notion of power by suggesting that power is what motivates (and not necessarily in a conscious or rational manner) individuals' "investments" in discursive positions. If at any one time there are several competing, even contradictory, discourses on sexuality—rather than a single, all-encompassing or monolithic, ideology—then what makes one take up a position in a certain discourse rather than another is an "investment" (this term translates the German *Besetzung,* a word used by Freud and rendered in English as *cathexis*), something between an emotional commitment and a vested interest, in the relative power (satisfaction, reward, payoff) which that position promises (but does not necessarily fulfill).

Hollway's is an interesting attempt to reconceptualize power in such a manner that agency (rather than choice) may be seen to exist for the subject, and especially for those subjects who have been (perceived as) "victims" of social oppression or especially disempowered by the discursive monopoly of power-knowledge. It not only may explain why, for example, women (who are people of one gender) have historically made different investments and thus have taken up different positions in gender and sexual practices and identities (celibacy, monogamy, non-monogamy, frigidity, sexual-role playing, lesbianism, heterosexuality, feminism, anti-feminism, postfeminism, etc.); but it may explain, as well, the fact that "other major dimensions of social difference such as class, race and age intersect with gender to favor or disfavor certain positions" (p. 239), as Hollway suggests. However, her conclusion that "every relation and every practice is a site of potential change as much as it is a site of reproduction" does not say what relation the potential for change in gender relations—if it is a change both in consciousness and in social reality—may bear to the hegemony of discourses.

How do changes in consciousness affect or effect changes in dominant discourses? Or, put another way, whose investments yield more relative power? For example, if we say that certain discourses and practices, even though marginal with regard to institutions, but nonetheless disruptive or oppositional (e.g., women's cinema and health collectives, Women's Studies' and Afro-American Studies' revisions of the literary canon and college curricula, the developing critique of colonial discourse), do have the power to "implant" new objects and modes of knowledge in individual subjects, does it follow that these oppositional discourses or counter-practices (as Claire Johnston called women's cinema in the early 1970s "counter-cinema") can become dominant or hegemonic? And if so, how? Or need they not become dominant in order for social relations to change? And if not, how will the social relations of gender change? I may restate these questions into one, as follows: If, as Hollway writes, "gender difference is . . . reproduced in day-to-day interactions in heterosexual couples, through the denial of the non-unitary, non-rational, relational character of subjectivity" (p. 252), what will persuade women to invest in other positions, in other sources of power capable of changing gender relations, when they have assumed the current position (of female in the couple), in the first place, because that position afforded them, as women, a certain relative power?

The point I am trying to make, much as I agree with Hollway in most of her argument, and much as I like her effort to redistribute power among most of us, is that to theorize as positive the "relative" power of those oppressed by current social relations necessitates something more radical, or perhaps more drastic, than she seems willing to stake. The problem is compounded by the fact that the investments studied by Hollway are secured and bonded by a heterosexual contract; that is to say, her object of study is the very site in which the social relations of gender and thus gender ideology are re-produced in everyday life. Any changes that may result therein, however they may occur, are likely to be changes in "gender difference," precisely, rather than changes in the social relations of gender: changes, in short, in the direction of more or less "equality" of women *to men*.

Here is, clearly in evidence, the problem in the notion of sexual difference(s), its conservative force limiting and working against the effort to rethink its very representations. I believe that to envision gender (men and women) otherwise, and to (re)construct it in terms other than those dictated by the patriarchal contract, we must walk out of the male-centered frame of reference in which gender and sexuality are (re)produced by the discourse of male sexuality—or, as Luce Irigaray has so well written it, of hom(m)osexuality. This essay would like to be a rough map of the first steps of the way out.

Taking up position in quite another frame of reference, Monique Wittig has stressed the power of discourses to "do violence" to people, a violence which is material and physical, although produced by abstract and scientific discourses as well as the discourses of the mass media.

> If the discourse of modern theoretical systems and social science exert[s] a power upon us, it is because it works with concepts which closely touch

us. . . . They function like primitive concepts in a conglomerate of all kinds
of disciplines, theories, and current ideas that I will call the straight mind.
(See *The Savage Mind* by Claude Lévi-Strauss.) They concern "woman,"
"man," "sex," "difference," and all of the series of concepts which bear this
mark, including such concepts as "history," "culture," and the "real." And
although it has been accepted in recent years that there is no such thing as
nature, that everything is culture, there remains within that culture a core of
nature which resists examination, a relationship excluded from the social in
the analysis—a relationship whose characteristic is ineluctability in culture, as
well as in nature, and which is the heterosexual relationship. I will call it the
obligatory social relationship between "man" and "woman."[24]

In arguing that the "discourses of heterosexuality oppress us in the sense
that they prevent us from speaking unless we speak in their terms" (p. 105),
Wittig is recovering the sense of the oppressiveness of power as it is
imbricated in institutionally controlled knowledges, a sense which has
somehow been lost in placing the emphasis on the Foucauldian view of
power as productive, *and hence as positive.* While it would be difficult to
disprove that power is productive of knowledges, meanings, and values, it
seems obvious enough that we have to make distinctions between the
positive effects and the oppressive effects of such production. And that is
not an issue for political practice alone, but, as Wittig forcefully reminds us,
it is especially a question to be asked of theory.

I will then rewrite my third proposition: *The construction of gender goes on
today through the various technologies of gender (e.g., cinema) and institutional
discourses (e.g., theory) with power to control the field of social meaning and thus
produce, promote, and "implant" representations of gender. But the terms of a
different construction of gender also exist, in the margins of hegemonic discourses.
Posed from outside the heterosexual social contract, and inscribed in micropolitical
practices, these terms can also have a part in the construction of gender, and their
effects are rather at the "local" level of resistances, in subjectivity and self-representation.* I will return to this last point in section 4.

In the last chapter of *Alice Doesn't,* I used the term *experience* to designate
the process by which, for all social beings, subjectivity is constructed. I
sought to define experience more precisely as a complex of meaning
effects, habits, dispositions, associations, and perceptions resulting from
the semiotic interaction of self and outer world (in C.S. Peirce's words). The
constellation or configuration of meaning effects which I call experience
shifts and is reformed continually, for each subject, with her or his continuous engagement in social reality, a reality that includes—and for women
centrally—the social relations of gender. For, as I began to argue in that
book, following through the critical insights of Virginia Woolf and Catharine MacKinnon, female subjectivity and experience are necessarily
couched in a specific relation to sexuality. And however insufficiently de-

veloped, that observation suggests to me that what I was trying to define with the notion of a complex of habits, associations, perceptions, and dispositions which en-genders one as female—what I was getting at was precisely the experience of gender, the meaning effects and self-representations produced in the subject by the sociocultural practices, discourses, and institutions devoted to the production of women and men. And it was surely not coincidental, then, that my analyses had been concerned with cinema, narrative, and theory. For these themselves, of course, are all technologies of gender.

Now, to assert that theory (a generic term for any theoretical discourse seeking to account for a particular object of knowledge, and in effect constructing that object in a field of meaning as its proper domain of knowledge, the domain being often called "discipline") is a technology of gender may seem paradoxical given the fact I have been lamenting for most of these pages; namely, that the theories that are available to help us map the passage from sociality to subjectivity, from symbolic systems to individual perception, or from cultural representations to self-representation—a passage in discontinuous space, I might say—are either unconcerned with gender or unable to conceive of a female subject.[25] They are unconcerned with gender, like Althusser's and Foucault's, or the earlier work of Julia Kristeva or of Umberto Eco; or else, if they do concern themselves with gender, as Freud's theory of psychoanalysis does (more than any other, in fact, with the exception of feminist theory), and if they do then offer a model of the construction of gender in sexual difference, nevertheless their map of the terrain between sociality and subjectivity is one that leaves the female subject hopelessly caught in patriarchal swamps or stranded somewhere between the devil and the deep blue sea. However, and this is my argument in the present book, *both* kinds of theories, and the fictions they inspire, contain and promote some representation of gender, no less than cinema does.

A case in point is Kaja Silverman's illuminating work on subjectivity and language in psychoanalysis. In arguing that subjectivity is produced through language, and that the human subject is a semiotic and therefore also a gendered subject, Silverman makes a valiant effort, in her words, "to create a space for the female subject within [its] pages, even if that space is only a negative one."[26] And indeed, in the Lacanian framework of her analysis, the issue of gender does not fit, and the female subject can be defined only vaguely as a "point of resistance" (p. 144, p. 232) to patriarchal culture, as "potentially subversive" (p. 233), or as structured negatively "in relation to the phallus" (p. 191). This negativity of woman, her lacking or transcending the laws and processes of signification, has a counterpart, in poststructuralist psychoanalytic theory, in the notion of femininity as a privileged condition, a nearness to nature, the body, the side of the maternal, or the unconscious. However, we are cautioned, this femininity is purely a representation, a positionality within the phallic model of desire and signification; it is not a quality or a property of women. Which all amounts to saying that woman, *as* subject of desire or of signification, is unrepresentable; or, better, that in the phallic order of patriarchal culture and in its theory, woman is unrepresentable except as representation.

But even when it diverges from the Lacanian version that is predominant in literary criticism and film theory, and when it does pose the question of how one becomes a woman (as does, for instance, object-relations theory, which has appealed to feminists as much as if not more than Lacan or Freud), psychoanalysis defines woman *in relation to* man, from within the same frame of reference and with the analytical categories elaborated to account for the psychosocial development of the male. That is why psychoanalysis does not address, cannot address, the complex and contradictory relation of women to Woman, which it instead defines as a simple equation: women = Woman = Mother. And that, as I have suggested, is one of the most deeply rooted effects of the ideology of gender.

Before I go on to consider the representations of gender that are contained in other current discourses of interest to feminism, I want to return briefly to my own position vis-à-vis the problem of understanding gender both through a critical reading of theory and through the shifting configurations of my experience as a feminist and a theorist. If I could not but see, although I was unable to formulate it in my earlier work, that cinema and narrative theories were technologies of gender,[27] it was not only that I had read Foucault and Althusser (they had said nothing about gender) and Woolf and MacKinnon (they had), but also that I had absorbed as my experience (through my own history and engagement in social reality and in the gendered spaces of feminist communities) the analytical and critical method of feminism, the *practice* of self-consciousness. For the understanding of one's personal condition as a woman in terms social and political, and the constant revision, reevaluation, and reconceptualization of that condition in relation to other women's understanding of their sociosexual positions, generate a mode of apprehension of all social reality that derives from the consciousness of gender. And from that apprehension, from that personal, intimate, analytical, and political knowledge of the pervasiveness of gender, there is no going back to the innocence of "biology."

That is why I find it impossible to share some women's belief in a matriarchal past or a contemporary "matristic" realm presided over by the Goddess, a realm of female tradition, marginal and subterranean and yet all positive and good, peace-loving, ecologically correct, matrilineal, matrifocal, non-Indo-European, and so forth; in short, a world untouched by ideology, class and racial struggle, television—a world untroubled by the contradictory demands and oppressive rewards of gender as I, and surely those women, too, have daily experienced it. On the other hand, and much for the same reasons, I find it equally impossible to dismiss gender either as an essentialist and mythical idea of the kind I have just described, or as the liberal-bourgeois idea encouraged by media advertisers: someday soon, somehow, women will have careers, their own last names and property, children, husbands, and/or female lovers according to preference—and all that without altering the existing social relations and the heterosexual structures to which our society, and most others, are securely screwed.

Even this scenario, which, honestly I must admit, looms often enough in the background of a certain feminist discourse on gender, even this Ideal State of gender equality is not sufficient to deter me from claiming gender as a radical issue for feminist theory. And so I come to the last of the four propositions.

4.

The ideal state of gender equality, as I have just described it, is an easy target for deconstructors. Granted. (Although it is not altogether a straw man, because it is a real representation, as it were: just go to the movies on your next date, and you may see it.) But besides the blatant examples of ideological representation of gender in cinema, where the technology's intentionality is virtually foregrounded on the screen; and besides psychoanalysis, whose medical practice is much more of a technology of gender than its theory, there are other, subtler efforts to contain the trauma of gender—the potential disruption of the social fabric and of white male privilege that could ensue if this feminist critique of gender as ideologico-technological production were to become widespread.

Consider, for one, the new wave of critical writings by men on feminism that have appeared of late. Male philosophers writing as woman, male critics reading as a woman, men on feminism—what is it all about? Clearly it is an *hommage* (the pun is too tempting not to save it), but to what end? For the most part in the form of short mentions or occasional papers, these works do not support or valorize within the academy the feminist project per se. What they valorize and legitimate are certain positions within academic feminism, those positions that accommodate either or both the critic's personal interests and male-centered theoretical concerns.[28]

As the introduction to a recent collection of essays on *Gender and Reading* remarks, there is evidence that men are "resisting readers" of women's fiction. More precisely, "it is not that men can't read women's texts; it is, rather, that they *won't.*"[29] As far as theory goes, the evidence is very easy to check by a quick glance through the index of names of any book that does not specifically identify itself as feminist. The poverty of references to both feminist and female critics there is so consistent that one may be tempted, as Elaine Showalter was, to welcome "the move to feminist criticism on the part of [prominent] male theorists."[30] And the temptation may be irresistible if, like the editors of *Gender and Reading,* one is concerned "that discussions of *gender difference* do not foreclose the recognition of individual variability and of *the common ground shared by all humans*" (p. xxix; emphasis added).

The limits and the liability of this view of gender as "gender difference" become especially apparent when, in one of the essays of the collection, which proposes "A Theory for Lesbian Readers," Jean Kennard finds herself in agreement with Jonathan Culler (quoting Showalter) and re-inscribes his-and-her words directly into her own: "Reading as a lesbian is not necessarily what happens when a lesbian reads. . . . The hypothesis of a *lesbian* reader [is what] changes our apprehension of a given text."[31] Ironically, or, I should rather say, thanks to poetic justice, this last statement contradicts and runs in the opposite direction of Kennard's own critical project, clearly stated a few pages earlier: "What I wish to suggest here is a theory of reading which will not oversimplify the concept of identification, which will not subsume lesbian difference under a universal female. . . . It is an attempt to suggest a way in which lesbians could reread and write about texts" (p. 66).

The irony is in that Culler's statement—in line with Derridean deconstruction, which is the context of his statement—is intended to make gender synonymous with discursive difference(s), differences that are effects of language or positions in discourse, and thus indeed independent of the reader's gender (this notion of difference was already mentioned à propos of Michèle Barrett's critique of it). What Kennard is suggesting, then, is that Culler can read not only as a woman but also as a lesbian, and that would "subsume lesbian difference" not only "under a universal female" but also under the universal male (which Jonathan Culler himself might not accept to represent, in the name of *différance*). The poetic justice is welcome in that Kennard's critical hunch and initial assumption (that lesbians read differently from committedly heterosexual women as well as men) are quite correct, in my opinion; only, they need to be justified, or rendered justice to, by other means than male theories of reading or Gestalt psychology (for in addition to Lacan and Derrida, via Culler, Kennard draws her theory of "polar reading" from Joseph Zinker's theory of opposing characteristics or "polarities"). For the purposes of the matter at hand, poetic justice may be impersonated by Tania Modleski's critical assessment of the Showalter-Culler "hypothesis":

> For Culler, each stage of feminist criticism renders increasingly problematic the idea of "women's experience." By calling this notion into question, Culler manages to clear a space for male feminist interpretations of literary texts. Thus, at one point he quotes Peggy Kamuf's remark about feminism as a way of reading, and he borrows a term, ironically enough, from Elaine Showalter in order to suggest that "reading as a woman" is ultimately not a matter of any actual reader's gender: over and over again, Culler speaks of the need for the critic to adopt what Showalter has called the "hypothesis" of a woman reader in lieu of appealing to the experience of real readers.[32]

Then, showing how Culler accepts Freud's account in *Moses and Monotheism*, and hence speculates that a literary criticism bent on ascertaining the *legitimate* meanings of a text must be seen as "patriarchal," Modleski suggests that Culler is himself patriarchal "just at the point when he seems to be most feminist—when he arrogates to himself and to other male critics the ability to read as women by 'hypothesizing' women readers" (p. 133). A *feminist* criticism, she concludes, should reject "the *hypothesis* of a woman reader" and instead promote the "actual female reader."[33]

Paradoxically, as I point out in chapter 2 with regard to Foucault's stance on the issue of rape, some of the more subtle attempts to contain this trauma of gender are inscribed in the theoretical discourses that most explicitly aim to deconstruct the status quo in the Text of Western Culture: antihumanist philosophy and Derridean deconstruction itself, as refashioned in literary and textual studies in the Anglo-American academy. In her analysis of the notion of femininity in contemporary French philosophy, Rosi Braidotti sees that notion as central to its foremost preoccupations: the critique of rationality, the demystification of unified subjectivity (the individual as subject of knowledge), and the investigation of the complicity between knowledge and power. The radical critique of subjectivity, she argues, "has become focused on a number of questions concerning the role and the status of 'femininity' in the conceptual frame of philosophic discourse."[34] This interest appears to be "an extraordinary co-occurrence of phenomena: the rebirth of the women's movement, on the one hand, and the need to reexamine the foundations of rational discourse felt by the majority of European philosophers," on the other. Braidotti then goes on to discuss the various forms that femininity assumes in the work of Deleuze, Foucault, Lyotard, and Derrida, and, concurrently, the consistent refusal by each philosopher to identify femininity with real women. On the contrary, it is only by giving up the insistence on sexual specificity (gender) that women, in their eyes, would be the social group best qualified (because they

are oppressed by sexuality) to foster a radically "other" subject, de-centered
and de-sexualized.

So it is that, by displacing the question of gender onto an ahistorical,
purely textual figure of femininity (Derrida); or by shifting the sexual basis
of gender quite beyond sexual difference, onto a body of diffuse pleasures
(Foucault) and libidinally invested surfaces (Lyotard), or a body-site of
undifferentiated affectivity, and hence a subject freed from (self-)represen-
tation and the constraints of identity (Deleuze); and finally by displacing
the ideology, but also the reality—the historicity—of gender onto this
diffuse, decentered, or deconstructed (but certainly not female) subject—
so it is that, paradoxically again, these theories make their appeal to
women, naming the process of such displacing with the term *becoming
woman (devenir-femme)*.

In other words, only by denying sexual difference (and gender) as
components of subjectivity in real women, and hence by denying the
history of women's political oppression and resistance, as well as the epistemological contribution of feminism to the redefinition of subjectivity and
sociality, can the philosophers see in "women" the privileged repository of
"the future of mankind." That, Braidotti observes, "is nothing but the old
mental habit [of philosophers] of thinking the masculine as synonymous
with universal . . . the mental habit of translating women into metaphor"
(pp. 34–35). That this habit is older, and so harder to break than the
Cartesian subject, may account for the predominant disregard, when it is
not outright contempt, that male intellectuals have for feminist theorizing,
in spite of occasional gestures in the direction of "women's struggles" or the
granting of political status to the women's movement. That should not, and
does not, prevent feminist theorists from reading, rereading and rewriting
their works.

On the contrary, the need for feminist theory to continue its radical
critique of dominant discourses on gender, such as these are, even as they
attempt to do away with sexual difference altogether, is all the more
pressing since the word *postfeminism* has been spoken, and not in vain. This
kind of deconstruction of the subject is effectively a way to recontain
women in femininity (Woman) and to reposition female subjectivity *in* the
male subject, however that will be defined. Furthermore, it closes the door
in the face of the emergent social subject which these discourses are pur-
portedly seeking to address, a subject constituted across a multiplicity of
differences in discursive and material heterogeneity. Again, then, I rewrite:
*If the deconstruction of gender inevitably effects its (re)construction, the question is,
in which terms and in whose interest is the de-re-construction being effected?*

Returning now to the problem I tried to elucidate in discussing Jean

Kennard's essay, the difficulty we find in theorizing the construction of subjectivity in textuality is greatly increased, and the task proportionately more urgent, when the subjectivity in question is en-gendered in a relation to sexuality that is altogether unrepresentable in the terms of hegemonic discourses on sexuality. and gender. The problem, which is a problem for all feminist scholars and teachers, is one we face almost daily in our work, namely, that most of the available theories of reading, writing, sexuality, ideology, or any other cultural production are built on male narratives of gender, whether oedipal or anti-oedipal, bound by the heterosexual contract; narratives which persistently tend to re-produce themselves in feminist theories. They *tend to*, and will do so unless one constantly resists, suspicious of their drift. Which is why the critique of all discourses concerning gender, including those produced or promoted as feminist, continues to be as vital a part of feminism as is the ongoing effort to create new spaces of discourse, to rewrite cultural narratives, and to define the terms of another perspective—a view from "elsewhere."

For, if that view is nowhere to be seen, not given in a single text, not recognizable as a representation, it is not that we—feminists, women—have not yet succeeded in producing it. It is, rather, that what we have produced is not recognizable, precisely, as a representation. For that "elsewhere" is not some mythic distant past or some utopian future history: it is the elsewhere of discourse here and now, the blind spots, or the space-off, of its representations. I think of it as spaces in the margins of hegemonic discourses, social spaces carved in the interstices of institutions and in the chinks and cracks of the power-knowledge apparati. And it is there that the terms of a different construction of gender can be posed—terms that do have effect and take hold at the level of subjectivity and self-representation: in the micropolitical practices of daily life and daily resistances that afford both agency and sources of power or empowering investments; and in the cultural productions of women, feminists, which inscribe that movement in and out of ideology, that crossing back and forth of the boundaries—and of the limits—of sexual difference(s).

I want to be very clear about this movement back and forth across the boundaries of sexual difference. I do *not* mean a movement from one space to another beyond it, or outside: say, from the space of a representation, the image produced by representation in a discursive or visual field, to the space outside the representation, the space outside discourse, which would then be thought of as "real"; or, as Althusser would say, from the space of ideology to the space of scientific and real knowledge; or again, from the symbolic space constructed by the sex-gender system to a "reality" external to it. For, clearly, no social reality exists for a given society outside of its particular sex-gender system (the mutually exclusive and exhaustive categories of male and female). What I mean, instead, is a movement from the space represented by/in a representation, by/in a discourse, by/in a sex-gender system, to the space not represented yet implied (unseen) in them.

A while ago I used the expression "space-off," borrowed from film theory: the space not visible in the frame but inferable from what the frame makes visible. In classical and commercial cinema, the space-off is, in fact, erased, or, better, recontained and sealed into the image by the cinematic rules of narrativization (first among them, the shot/reverse-shot system). But avant-garde cinema has shown the space-off to exist concurrently and alongside the represented space, has made it visible by remarking its absence in the frame or in the succession of frames, and has shown it to include not only the camera (the point of articulation and perspective from which the image is constructed) but also the spectator (the point where the image is received, re-constructed, and re-produced in/as subjectivity).

Now, the movement in and out of gender as ideological representation, which I propose characterizes the subject of feminism, is a movement back and forth between the representation of gender (in its male-centered frame of reference) and what that representation leaves out or, more pointedly, makes unrepresentable. It is a movement between the (represented) discursive space of the positions made available by hegemonic discourses and the space-off, the elsewhere, of those discourses: those other spaces both discursive and social that exist, since feminist practices have (re)constructed them, in the margins (or "between the lines," or "against the grain") of hegemonic discourses and in the interstices of institutions, in counter-practices and new forms of community. These two kinds of spaces are neither in opposition to one another nor strung along a chain of signification, but they coexist concurrently and in contradiction. The movement between them, therefore, is not that of a dialectic, of integration, of a combinatory, or of *différance*, but is the tension of contradiction, multiplicity, and heteronomy.

If in the master narratives, cinematic and otherwise, the two kinds of spaces are reconciled and integrated, as man recontains woman in his (man)kind, his hom(m)osexuality, nevertheless the cultural productions and micropolitical practices of feminism have shown them to be separate and heteronomous spaces. Thus, to inhabit both kinds of spaces at once is to live the contradiction which, I have suggested, is the condition of feminism here and now: the tension of a twofold pull in contrary directions— the critical negativity of its theory, and the affirmative positivity of its politics—is both the historical condition of existence of feminism and its theoretical condition of possibility. The subject of feminism is en-gendered there. That is to say, elsewhere.

Notes

I wish to thank my students in the History of Consciousness seminar in "Topics in Feminist Theory: Technologies of Gender" for their comments and observations, and my colleague Hayden White for his careful reading of this essay, all of which helped me formulate more clearly some of the issues discussed here.

1. For further discussion of these terms, see Teresa de Lauretis, ed., *Feminist Studies/Critical Studies* (Bloomington: Indiana University Press, 1986), especially the essays by Sondra O'Neale and Mary Russo.

2. Michel Foucault, *The History of Sexuality, Vol. I: An Introduction*, trans. Robert Hurley (New York: Vintage Books, 1980), p. 127.

3. I need not detail other well-known exceptions in English usage, such as ships' and automobiles' and countries' being feminine. See Dale Spender, *Man Made Language* (London: Routledge & Kegan Paul, 1980), for a very useful survey of the issues raised in Anglo-American feminist sociolinguistic research. On the philosophical issue of gender in language, and especially its subversion in practices of writing by the strategic employ of personal pronouns, see Monique Wittig, "The Mark of Gender," *Feminist Issues* 5, no. 2 (Fall 1985): 3–12.

4. See Sherry B. Ortner and Harriet Whitehead, *Sexual Meanings: The Cultural Construction of Gender and Sexuality* (Cambridge: Cambridge University Press, 1981). The term *sex/gender system* was first used by Gayle Rubin, "The Traffic in Women: Notes toward a Political Economy of Sex," in *Toward an Anthropology of Women*, ed. Rayna Reiter (New York: Monthly Review Press, 1975), pp. 157–210.

5. Jane F. Collier and Michelle Z. Rosaldo, "Politics and Gender in Simple Societies," in Ortner and Whitehead, *Sexual Meanings*, p. 275. In the same volume, see also Sherry B. Ortner, "Gender and Sexuality in Hierarchical Societies," pp. 359–409.

6. Louis Althusser, "Ideology and Ideological State Apparatuses (Notes Towards an Investigation)," in *Lenin and Philosophy* (New York: Monthly Review Press, 1971), p. 165. Subsequent references to this work are included in the text.

7. Cf. *The Woman Question: Selections from the Writings of Karl Marx, Frederick Engels, V. I. Lenin, Joseph Stalin* (New York: International Publishers, 1951).

8. A clear exposition of the theoretical context of Althusser's subject in ideology can be found in Catherine Belsey, *Critical Practice* (London: Methuen, 1980), pp. 56–65. In Lacan's theory of the subject, 'the woman' is, of course, a fundamental category, but precisely as 'fantasy' or 'symptom' for the man, as Jacqueline Rose explains: "Woman is constructed as an absolute category (excluded and elevated at one and the same time), a category which seems to guarantee that unity on the side of the man. . . . The problem is that once the notion of 'woman' has been so relentlessly exposed as a fantasy, then any such question [the question of her own *jouissance*] becomes an almost impossible one to pose" (Jacques Lacan, *Feminine Sexuality*, ed. Juliet Mitchell and Jacqueline Rose [New York: W. W. Norton, 1982], pp. 47–51). On both Lacan's and Althusser's subjects together, see Stephen Heath, "The Turn of the Subject," *Cine-Tracts*, no. 8 (Summer-Fall 1979): 32–48.

9. Michèle Barrett, "Ideology and the Cultural Production of Gender," in *Feminist Criticism and Social Change*, ed. Judith Newton and Deborah Rosenfelt (New York: Methuen, 1985), p. 74.

10. Parveen Adams, "A Note on the Distinction between Sexual Division and Sexual Differences," *m/f*, no. 3 (1979): 52 [quoted in Barrett, p. 67].

11. Joan Kelly, *Women, History, and Theory* (Chicago: University of Chicago Press, 1984), p. 58. Subsequent references to this work are included in the text.

12. See, for example, Patricia Hill Collins, "The Emerging Theory and Pedagogy of Black Women's Studies," *Feminist Issues* 6, no. 1 (Spring 1986): 3–17; Angela Davis, *Women, Race, and Class* (New York: Random House, 1981); and Bell Hooks,

Ain't I a Woman: Black Women and Feminism (Boston: Long Haul Press, 1981).

13. Teresa de Lauretis, *Alice Doesn't: Feminism, Semiotics, Cinema* (Bloomington: Indiana University Press, 1984).

14. On the feminist critique of science, Evelyn Fox Keller, *Reflections on Gender and Science* (New Haven, Conn.: Yale University Press, 1985), states: "A feminist perspective on science confronts us with the task of examining the roots, the dynamics, and consequences of . . . what might be called the 'science-gender system'. It leads us to ask how ideologies of gender and science inform each other in their mutual construction, how the construction functions in our social arrangements, and how it affects men and women, science and nature" (p. 8). Moving from "the woman question" in science to survey the distinct epistemologies that inform the feminist critique of science, Sandra Harding, *The Science Question in Feminism* (Ithaca, N.Y.: Cornell University Press, 1986), raises some crucial theoretical questions regarding the relations "between knowing and being, between epistemology and metaphysics" and the alternatives "to the dominant epistemologies developed to justify science's modes of knowledge-seeking and ways of being in the world" (p. 24). "The feminist criticisms of science," she argues, "have produced an array of conceptual questions that threaten both our cultural identity as a democractic and socially progressive society and our core personal identities as gender-distinct individuals" (pp. 28–29). A further reference is appropriate in this context: Mary Ann Warren, *Gendercide* (Totowa, N.J.: Rowman & Allanheld, 1985), a study of the developing "technology of sex selection," as reviewed by Shelley Minden in *The Women's Review of Books*, February 1986, pp. 13–14.

15. *This Bridge Called My Back* was originally published by Persephone Press in 1981. It is now available in its second edition, reprinted by Kitchen Table: Women of Color Press (New York, 1983).

16. See, for example, Cheryl Clark, "Lesbianism: An Act of Resistance," and Mirtha Quintanales, "I Paid Very Hard for My Immigrant Ignorance," both in *This Bridge Called My Back;* Cherríe Moraga, "From a Long Line of Vendidas," and Sheila Radford-Hill, "Considering Feminism as a Model for Social Change," both in de Lauretis, *Feminist Studies/Critical Studies;* and Elly Bulkin, Minnie Bruce Pratt, and Barbara Smith, *Yours in Struggle: Three Feminist Perspectives on Anti-Semitism and Racism* (Brooklyn, N.Y.: Long Haul Press, 1984).

17. Foucault, *The History of Sexuality*, p. 116. The preceding paragraph also appears in another essay in this volume, "The Violence of Rhetoric," written prior to this essay, where I first considered the applicability of Foucault's notion of a technology of sex to the construction of gender. I wrote: "Illuminating as his work is to our understanding of the mechanics of power in social relations, its critical value is limited by his unconcern for what, after him, we might call the 'technology of gender'—the techniques and discursive strategies by which gender is constructed."

18. For example, Mary Poovey, " 'Scenes of an Indelicate Character': The Medical 'Treatment' of Victorian Women," *Representations*, no. 14 (Spring 1986): 137–68; and Mary Ann Doane, "Clinical Eyes: The Medical Discourse," a chapter in her book *The Desire to Desire: The "Woman's Film" of the 1940s* (Bloomington: Indiana University Press, 1987).

19. Although more detailed references to feminist work in film may be found in *Alice Doesn't*, I want to mention two fundamental critical texts, both published in 1975 (the year in which Foucault's *Surveiller et Punir* [Discipline and Punish] first appeared in France): Laura Mulvey, "Visual Pleasure and Narrative Cinema," *Screen* 16, no. 3 (August 1975): 6–18; and Stephen Heath, "Narrative Space," now in *Questions of Cinema* (Bloomington: Indiana University Press, 1981), pp. 19–75.

20. Teresa de Lauretis and Stephen Heath, eds., *The Cinematic Apparatus* (London: Macmillan, 1980).

21. In the single film text, but always by way of the entire apparatus, including cinematic genres, the "film industry," and the whole "history of the cinema-machine," as Stephen Heath has defined it ("The Cinematic Apparatus: Technology as Historical and Cultural Form," in de Lauretis and Heath, *The Cinematic Apparatus*, p. 7).

22. Lucy Bland, "The Domain of the Sexual: A Response," *Screen Education*, no. 39 (Summer 1981): 56. Subsequent references to this work are included in the text.

23. Julian Henriques, Wendy Hollway, Cathy Urwin, Couze Venn, and Valerie Walkerdine, *Changing the Subject: Psychology, social regulation and subjectivity* (London: Methuen, 1984). Subsequent references to this work are included in the text.

24. Monique Wittig, "The Straight Mind," *Feminist Issues*, no. 1 (Summer 1980): 106–107. Subsequent references to this work are included in the text.

25. It may also sound paradoxical to assert that theory is a social technology in view of the common belief that theory (and similarly science) is the opposite of technique, empirical know-how, "hands-on" expertise, practical or applied knowledge—in short, all that is associated with the term *technology*. But I trust that everything said so far in the essay absolves me from the burden of again defining what I mean by technology.

26. Kaja Silverman, *The Subject of Semiotics* (New York: Oxford University Press, 1983), p. 131. Subsequent references to this work are included in the text.

27. I find that I wrote the following, for example: "Narrative and cinema solicit women's consent and by a surplus of pleasure hope to seduce women into femininity" (*Alice Doesn't*, p. 10).

28. See Elaine Showalter, "Critical Cross-Dressing: Male Feminists and the Woman of the Year," *Raritan* 3, no. 2 (1983): 130–49; Gayatri Chakravorty Spivak, "Displacement and the Discourse of Woman," in *Displacement: Derrida and After*, ed. Mark Krupnick (Bloomington: Indiana University Press, 1983), pp. 169–95; Mary Russo, "Female Grotesques: Carnival and Theory," in de Lauretis, *Feminist Studies/Critical Studies*, pp. 213–229; and Alice Jardine et al., eds., *Men on Feminism* (New York: Methuen, 1987).

29. Elizabeth A. Flynn and Patrocinio P. Schweickart, eds., *Gender and Reading: Essays on Readers, Texts, and Contexts* (Baltimore: Johns Hopkins University Press, 1986), p. xviii. This passage in the introduction refers specifically to the essay by Judith Fetterley "Reading about Reading," pp. 147–64. Subsequent references to this volume are included in the text. The programmatic emphasis of that refusal is corroborated by the historical evidence that Sandra Gilbert and Susan Gubar bring to document "the reaction-formation of intensified misogyny with which male [modernist] writers greeted the entrance of women into the literary marketplace" since the end of the nineteenth century, in their essay "Sexual Linguistics: Gender, Language, Sexuality," *New Literary History* 16, no. 3 (Spring 1985): 524.

30. Showalter, "Critical Cross-Dressing," p. 131. However, as Gilbert and Gubar also point out, such a move is not unprecedented or necessarily disinterested. It may well be—and why not?—that the effort of European (male) writers since the Middle Ages to transform the *materna lingua*, or mother tongue (the vernacular), into a cultivated *patrius sermo*, or father speech (in Walter Ong's terms), as a more suitable instrument for art, has been an effort to cure what Gilbert and Gubar call "the male linguistic wound": "Mourning and waking a lost *patrius sermo*, male modernists and postmodernists transform the maternal vernacular into a new morning of patriarchy in which they can wake the old powers of the 'Allfather's' Word" (Gilbert and Gubar, "Sexual Linguistics," pp. 534–35).

31. Jean E. Kennard, "Ourselves behind Ourselves: A Theory for Lesbian Readers," in Flynn and Schweickart, *Gender and Reading*, p. 71. Here Kennard is quoting and readapting (by replacing the word *woman* with the word *lesbian*) from Jonathan

Culler, *On Deconstruction: Theory and Criticism after Structuralism* (Ithaca, N.Y.: Cornell University Press, 1982), pp. 49 and 50; on p. 50, Culler himself is quoting from Showalter.

32. Tania Modleski, "Feminism and the Power of Interpretation: Some Critical Readings," in de Lauretis, *Feminist Studies/Critical Studies*, p. 132. Subsequent references to this work are included in the text. See also, in the same volume, Nancy K. Miller, "Changing the Subject: Authorship, Writing, and the Reader," pp. 102–120.

33. Modleski's "actual female reader" seems to parallel Kennard's "individual lesbian readers." For example, and I quote from her conclusion, Kennard states: "Polar reading, then, is not a theory of lesbian reading, but a method particularly appropriate to lesbian readers" (p. 77). This sentence, however, is also put into question by the author's preoccupation, a few lines above, with satisfying all possible readers: "Polar reading permits the participation of any reader in any text and thus opens up the possibility of enjoying the widest range of literary experience." In the end, this reader remains confused.

34. Rosi Braidotti, "Modelli di dissonanza: donne e/in filosofia," in Patrizia Magli, ed., *Le donne e i segni* (Urbino: Il lavoro editoriale, 1985), p. 25. Although, as I understand, an English version of this paper is available, this and subsequent references included in the text are to the Italian version, in my translation.

2

THE VIOLENCE OF RHETORIC
Considerations on Representation and Gender

> Older women are more skeptical in their
> heart of hearts than any man; they believe
> in the superficiality of existence as in its
> essence, and all virtue and profundity is to
> them merely a way to cover up this "truth,"
> a very welcome veil over a *pudendum*—in
> other words, a matter of decency and
> shame, and nothing more!
> —FRIEDRICH NIETZSCHE, *The Gay Science*

> Even the healthiest woman runs a zigzag
> course between sexual and individual life,
> stunting herself now as a person, now as a
> woman.
> —LOU ANDREAS-SALOMÉ, *Zur Psychologie
> der Frau*

Woman's skepticism, Nietzsche suggests, comes from her disregard for truth. Truth does not concern her. Therefore, paradoxically, woman becomes the symbol of Truth, of that which constantly eludes man and must be won, which lures and resists, mocks and seduces, and will not be captured. This skepticism, this truth of nontruth, is the "affirmative woman" Nietzsche loved and was, Derrida suggests. It is the philosophical position Nietzsche himself occupies and speaks from—a position which Derrida locates in the terms of a rhetoric, "between the 'enigma of this solution' and the 'solution of this enigma'" (1976b, p. 51).[1] The place from where he speaks, the locus of his enunciation, is a constantly shifting place

Written in 1983–84 as a contribution to the special issue of *Semiotica* on "The Rhetoric of Violence" edited by Nancy Armstrong. First published in *Semiotica* 54, nos. 1–2 (1985), with the dedication "To Umberto Eco." Reprinted here with some changes in editorial style and format.

within discourse (philosophy), a rhetorical function and construct; and a construct which—call it *différance*, displacement, negativity, internal exclusion, or marginality—has become perhaps the foremost rhetorical trope of recent philosophical speculation. However, in speaking from that place, from the position of woman, Nietzsche need not "stunt" himself "now as a person, now as a woman," as his contemporary and sometime friend Lou Andreas-Salomé admittedly did.[2] The difference between them, if I may put it bluntly, is not *différance* but gender.

If Nietzsche and Derrida can occupy and speak from the position of woman, it is because that position is vacant and, what is more, cannot be claimed by women. To anticipate a point that will be elaborated later on, I simply want to suggest that while the question of woman for the male philosophers is a question of style (of discourse, language, writing—of philosophy), for Salomé, as in most present-day feminist thinking, it is a question of gender—of the social construction of "woman" and "man," and the semiotic production of subjectivity. And whereas both style and gender have much to do with rhetoric, the latter (as I use the term and will attempt to articulate it) has also much to do with history, practices, and the imbrication of meaning with experience; in other words, with the mutually constitutive effects in semiosis of what Peirce called the "outer world" of social reality and the "inner world" of subjectivity.

With that in mind, let me then step into the role of Nietzsche's older woman and cast my considerations on the semiotic production of gender between the rhetoric of violence and the violence of rhetoric.

The very notion of a "rhetoric of violence," from which this volume departs, presupposes that some order of language, some kind of discursive representation is at work not only in the concept "violence" but in the social practices of violence as well. The (semiotic) relation of the social to the discursive is thus posed from the start. But once that relation is instated, once a connection is assumed between violence and rhetoric, the two terms begin to slide, and, soon enough, the connection will appear to be reversible. From the Foucauldian notion of a rhetoric of violence, an order of language which speaks violence—names certain behaviors and events as violent, but not others, and constructs objects and subjects of violence, and hence violence as a social fact—it is easy to slide into the reverse notion of a language which, itself, produces violence. But if violence is in language, before if not regardless of its concrete occurrences in the world, then there is also a violence of rhetoric, or what Derrida has called "the violence of the letter" (1976a, pp. 101–140).

I will contend that both views of the relation between rhetoric and violence contain and indeed depend on the same representation of sexual difference, whether they assume the "fact" of gender or, like Derrida, deny it; and further, that the representation of violence is inseparable from the notion of gender, even when the latter is explicitly "deconstructed" or, more exactly, indicted as "ideology." I contend, in short, that violence is en-gendered in representation.

Violence En-gendered

In reviewing the current scholarship on family violence, Wini Breines and Linda Gordon begin by saying: "Only a few decades ago, the term 'family violence' would have had no meaning: child abuse, wife beating, and incest would have been understood but not recognized as serious social problems" (1983, p. 490). In particular, while child abuse had been "dis-covered" as far back as the 1870s, but later lost visibility, social science research on wife beating (more often called "spouse abuse" or "marital violence") is altogether recent; and incest, though long labeled a crime, was thought to be rare and, in any event, not related to (family) violence. In other words, the concept of a form of violence institutionally inherent—if not quite institutionalized—in the family, did not exist as long as the expression "family violence" did not.

Breines and Gordon, a sociologist and a historian, are keenly aware of the semiotic, discursive dimension of the social. Thus, they go on to argue, if the great majority of scholarly studies still come short of a coherent understanding of family violence as a social problem, the reason is that, with the exception of feminist writers, clinicians, and a few male empirical researchers, the work in this area fails to analyze the terms of its own inquiry, especially terms such as *family, power,* and *gender.* For, Breines and Gordon maintain, violence between intimates must be seen in the wider context of social power relations; and gender is absolutely central to the family. In fact, we may add, it is as necessary to the constitution of the family as it is itself, in turn, forcefully constructed and inevitably re-produced by the family. Moreover, they continue, institutions such as the medical and other "helping professions" (e.g., the police and the judiciary) are complicit, or at least congruent, with "the social construction of batter-ing." For example, a study (Stark, Flitcraft, and Frazier 1979) of how the emergency room of a city hospital treated women for injuries or symptoms while completely ignoring the causes, if the injuries resulted from batter-ing, shows how the institution of medicine "coerce[s] women who are appealing for help back into the situations and relationships that batter them. It shows a system taking women who were hit, and turning them into battered women" (1983, p. 519).

The similarity of this critical position with that of Michel Foucault, himself a social historian, is striking, though no reference is made to his works (among them, *Discipline and Punish* and *The History of Sexuality* would be quite germane). But what the similarity makes apparent and even more striking is the difference of the two positions; that difference being, again, gender—not only the notion of gender, which is pivotal to the argument of Breines and Gordon, and largely irrelevant to Foucault's, but also, I will dare say, the gender of the authors. For it is feminism, the historical practice of the women's movement and the discourses which have emerged from it—such as the collective speaking, confrontation, and reconceptualization of the female's experience of sexuality—that inform the epistemological perspective of Breines and Gordon. They refute the idea that all violence is of similar origin, whether that origin be located in the individual (deviance) or in an abstract, transhistorical notion of society ("a sick society"). And they counter the dominant representation of violence as a "breakdown in social order" by proposing instead that violence is the sign of "a power struggle for the *maintenance* of a certain kind of social order" (1983, p. 511). But which kind of social order is in question, to be maintained or to be dismantled, is just what is at stake in the discourse on family violence. It is also where Breines and Gordon differ from Foucault.

As they see it, both the intrafamily and the gender-neutral methodological perspectives on incest, for instance, which are often found combined, are motivated by the desire to explain away a reality too uncomfortable or threatening to nonfeminists. (In spite of the agreement among statistical studies that, in cases of incest as well as child sexual abuse, 92% of the victims are females and 97% of the assailants are males, "predictably enough, until very recently the clinical literature ignored this feature of incest, implying that, for example, mother-son incest was as prevalent as father-daughter incest" [1983, p. 523].) Such studies not only obscure the actual history of violence against women, but by disregarding the feminist critique of patriarchy, they effectively discourage analysis of family violence from a context of both societal and *male* supremacy. Following up on the insights provided by Breines and Gordon, one can see that this is undoubtedly the rhetorical function of gender-neutral expressions such as "spouse abuse" or "marital violence," which at once imply that both spouses may equally engage in battering the other, and subtly hint at the writer's or speaker's non-partisan stance of scientific and moral neutrality. Put another way, even as those studies purport to remain innocent of the ideology or of the rhetoric of violence, they cannot avoid and indeed purposefully engage in the violence of rhetoric.

Foucault, on his part, is well aware of the paradox. The social, as he envisions it, is a field of forces, a crisscrossing of practices and discourses involving relations of power. With regard to the latter, individuals, groups, or classes assume variable positions, exercising at once power and resistance in an interplay of non-egalitarian but mobile, changeable relations; for the very existence of power relations "depends on a multiplicity of points of resistance . . . present everywhere in the power network" (Foucault 1980, p. 94). Both power and resistance, then, operate concurrently in "the strategic field" which constitutes the social, and both traverse or spread across—rather than inhere in or belong to—institutions, social stratifications, and individual unities. However, it is power, not resistance or negativity, that is the positive condition of knowledge. Far from being an agency of repression, power is a productive force that weaves through the social body as a network of discourses and generates simultaneously forms of knowledge and forms of subjectivity, or what we call social subjects. Here, one would think, the rhetoric of power and the power of rhetoric are one and the same thing. Indeed, he writes,

> this history of sexuality, or rather this series of studies concerning the historical relationships of power and the discourse on sex is, I realize, a circular project in the sense that it involves two endeavors that refer back to one another. We shall try to rid ourselves of a juridical and negative representation of power, and cease to conceive of it in terms of law, prohibition, liberty, and sovereignty. But how then do we analyze what has occurred in recent history with regard to this thing—seemingly one of the most forbidden areas of our lives and bodies—that is sex? How, if not by way of prohibition and blockage, does power gain access to it? (1980, p. 90)

His answer posits the notion of a "technology" of sex, a set of "techniques for maximizing life" (1980, p. 123) developed and deployed by the bourgeoisie since the end of the eighteenth century in order to ensure its class survival and continued hegemony. Those techniques involved the elaboration of discourses (classification, measurements, evaluation, etc.) about four privileged "figures" or objects of knowledge: the sexualization of children and the female body, the control of procreation, and the psychiatrization of anomalous sexual behavior as perversion. These discourses—which were implemented through pedagogy, medicine, demography, and economics, were anchored or supported by the institutions of the state, and became especially focused on the family—served to disseminate and to "implant" those figures and modes of knowledge into each individual, family, and institution. This technology "made sex not only a secular concern but a concern of the state as well; to be more exact, sex became a matter that required the social body as a whole, and virtually all of its individuals, to place themselves under surveillance" (1980, p. 116).

Sexuality, then, is not a property of bodies or something originally existent in human beings, but the product of that technology. What we call sexuality, Foucault states, is "the set of effects produced in bodies, behaviors, and social relations" by the deployment of "a complex political technology" (1980, p. 127), which is to say, by the deployment of sexuality. The analysis is in fact circular, however attractive or fitting. Sexuality is produced discursively (institutionally) by power, and power is produced institutionally (discursively) by the deployment of sexuality. Such a representation, like Foucault's view of the social, leaves no event or phenomenon out of the reach of *its* discursive power; nothing escapes from the discourse of power, nothing exceeds the totalizing power of discourse. His conclusion, therefore, is at best paradoxical. "We must not think that by saying yes to sex, one says no to power. . . . The rallying point for the counterattack against the deployment of sexuality ought not to be sex-desire, but bodies and pleasures" (1980, p. 157)—as if bodies and pleasures existed apart from the discursive order, from language or representation. But then they would exist in a space which his theory precisely locates outside the social.

I have suggested elsewhere that there may be a discrepancy between Foucault's theory and radical politics (his interventions in issues of capital punishment, prison revolts, psychiatric clinics, judiciary scandals, etc.), a discrepancy which can be accounted for by a contradiction perhaps inescapable at this time in history: the twin and opposite pull exerted on any progressive or radical thinker by the positivity of political action, on one front, and the negativity of critical theory, on the other. The contradiction is most evident, for me, in the efforts to elaborate a feminist theory of culture, history, representation, or subjectivity. Since feminism begins at home, so to speak, as a collective reflection on practice, on experience, on the personal as political, and on the politics of subjectivity, a feminist theory exists as such only insofar as it refers and constantly comes back to these issues. The contradictory pressure toward affirmative political action (the "counterattack") and toward the theoretical negation of patriarchal culture and social relations is glaring, unavoidable, and probably even constitutive of the specificity of feminist thought. In Foucault, the effect of that discrepancy (if my hypothesis is correct) has prompted charges of "paradoxical conservatism."[3]

For example, his political stance on the issue of rape, in the context of the reform of criminal law in France, has been criticized by French feminists as more subtly pernicious than the traditional, "naturalist" ideology. Arguing for the decriminalization (and the desexualization) of rape, in a volume published in 1977 by the Change collective with the title *La folie encerclée*, Foucault proposed that rape should be treated as an act of violence like any other, an act of aggression rather than a sexual act. A similar position was also held by some American feminists (e.g., Brownmiller 1975), though with the opposite intent with regard to its juridical implications, and has been acutely criticized within American feminism: "Taking rape from the realm of 'the sexual,' placing it in the realm of 'the violent,' allows one to be against it without raising any questions about the extent to which the institution of heterosexuality has defined force as a normal part of [(hetero)sexual relations]" (MacKinnon 1979, p. 219). In the terms of Foucault's theoretical analysis, his proposal may be understood as an effort to counter the technology of sex by breaking the bond between sexuality and crime; an effort to enfranchise sexual behaviors from legal punishment, and so to render the sexual sphere free from intervention by the state. Such a form of "local resistance" on behalf of the men imprisoned on, or subject to, charges of rape, however, would paradoxically but practically work to increase and further to legitimate the *sexual* oppression of women. As Monique Plaza puts it, it is a matter of "our costs and their benefits." For what is rape if not a sexual practice, she asks, an act of *sexual* violence? While it may not be exclusively practiced on women, "rape is sexual essentially because it rests on the very social difference between the sexes. . . . It is *social sexing* which is latent in rape. If men rape women, it is precisely because they are women in a social sense"; and when a male is raped, he too is raped "as a woman" (Plaza 1980, p. 31).

This allows us to unravel the contradiction at the heart of Foucault's modest proposal, a contradiction which his analysis of sexuality does not serve to resolve: to speak against sexual penalization and repression, in our society, is to uphold the sexual oppression of women, or, better, to uphold the practices and institutions that produce "woman" in terms of the sexual, and then oppression in terms of gender. (Which, of course, is not to say that oppression is not also produced in other terms.) To release "bodies and pleasures" from the legal control of the state, and from the relations of power exercised through the technology of sex, is to affirm and perpetuate the present social relations which give men rights over women's bodies. To decriminalize rape is, as Plaza states—making full use of the rhetoric of violence in her political confrontation with Foucault—to "defend the rights of the rapists . . . from the position of potential rapist that you are 'subjected' to by your status as a man" (1980, p. 33). Here Plaza sharply identifies the problem in Foucault's own "enunciative modality" (defined in Foucault 1972); that is to say, the place or sociosexual position from which he speaks, that of the male or male-sexed subject. For sexuality, not only in the general and traditional discourse but in Foucault's as well, is construed not as gendered (as having a male form and a female form) but simply as male. Even when it is located, as it very often is, *in* the woman's body, sexuality is an attribute or property of the male. It is in this sense, in light of that "enunciative modality" common to all the accepted discourses in Western culture (but not only there), that Adrienne Rich's notion of "compulsory heterosexuality" acquires its profoundest resonance and productivity. And in this sense her argument is not at the margins of feminism, as she seems to fear, but quite central to it (Rich 1980).

The historical fact of gender, the fact that it exists in social reality, that it has concrete existence in cultural forms and actual weight in social relations, makes gender a political issue that cannot be evaded or wished away, much as one would want to, be one male or female. For even as we agree that sexuality is socially constructed and overdetermined, we cannot deny the particular specification of gender that is the issue of that process; nor can we deny that precisely such process finally positions women and men in an antagonistic and asymmetrical relation. The interests of men and women, or, in the case in question earlier, of rapists and their victims, are exactly opposed in the practices of social reality, and cannot be reconciled rhetorically. That is the blind spot in Foucault's radical politics and anti-humanist theory, both of which must and do appeal to feminists as valuable contributions to the critique of ideology (see, for example, Martin [1982] and Doane, Mellencamp, and Williams [1984]). Therefore, illuminating as his work is to our understanding of the mechanics of power in social relations, its critical value is limited by his unconcern for what, after him, we might call "the technology of gender"—the techniques and discursive strategies by which gender is constructed and hence, as I argue, violence is en-gendered.

But there may be another chestnut in the fire, another point at issue. To say that (A) the concept of "family violence" did not exist before the expression came into being, as I said earlier, is not the same as saying that (B) family violence did not exist before "family violence" became part of the discourse of social science. The enormously complex relation binding expression, content, and referent (or sign, meaning, and object) is what makes (A) and (B) not the same. It seems to me that of the three—the concept, the expression, and the violence—only the first two belong to Foucault's discursive order. The third is somewhere else, like "bodies and pleasures," outside the social. Now, for those of us whose bodies and whose pleasures are out there, where the violence is (in that we have no language, enunciative position, or power apparati to speak them), the risk of saying yes to sex-desire and power is relatively small, and amounts to a choice between the devil and the deep blue sea. If we then want to bring our bodies and our pleasures closer, where we might see what they are like; better still, where we might represent them from another perspective, construct them with another standard of measurement, or understand them within other terms of analysis; in short, if we want to attempt to know them, we have to leave Foucault and turn, for the time being, to Peirce.

For Peirce, the object has more weight, as it were. The real, the physical world and empirical reality are of greater consequence to the human activity of semiosis, as outlined by Charles Sanders Peirce, than they are to the symbolic activity of signification, as defined in Saussure's theory of language and reelaborated in contemporary French thought. Saussure's insistence on the arbitrary or unmotivated nature of the linguistic sign caused semiology to extend the categorical distinction between language (*langue*, the language system) and reality to all forms and processes of representation, and thus to posit an essential discontinuity between the orders of the symbolic and the real. Thereafter, not only would the consideration of the referent be no longer pertinent—or even possible—to the account of signification processes; but the different status of the signifier and the signified would be questioned. The signified would be seen as either inaccessible, separated from the signifier by the "bar" of repression (Lacan 1966, p. 497), or equally engaged in the "play of differences" that make up the system of signifiers and the domain of signification (Derrida 1976a, p. 7). The work of the sign, in brief, would have no reference and no purchase on the real. For Peirce, on the other hand, the "outer world" enters into semiosis at both ends of the signifying process: first through the object, more specifically the "dynamic object," and second through the final interpretant. That complicates the picture in which a signifier would immediately correspond to a signified (Saussure) or merely refer to another signifier (Lacan, Derrida). Take the famous definition:

> A sign, or representamen, is something which stands to somebody for something in some respect or capacity. It addresses somebody, that is, it creates in the mind of that person an equivalent sign, or perhaps a more developed sign. That sign which it creates I call the *interpretant* of the first sign. The sign stands for something, its *object*. It stands for that object, not in all respects, but in reference to a sort of idea, which I have sometimes called the *ground* of the representation. (Peirce 2.228)

As Umberto Eco observes in his brilliant essay "Peirce and the Semiotic Foundations of Openness" (1979, pp. 175–99), the notions of meaning, ground, and interpretant all pertain in some degree to the area of the signified, while interpretant and ground also pertain in some degree to the area of the referent (object). Moreover, Peirce distinguishes between the dynamic object and the immediate object, and it is the notion of ground that sustains the distinction. The dynamic object is external to the sign: it is that which "by some means contrives to determine the sign to its representation" (4.536). The immediate object, instead, is internal; it is an "Idea" or a "mental representation," "the object as the sign itself represents it" (4.536).

From the analysis of the notion of "ground" (a sort of context of the sign, which makes pertinent certain attributes or aspects of the object and thus is already a component of meaning), Eco argues that not only does the sign in Peirce appear as a textual matrix; the object, too, "is not necessarily a thing or a state of the world but a rule, a law, a prescription: it appears as the operational description of a set of possible experiences" (1979, p. 181).

> Signs have a direct connection with Dynamic Objects only insofar as objects determine the formation of a sign; on the other hand, signs only "know" Immediate Objects, that is, meanings. There is a difference between the *object of which a sign is a sign* and the *object of a sign:* the former is the Dynamic Object, a state of the outer world; the latter is a semiotic construction. (Eco 1979, p. 193).

But the immediate object's relation to the representamen is established by the interpretant, which is itself another sign, "perhaps a more developed sign." Thus, in the process of unlimited semiosis, the nexus object-sign-meaning is a series of ongoing mediations between "outer world" and "inner" or mental representations. The key term, the principle that supports the series of mediations, is of course the interpretant.

As Peirce sees it, "the problem of what the 'meaning' of an intellectual concept is can only be solved by the study of the interpretants, or proper significate effects, of signs" (5.475). He then describes three general classes.

(1) "The first proper significate effect of a sign is a *feeling* produced by it." This is the *emotional* interpretant. Although its "foundation of truth" may be slight at times, often it remains the only effect produced by a sign, such as, for example, the performance of a piece of music.

(2) When a further significate effect is produced, however, it is "through the mediation of the emotional interpretant"; and this second type of meaning effect he calls the *energetic* interpretant, for it involves an "effort," which may be a muscular exertion but is more usually a mental effort, "an exertion upon the Inner World."

(3) The third and final type of meaning effect that may be produced by the sign, through the mediation of the former two, is "a *habit-change*": "a modification of a person's tendencies toward action, resulting from previous experiences or from previous exertions." This is the "ultimate" interpretant of the sign, the effect of meaning on which the process of semiosis, in the instance considered, comes to rest. "The real and living logical conclusion *is* that habit," Peirce states, and designates the third type of significate effect, the *logical* interpretant. But immediately he adds a qualification, distinguishing this logical interpretant from the concept or "intellectual" sign:

> The concept which is a logical interpretant is only imperfectly so. It some-what partakes of the nature of a verbal definition, and is as inferior to the

habit, and much in the same way, as a verbal definition is inferior to the real definition. The deliberately formed, self-analyzing habit—self-analyzing because formed by the aid of analysis of the exercises that nourished it—is the living definition, the veritable and final logical interpretant. (5.491)

The final interpretant, then, is not "logical" in the sense in which a syllogism is logical, or because it is the result of an "intellectual" operation such as deductive reasoning. It is logical in that it is "self-analyzing," or, we might say, in that it makes sense of the emotion and muscular/mental effort which preceded it by providing a conceptual representation of that effort. Such a representation is implicit in the notion of habit as a "tendency toward action" and in the solidarity of habit and belief (5.538)

Peirce's formulation of the ultimate interpretant maps another path or a way back from semiosis to reality. For Eco, it provides the "missing link" between signification and concrete action. The final interpretant, he states, is not a Platonic essence or a transcendental law of signification but a result, as well as a rule: "To have understood the sign as a rule through the series of its interpretants means to have acquired the habit to act according to the prescription given by the sign. . . . The action is the place in which the *haecceitas* ends the game of semiosis" (1979, pp. 194–95). But we should go further in our reading of Peirce, and so enter into a territory where Eco fears to tread, the terrain of subjectivity.

When Peirce speaks of habit as the result of a process involving emotion, muscular and mental exertion, and some kind of conceptual representation (the "final logical interpretant"), he is thinking of individual persons as the subject of such process. If the modification of consciousness, the habit or habit-change, is indeed the meaning effect, the "real and living" conclusion of each single process of semiosis, then where "the game of semiosis" ends, time and time again, is not exactly "concrete action," as Eco sees it, but a person's (subjective) disposition, a readiness (to action), a set of expectations. For the chain of meaning comes to a halt, however temporarily, by anchoring itself to somebody, to some body, an individual subject.[4] Thus, as we use signs or produce interpretants, their significate effects must pass through each of us, each body and each consciousness, before they may produce an effect or an action upon the world. Finally, then, the individual's habit as a semiotic production is both the result and the condition of the social production of meaning.

Clearly, this reading of Peirce points toward a possible elaboration of semiotics as a theory of culture that hinges on a historical, materialist, *and* gendered subject—a project that cannot be pursued here. What I wish to stress, for the sake of the present discussion, is the sense of a certain weight of the object in semiosis, an overdetermination wrought into the work of the sign by the real, or what we take as reality, even if it is itself already an

interpretant; and hence the sense that experience (habit), however mis-
recognized or misconstrued, is indissociable from meaning; and therefore
that practices—events and behaviors occurring in social formations—weigh
in the constitution of subjectivity as much as does language. In that sense,
too, violence is not simply "in" language or "in" representation, but it also
thereby en-gendered.

Violence and Representation

When one first surveys the representations of violence in general terms,
there seem to be two kinds of violence with respect to its object: male and
female. I do not mean that the "victims" of such kinds of violence are men
and women, but rather that the object on which or to which the violence is
done is what establishes the meaning of the represented act; and that object
is perceived or apprehended as either feminine or masculine. An obvious
example of the first instance is "nature," as in the expression "the rape of
nature," which at once defines nature as feminine, and rape as violence
done to a feminine other (whether its physical object be a woman, a man, or
an inanimate object). Speculating on the particular rhetoric of violence that
permeates the discourse in which scientists describe their encounter with
the unknown, Evelyn Fox Keller finds a recurrent thematics of conquest,
domination, and aggression reflecting a "basic adversarial relation to the
object of study."

> Problems, for many scientists, are things to be 'attacked,' 'licked' or 'con-
> quered.' If more subtle means fail, then one resorts to 'brute force,' to the
> 'hammer and tongs' approach. In the effort to 'master' nature, to 'storm her
> strongholds and castles,' science can come to sound like a battlefield. Some-
> times, such imagery becomes quite extreme, exceeding even the conventional
> imagery of war. Note, for example, the language in which one scientist
> describes his pursuit: 'I liked to follow the workings of another mind
> through these minute, teasing investigations to see a relentless observer get
> hold of Nature and squeeze her until the sweat broke out all over her and her
> sphincters loosened' (Keller 1983, p. 20).

The "genderization of science," as Keller calls the association of scientific
thought with masculinity and of the scientific domain with femininity, is a
pervasive metaphor in the discourse of science, from Bacon's prescription
of "a chaste and lawful marriage between Mind and Nature" to Bohr's
chosen emblem, the yin-yang symbol, for his coat of arms (Keller 1978,
pp. 413 and 432). It is a compelling representation, whose effects for the
ideology and the practice of science, as well as for the subjectivity of
individual scientists, are all the more forceful since the representation is

treated as a myth; that is to say, while the genderization of science is admitted and encouraged in the realm of common knowledge, it is simultaneously denied entry or currency in the realm of formal knowledge (Keller 1978, p. 410). Such is the case not only in the "hard" sciences, so-called, but also more often than not in the "softer" disciplines and even, ironically enough, in the study of myth.

The other kind of violence is that which in *Violence and the Sacred* René Girard has aptly called "violent reciprocity," the acting out of "rivalry" between brothers or between father and son, and which is socially held in check by the institution of kinship, ritual, and other forms of mimetic violence (war and sport come immediately to mind). The distinctive trait here is the "reciprocity" and thus, by implication, the equality of the two terms of the violent exchange, the "subject" and the "object" engaged in the rivalry; and consequently the masculinity attributed, in this particular case, to the object. For the subject of the violence is always, by definition, masculine; "man" is by definition the subject of culture and of any social act.[5]

In the mythical text, for example, according to Lotman's theory of plot typology, there are only two characters, the hero and the obstacle or boundary. The first is the mythical subject, who moves through the plot-space establishing differences and norms. The second is but a function of that space, a marker of boundary, and therefore inanimate even when anthropomorphized.

> Characters can be divided into those who are mobile, who enjoy freedom with regard to plot-space, who can change their place in the structure of the artistic world and cross the frontier, the basic topological feature of this space, and those who are immobile, who represent, in fact, a function of this space. Looked at typologically, the initial situation is that a certain plot-space is divided by a *single* boundary into an internal and an external sphere, and a *single* character has the opportunity to cross that boundary. . . . Inasmuch as closed space can be interpreted as 'a cave', 'the grave', 'a house', 'woman' (and, correspondingly, be allotted the features of darkness, warmth, dampness), entry into it is interpreted on various levels as 'death', 'conception', 'return home' and so on; moreover all these acts are thought of as mutually identical. (Lotman 1979, pp. 167–68)

In the mythical text, then, the hero must be male regardless of the gender of the character, because the obstacle, whatever its personification (sphinx or dragon, sorceress or villain), is morphologically female—and indeed, simply, the womb, the earth, the space of his movement. As he crosses the boundary and "penetrates" the other space, the mythical subject is constructed as human being and as male; he is the active principle of culture, the establisher of distinction, the creator of differences. Female is what is not susceptible to transformation, to life or death; she (it) is an element of plot-space, a topos, a resistance, matrix and matter.

Narrative cinema, too, performs a similar inscription of gender in its visual figuration of the masculine and the feminine positions. The woman, fixed in the position of icon, spectacle, or image to be looked at, bears the mobile look of both the spectator and the male character(s). It is the latter who commands at once the action and the landscape, and who occupies the position of subject of vision, which he relays to the spectator. As Laura Mulvey shows in her analysis of the complex relations of narrative and visual pleasure, "sadism demands a story" (1975, p. 14). Thus, if Oedipus has become a paradigm of human life and error, narrative temporality and dramatic structure, one may be entitled to wonder whether that is purely due to the artistry of Sophocles or the widespread influence of Freud's theory of human psychic development in our culture; or whether it might not also be due to the fact that, like the best of stories and better than most, the story of Oedipus weaves the inscription of violence (and family violence, at that) into the representation of gender.

I will now turn to two celebrated critical texts, which exemplify two discursive strategies deployed in the construction of gender and two distinctive rhetorical configurations of violence. The first is Lévi-Strauss's reading, in "The Effectiveness of Symbols" (Lévi-Strauss 1967), of a Cuna incantation performed to facilitate difficult childbirth; a reading which prompts him to make a daring parallel between shamanistic practices and psychoanalysis, and allows him to elaborate his crucial notion of the unconscious as symbolic function. The shaman's cure consists, he states, "in making explicit a situation originally existing on the emotional level and in rendering acceptable to the mind pains which the body refuses to tolerate" by provoking an experience "through symbols, that is, through meaningful equivalents of things meant which belong to a another order of reality" (1967, pp. 192 and 196). Whereas the arbitrary pains are alien and unacceptable to the woman, the supernatural monsters evoked by the shaman in his symbolic narrative are part of a coherent system on which the native conception of the universe is founded. By calling upon the myth, the shaman reintegrates the pains within a conceptual and meaningful whole, and "provides the sick [sic] woman with a *language*, by means of which unexpressed, and otherwise inexpressible, psychic states can be immediately expressed" (1967, p. 193). Both the shaman's cure and psychoanalytic therapy, argues Lévi-Strauss, albeit with an inversion of all the elements, are done by means of a manipulation carried out through symbols which constitute a meaningful code, a language.

Let us consider now the structure of the myth in question and the performative value of the shaman's narrative. For, after all, the incantation is a ritual, though based on myth. It has, that is, a practical purpose: it seeks to effect a physical, somatic transformation in its addressee. The main actors are the shaman, performing the incantation, and the woman in labor whose body is to undergo the transformation, to become actively engaged in expelling the full-grown fetus and bringing forth the child. In the myth which subtends the incantation, one would think, the hero must be a woman or at least a female spirit, goddess, or totemic ancestor. But it is not so. Not only is the hero a male, personified by the shaman, as are his helpers, also symbolized with decidedly phallic attributes; and not only is the incantation intended to effect the childbearing woman's identification with the male hero in his struggle with the villain (a *female* deity who has taken possession of the woman's body and soul). But, more important, the incantation aims at detaching the woman's identification or perception of self from her own body. It seeks to sever her identification with a body which she must come to perceive precisely as a space, the territory in which the battle is waged. The hero's victory then results in his recapturing the woman's soul, and his descent through the landscape of her body symbolizes the (now) unimpeded descent of the fetus along the birth canal.

The effectiveness of symbols, the work of the symbolic function in the unconscious, would thus effect a splitting of the female subject's identification into the two mythical positions of hero (the human subject) and boundary (spatially fixed object or personified obstacle—her body). The doubt that the apprehension of one's body or oneself as obstacle, landscape, or battlefield may not "provide the . . . woman with a language" does not cross the text. But whether or not this construct would "make sense" to the Cuna woman for whose benefit the ritual is presumably performed, Lévi-Strauss's interpretation must be acceptable in principle to Lotman, Girard, and any others who look on the history of the human race from the anthropological perspective and within an epistemology wherein "biological" sexual difference is the ground (in Peirce's term) of gender. In that perspective, woman remains outside of history. She is Mother and Nature, matrix and matter, "an equivalent more universal than money," as Lea Melandri accurately phrased it (1977, p. 27). The discourse of the sciences of man constructs the object as female and the female as object. That, I suggest, is its rhetoric of violence, even when the discourse presents itself as humanistic, benevolent, or well-intentioned.

Indeed, Derrida criticizes Lévi-Strauss's paternalistic attitude toward his objects of study (the Nambikwara), as well as the naiveté by which he regards them as an "innocent" people because they have no written language. In such a community, described in the autobiographical *Tristes Tropiques*, violence would be introduced by Western civilization, and actually erupts as the anthropologist (Lévi-Strauss himself, who recounts the event) teaches a group of children how to write. The "revenge" of one little girl, struck by another during the "Writing Lesson," consists in revealing to the anthropologist the "secret" of the other girl's proper name, which the Nambikwara are not allowed to use. What is ingenuous, for Derrida, is Lévi-Strauss's ostensible belief that writing is merely the phonetic notation of speech, and that violence is an effect of written language (civilization) rather than of language as such; for "all societies capable of producing, that is to say of obliterating, their proper names, and of bringing classificatory difference into play, practice writing in general" (Derrida 1976a, p. 109).

> To name, to give names that it will on occasion be forbidden to pronounce, such is the originary violence of language which consists in inscribing within a difference, in classifying, in suspending the vocative absolute. To think the unique *within* the system, to inscribe it there, such is the gesture of the arche-writing: arche-violence, loss of the proper, of absolute proximity, of self-presence. . . . Out of this arche-violence, forbidden and therefore confirmed by a second violence that is reparatory, protective, instituting the 'moral,' prescribing the concealment of writing and the effacement and obliteration of the so-called proper name which was already dividing the proper, a third violence can *possibly* emerge or not (an empirical possibility) within what is commonly called evil, war, indiscretion, rape; which consists of revealing by effraction the so-called proper name, the originary violence which has severed the proper from its property and its self-sameness [*propété*]. (1976a, p. 112).

Empirical or common violence (and we cannot help remarking the text's own classificatory play in the listing of signifiers: evil, war, indiscretion, rape) is "more complex" than the other two levels to which it refers, namely, arche-violence and law. Unfortunately for us, however, Derrida is not concerned to analyze it or to suggest why, how, or when it may possibly emerge. He only implies that the emergence of empirical violence, the fact of violence in society, is no accident, though Lévi-Strauss would need to see it as an accident in order to maintain his belief in the natural innocence and goodness of the primitive culture. From Rousseau and the eighteenth century, Derrida concludes, Lévi-Strauss has inherited an archaeology which "is also a teleology and an eschatology": "The dream of a full and immediate presence closing history [suppresses] contradiction and difference" (1976a, p. 115).

The rhetorical construct of a "violence of the letter," the originary violence which preempts presence, identity, and property or propriety, is perhaps more accessible in another of Derrida's own works, *Spurs*, where he performs a reading of Nietzsche and, with him, addresses just what he claimed that Lévi-Strauss suppressed—contradiction and difference. This could be my second textual *exemplum*, whereby to illustrate what I earlier called the violence of rhetoric. It would support my contention that, while Derrida's discourse denies the fact of gender, its "becoming woman" depends on the same construct of sexual difference precisely if naively and traditionally articulated by Lévi-Strauss (1969).

Were I to do so, however, I would earn Derrida's contempt for "those women feminists so derided by Nietzsche," I would put myself in the position of one "who aspires to be like a man," who "seeks to castrate" and "wants a castrated woman" (Derrida 1976b, p. 53). I shall not do so, therefore. Decency and shame prevent me, though nothing more. I shall instead approach Derrida's text obliquely—a gesture the philosopher may not find displeasing—by way of another's reading, or a quadruple displacement, if you will.

"The discourse of man," writes Gayatri Spivak, "is in the metaphor of woman" (1983, p. 169). The problem with phallocentrism "is not merely one of psycho-socio-sexual behavior [as, we recall, Foucault would have it] but of the production and consolidation of reference and meaning" (1983, p. 169). Derrida's critique of phallocentrism—deconstruction—takes the woman as "model" for the deconstructive discourse. It takes the woman as model because, as Spivak reads (Derrida reading) Nietzsche, the woman can fake an orgasm, while the man cannot:

> Women impersonate themselves as having an orgasm even at the time of orgasm. Within the historical understanding of women as incapable of orgasm, Nietzsche is arguing that impersonating is woman's only sexual pleasure. (Spivak 1983, p. 170)

Thus, in what appears to me as a case of inscribing gender with a vengeance, Derrida searches for the name of the mother in *Glas;* elsewhere, he uses the "name of woman" to question the "we-men" of the philosophers (1983, p. 173); and *Dissemination* takes the hymen as figure for the text, the undecidability of meaning, the "law of the textual operation—of reading, writing, philosophizing" (1983, p. 175).

Deconstruction thus effects "a feminization of the practice of philosophy," Spivak observes (with a phrase that reminds me immediately of Keller's "genderization of science"), adding that she does not regard it as "just another example of the masculine use of woman as instrument of self-assertion" (1983, p. 173). For if man can never "fully disown his status as subject," and if desire must still "be expressed as man's desire," yet the deconstructor's enterprise—seeking his own displacement "by taking the woman as object or figure"—is an "unusual and courageous" one. Regretfully, one must infer, Spivak is led to admit that the question of woman, asked in the way Nietzsche and Derrida ask it, "is *their* question, not *ours*" (1983, p. 184). Then she suggests, "with respect," that such a feminization

of philosophy as serves the male deconstructor "might find its most adequate legend in male homosexuality defined as criminality, and that it
cannot speak for the woman" (1983, p. 177). One can only conclude that,
insofar as the "deconstructor" is a woman, the value of that critical practice
("the 'patriarchy's' own self-critique") is at best ambiguous. We can produce,
as Spivak recommends, "useful and scrupulous fake readings in the place
of the passively active fake orgasm" (1983, p. 186), but we will not have
come at all closer to understanding, representing, or reconstructing our
bodies and our pleasures otherwise.

For the female subject, finally, gender marks the limit of deconstruction,
the rocky bed (so to speak) of the "abyss of meaning." Which is not to say
that woman, femininity, or femaleness is any more or any less outside
discourse than anything else is. This is precisely the insistent emphasis of
feminist criticism: gender must be accounted for. It must be understood
not as a "biological" difference that lies before or beyond signification, or as
a culturally constructed object of masculine desire, but as semiotic difference—a different production of reference and meaning such as, not
Derrida and not Foucault, but possibly Peirce's notion of semiosis may allow
us to begin to chart. Clearly, the time of "replacing feminist criticism"
(Kamuf 1982) has not come.

Notes

1. In Barbara Harlow's translation of *Spurs,* the quotations from Nietzsche incorporated in Derrida's text are given in the words of the English translation by
Thomas Common (*Joyful Wisdom* [New York: Frederick Ungar, 1960]). I have
preferred to use Walter Kaufmann's translation in *The Gay Science* (1974), both
below and, somewhat modified, in my epigraph above, which is from paragraph 64.
In the passage cited by Derrida from *Die fröhliche Wissenschaft* (paragraph 71, "On
female chastity"), Nietzsche is speaking of the contradiction which upper-class
women, reared in total ignorance of sexuality, must encounter at the moment of
marriage. From their supposed ignorance of sex, Nietzsche mockingly laments,
women are "hurled, as by a gruesome lightning bolt, into reality and knowledge, by
marriage—precisely by the man they love and esteem most! To catch love and
shame in a contradiction and to be forced to experience at the same time delight,
surrender, duty, pity, terror, and who knows what else, in the face of the unexpected neighborliness of god and beast! . . . Even the compassionate curiosity of the
wisest student of humanity is inadequate for guessing how this or that woman
manages to accommodate herself to *this solution of the riddle,* and to *the riddle of a
solution,* and what dreadful, far-reaching suspicions must stir in her poor, unhinged
soul—and how the ultimate philosophy and skepsis of woman casts anchor at this
point!" I have italicized the phrases which Derrida takes out of context and recasts
in the frame of his interpretation of Nietzsche. As will be discussed later, Derrida
reads in Nietzsche a progressive valorization of woman as a self-affirming power, "a
dissimulatress, an artist, a dionysiac"; and this is the "affirmative woman" that
Derrida takes as his model for "writing," for the critical operation of questioning,
doubting, or "deconstructing" all truths.

2. For an interesting discussion of Salomé's writing, figure, and historiographical "legend" from the perspective of present-day feminism, see Martin (1982). The quotation from Salomé's *Zur Psychologie der Frau*, which appears at the beginning of this essay, is cited in Martin (1982, p. 29).

3. "Paradoxical conservatism," I have argued, "is a very appropriate phrase for a major theoretician of social history who writes of power and resistance, bodies and pleasures and sexuality as if the ideological structures and effects of patriarchy had nothing to do with history, as if they had no discursive status or political implications. The rape and sexual extortion performed on little girls by young and adult males is a 'bit of theatre,' a petty 'everyday occurrence in the life of village sexuality,' purely 'inconsequential bucolic pleasures' [Foucault 1980, pp. 31–32]. What really matters to the historian is the power of institutions, the mechanisms by which these bits of theatre become, he claims, pleasurable for the individuals involved—the men *and* the women, former little girls—who thus become complicit with those institutional apparati" (de Lauretis 1984, p. 94). This passage, which I take the liberty of reprinting here, occurs in the context of my analysis of a film, Nicolas Roeg's *Bad Timing: A Sensual Obsession* (1980), in light of some of Foucault's ideas. The film is an interesting study of "marital violence," and an excellent visual-narrative text for a discussion of violence, representation, and gender.

4. My reading of Peirce's definition of the sign, and thus of the relationship of sign and subject, bears a comparison with Lacan's ostensibly antithetical formula ("a signifier represents a subject for another signifier"). I must again refer interested readers to chapter 6 of my book (1984) *Semiotics and Experience*, where a fuller discussion of Eco is also to be found.

5. Studies in language usage demonstrate that, if the term *man* includes women (while the obverse is not true, for the term *woman* is always gendered, i.e., sexually connoted), it is only to the extent that, in the given context, women are (to be) perceived as nongendered "human beings," and thus as man [see Spender (1980)]. For example, Lévi-Strauss's theory of kinship (1969) is based on the thesis that women are both like men and unlike men: they are human beings (like men), but their special function in culture and society is to be exchanged and circulated among men (unlike men). Because of their "value" as means of sexual gratification and reproduction, women are the means—objects and signs—of social communication (among human beings). Nevertheless, as he is unwilling to exclude women from humanity or "mankind," he compromises by saying that women are also human beings, although in the symbolic order of culture they do not speak, desire, or produce meaning *for themselves,* as men do, by means of the exchange of women. One can only conclude that, insofar as women are human beings, they are (like) men.

References

Andreas-Salomé, Lou (1978). *Zur Psychologie der Frau*, ed. Gisela Brinker-Gabler. Frankfurt am Main: Fischer Taschenbuch Verlag.

Breines, Wini and Linda Gordon (1983). "The New Scholarship on Family Violence." *Signs: A Journal of Women in Culture and Society* 8, no. 3: 490–531.

Brownmiller, Susan (1975). *Against Our Will: Men, Women, and Rape.* New York: Simon & Schuster.

Change (1977). *La folie encerclée.* Paris: Seghers/Laffont.

de Lauretis, Teresa (1984). *Alice Doesn't: Feminism, Semiotics, Cinema.* Bloomington: Indiana University Press.

50 Technologies of Gender

Derrida, Jacques (1976a). *Of Grammatology*, trans. Gayatri Chakravorty Spivak. Baltimore and London: Johns Hopkins University Press.

———. (1976b). *Éperons: Les styles de Nietzsche*. Venice: Corbo e Fiore. [This is a four-language edition; the English translation is by Barbara Harlow.]

Doane, Mary Ann, Patricia Mellencamp, and Linda Williams, eds., (1984). *Re-vision: Essays in Feminist Film Criticism*. Frederick, Md.: University Publications of America and the American Film Institute.

Eco, Umberto (1979). *The Role of the Reader: Explorations in the Semiotics of Texts*. Bloomington and London: Indiana University Press.

Foucault, Michel (1972). *The Archaeolology of Knowledge*, trans. A. M. Sheridan Smith. London.

———. (1980). *The History of Sexuality, Vol. I: An Introduction*, trans. Robert Hurley. New York: Vintage Books.

Girard, René (1977). *Violence and the Sacred*, trans. Patrick Gregory. Baltimore and London: Johns Hopkins University Press.

Kamuf, Peggy (1982). "Replacing Feminist Criticism." *Diacritics* 12: 42–47.

Keller, Evelyn Fox (1978). "Gender and Science." *Psychoanalysis and Contemporary Thought* (September): 409–433.

———. (1983). "Feminism as an Analytic Tool for the Study of Science." *Academe* (September–October): 15–21.

Lacan, Jacques (1966). *Écrits*. Paris: Éditions du Seuil.

Lévi-Strauss, Claude (1961). *Tristes Tropiques*, trans. John Russell. New York.

———. (1967). *Structural Anthropology*, trans. Claire Jacobson and Brooke Grundfest Schoept. Garden City, N.Y.: Anchor Books.

———. (1969). *The Elementary Structures of Kinship*, trans. James Harle Bell, John Richard von Sturmer, and Rodney Needham. Boston: Beacon Press.

Lotman, Jurij (1979). "The Origin of Plot in the Light of Typology," trans. Julian Graffy. *Poetics Today* 1, nos. 1–2: 161–84.

MacKinnon, Catharine (1979). *Sexual Harassment of Working Women: A Case of Sex Discrimination*. New Haven, Conn.: Yale University Press.

Martin, Biddy (1982). "Feminism, Criticism, and Foucault." *New German Critique*, no. 27: 3–30.

Melandri, Lea (1977). *L'infamia originaria*. Milan: Edizioni L'Erba Voglio.

Mulvey, Laura (1975). "Visual Pleasure and Narrative Cinema." *Screen* 16, no. 3: 6–18.

Nietzsche, Friedrich (1974). *The Gay Science*, trans. Walter Kaufmann. New York: Vintage Books.

Peirce, Charles Sanders (1931–1958). *Collected Papers*, vols. 1–8. Cambridge, Mass.: Harvard University Press. [Cited in the text by volume number followed by paragraph number.]

Plaza, Monique (1980). "Our Costs and Their Benefits," trans. Wendy Harrison. *m/f*, no 4: 28–39. [Originally in *Questions féministes*, no. 3 (May 1978).]

Rich, Adrienne (1980). "Compulsory Heterosexuality and Lesbian Existence." *Signs: A Journal of Women in Culture and Society* 5, no. 4: 631–60.

Spender, Dale (1980). *Man Made Language*. London: Routledge & Kegan Paul.

Spivak, Gayatri Chakravorty (1983). "Displacement and the Discourse of Woman." In *Displacement: Derrida and After*, ed. Mark Krupnick, pp. 169–95. Bloomington: Indiana University Press.

Stark, Evan, Anne Flitcraft, and William Frazier (1979). "Medicine and Patriarchal Violence: The Social Construction of a 'Private' Event." *International Journal of Health Services* 9, no. 3: 461–93.

3

GAUDY ROSE
Eco and Narcissism

Scene i. The Balcony

What's in a name? asks Juliet, who is a woman and knows the tide, the ebb and flow, the pull of the real. Eco answers her question simply, yet implicating the whole of philosophy and the vicissitudes of Western epistemology: everything and nothing. *Stat rosa pristina nomine. Nomina nuda tenemus.*[1] But Juliet's, of course, was a rhetorical question, and Eco's answer is not what she wants. We leave Juliet at the balcony unfulfilled, as she must be, and go on to scene two.

Scene ii. The Garden

Imagine now Adam and Eve in the garden of Eden, naked, without guilt and (naturally, you might think) without language. But no, these Adam and Eve do have a kind of language, a rudimentary code made up of two sounds which combine to form a restricted set of signifiers and their corresponding semantic units or signifieds. The sounds are A and B, and with them Adam and Eve express their appreciation of the lush nature that surrounds them. Theirs is a happy life, unmarred by conflict or uncertainty, a world of simple, lasting values. Things are either edible or inedible, good or bad, beautiful or ugly, red or blue. But one day God speaks, and he says:

Written in various versions, English and Italian, between 1983 and 1985. A first English version, with a different title, was presented at the symposium "The Question of the Postmodern: Literature/Criticism/Culture" organized by Michael Hays at Cornell University in April 1977. First published in the present expanded version as a contribution to the special issue of *SubStance*, no. 47 (1985), on Eco's *The Name of the Rose*. Reprinted here with minor changes in editorial style and format.

BAAAB.BAB—BAAAB.BAAB
(apple inedible, apple bad)

That is, he proclaims that the apple, which they considered beautiful, edible, and good (because it is red), and therefore a yes, is actually a no, in fact a no-no (in the Edenic language, evil—the serpent—is BB). God thus introduces a contradiction in their semantic universe, one which will cause a major crisis in the Garden. For at that very moment Adam and Eve, who cannot doubt the truth of God's assertion since he is AA *par excellence* ("I am that I am," or you might say the transcendental signified), realize that denotation may be in contrast with connotation and, what is even more astonishing to them, that contradiction or ambiguity on the semantic level brings about the possibility of making new expressive forms, new signifiers; for example, of saying and writing "bluered" (BAAAAABABBBBBA). They are literally fascinated by the unusual sound of the new sequence. They repeat it over and over, not even looking at the apple: for the very first time, they are looking at words instead of things.

And so it happens that Adam and Eve come to taste the pleasure of the text, to know desire in language. And they begin to invent new word forms: they write *red* with blueberry juice, line up words in columns or with graphic emphasis, discover rhyme, rhythm, anaphora, *recitar cantando, parole in libertà*, and concrete poetry. In short, together with the arbitrariness of the sign, they have found out the structure of the code and so can instantaneously retrace the history of poetics. Adam rediscovers, after Jakobson, the poetic function of language and experiences Derrida's Heideggerian penchant for false etymologies. The thought crosses his mind that *nomina sunt numina,* the gods speak through language, and language is therefore part of nature, not of the superstructure; and he feels closer to God and his eternal laws. Closer to God than Eve, in fact, and that, he believes, must be *the* difference. On her part, Eve has other reasons to pursue linguistics and poetics: the meeting with the serpent has intimated the existence of prelinguistic factors in the semiotic domain, and she is now deeply engaged in *sémanalyse.*

To make a long story short, whether or not Adam will eat the apple offered or not by Eve is finally irrelevant. They have left the Garden since the moment they began to play with language and discovered that the univocal correspondence between signifiers and signifieds presumed by the Edenic code did not exist. At that moment, too, history began. For in His wish to test His creatures by instituting a prohibition, and by affirming His own Authority and the positivity of His Enunciation, God introduced a contradiction in the natural order of things, and that contradiction produced a condition of perpetual scrambling in the semiotic order. One moral of the story might be, God made a mistake. But there are at least two other equally possible hypotheses: 1) that God did not make a mistake but, rather, having read Lévi-Strauss, purposely instituted the universal taboo in order to create culture; or 2) that God did not exist, and the myth of the interdiction was arrived at later as a rationalization or *a posteriori* explanation of the event.

That is roughly the sense of an essay which Eco published in 1971 with the title "Generazione di messaggi estetici in una lingua edenica."[2] It was included in *Le forme del contenuto*, a book that marks the transition from the aesthetic and broadly philosophical concerns of *Opera aperta* (1962) and *La struttura assente* (1968) to the more formally defined inquiry of *A Theory of Semiotics* (1976). The essay itself, however, is representative of a third type of discourse, with which only the Italian readers of Eco are familiar, that of his journalistic writings—political commentary, essays in popular culture, reviews, interviews, and interventions in nearly all aspects of Italian life and mores. It is also exemplary of a particular form of the semiotic imagination which shapes all of Eco's writing, from the most abstract and theoretical to the most occasional and fictional.

This Genesis *sub specie semiotica* belongs neither to the former nor to the latter genre, but is constructed, according to the author, as a laboratory model, a practical demonstration of the work of semiosis, of the mechanics of the open work, of the aesthetic use of codes, and especially of invention as a mode of sign production. At the same time it is also a demonstration of the work of semiotics—as Eco sees it—as a potentially demystifying practice of signs, a sort of permanent critique of ideologies. But even more, the essay demonstrates the pleasure of both semiosis and semiotics: the first as pure play, *jouissance*, sense of wonder, Marino's *meraviglia;* the second as self-vindication or affirmation of the human(istic) subject who, by the semiotic activity, enters into a play-off with God, so to speak, and rather than cursing or repressing him, can scale him down to human size and transcode his mighty thunder into bleat or babble (BAAAB.BAB).

Not inconsistently, then, will Eco maintain in later works that semiotics is "a theory of the lie" and man the only animal capable of both lying and laughing.[3] A text is thus always a lie, often premeditated, and its greatest force is laughter. Long before writing the novel which turns on the quest for the mysterious Ur-text on comedy, the text of the truth of laughter, Eco had written of De Amicis's popular feuilleton *Cuore:* "Either one laughs at [the bourgeois] Order from within, or one must curse it from without; either one feigns to accept it so as to be able to expose it, or one feigns to reject it only to bring it about again in other forms; either one is Rabelais or one is Descartes."[4] In *The Name of the Rose*, I will suggest, Eco would want to be both.

If there is one text to which the designation of writing as a premeditated lie applies, that must be *The Name of the Rose*, a novel built in the vast laboratory of his critical studies and politico-cultural activities of over two decades, and properly a "summation" of the particular vision of history and culture, cognition and creativity, the world and the text, that emerges with consistency from his entire work. For this novel by (let us not forget) the disciple and admirer of Aquinas is also intended to be a narrative *summa*— the novel most novelistic, the mystery most insoluble, the *Bildungsroman* most picaresque, the text most intertextual, the manuscript found, not just in a bottle but in a Chinese box. At the same time, this is also the most "personal" of Eco's works, in the sense in which only narrative fiction, or narrativity in fiction, can be. For, however well contained by an elaborate scaffolding of narrative and metanarrative codes, the writer's affective investment comes through the fiction as sure as daylight; and in the histor-ical scenario, barely dissimulated by the scholar's astute manipulation of the rules of the genre, one can distinctly glimpse the trappings of another scene.

History and story, the public record of interpreted events and their traces in a subject's personal history, do not always fit so smoothly together. For some, indeed, they clash—Elsa Morante, for one, as *La storia* painfully testifies—producing ruptures and tears in the fabric of both life and text.[5] But here, in this "tale of books" (p. 5), personal and critical history merge in the literary topoi of the journey, the sentimental education, the descent into Hades, the remembrance of things past, the wake of reason; here the political inquest and the mythical quest are twined securely with the So-cratic dialogue, the *conte à la* Voltaire, the Conan Doyle mystery story. Our scene iii, then, is the library, as the novel opens with "naturally, a man-uscript."

Scene iii. The Library

In what appears to be the realm of historical fact, someone (presumably Eco) is handed a book by someone else (unspecified) "on August 16, 1968." The book purports to be the 1842 French translation of a seventeenth-century Latin edition of a manuscript written in Latin by a German monk toward the end of the fourteenth century. The first someone, having left Prague when "six days later Soviet troops invaded that unhappy city" (p. 1), meets up with his "beloved" in Vienna, and together they travel up the Danube to the monastery of Melk, where the presumed author of the manuscript had lived. There, not only is the original manuscript not to be found, but the French book also disappears "one tragic night," abducted by the "beloved," neither one ever to be seen again. By January 1980, the first someone has decided to publish *his* own manuscript, a modern Italian translation of the memoirs of Adso of Melk. Why? "Let us say it is an act of love. Or, if you like, a way of ridding myself of numerous, persistent obsessions" (p. 5).

Adso's memoirs, written by the Benedictine monk toward the end of his life, at the close of the century, relate events that happened in his youth, in A.D. 1327. His manuscript begins with a Prologue, and the Prologue begins with the words of John, *"In principio erat Verbum,"* "In the beginning was the Word and the Word was with God, and the Word was God." Then the narration of the events, divided into seven days (chapters) and told by Adso in the first person, begins with what may well appear to us as a quotation from *Peanuts,* the beginning of Snoopy's novel-in-progress: "It was a beautiful morning at the end of November" (p. 21). The three embedded beginnings contain and imbricate three references, three registers of discourse—the literary-historical, the theologico-philosophical, and the popular-cultural—which are not only the major areas of Eco's critical work but also the field of his writing practice. This is, in short, his semiotic and poetic manifesto. This text, we are to understand, demonstrates how Pierre Menard, in Borges's story, wrote his *Don Quixote.*[6] It is a novel made up almost entirely of other texts, of tales already told, of names either well known or sounding as if they should be known to us from literary and cultural history; a medley of famous passages and obscure quotations, specialized lexicons and subcodes (narrative, iconographic, literary, architectural, bibliographical, pharmaceutical, et cetera), and characters cut out in strips from a generic world encyclopedia.

Here are some. An abbot by the name of Abo; a fiftyish Franciscan monk and former inquisitor, Brother William of Baskerville, given to chewing grass in moments of nervous tension; and a young novice, his disciple and scribe, named Adso, who is often addressed by his better as "my dear Adso." Thus forewarned, the reader who will go and reread *The Hound of the Baskervilles* will find there not only the same investigative and inferential structure governing *The Name of the Rose,* not only the dry humor and the ambiguous relationship that binds Sherlock and Watson, like William and Adso, in an affectionate, homoerotic, master-slave dialectic; but even the exact physical description of characters (e.g., Dr. Mortimer) and locations (the castle, Baskerville Hall) which Eco lifts from Conan Doyle and inserts into his text unchanged. In the English novel, the ancient curse haunting the present owners of the castle is inscribed in an eighteenth-century manuscript; in Eco's, a manuscript more ancient and more elusive is responsible for the murders most foul evenly distributed one in each day or unit of narration. And just as Watson begins his story describing Sherlock

Holmes and Dr. Mortimer, so does Adso describe his beloved master in almost the same words and certainly with the same loving attention to his body, his hands, his look.

Further, both novels open with a feat of deductive brilliance: the large quantity of information Sherlock is able to infer from Dr. Mortimer's walking stick is more than matched by the detailed description of the abbot's horse, which William can produce from the bare evidence of a few marks left by its passage on the ground and adjacent shrubs. Here Eco appropriates almost verbatim an episode from Voltaire's *Zadig*—about the queen's dog and the king's horse—which is often cited as an example of semiotic inference, but he coyly goes one step beyond the great Encyclopedist by making his hero deduce the very name of the horse:

> "All right," I said, "but why Brunellus?"
>
> "May the Holy Ghost sharpen your mind, son!" my master exclaimed. "What other name could he possibly have? Why, even the great Buridan, who is about to become rector in Paris, when he wants to use a horse in one of his logical examples, always calls it Brunellus."
>
> This was my master's way. He not only knew how to read the great book of nature [as Voltaire's hero did], but also knew the way monks read the books of Scripture, and how they thought through them. (pp. 24–25)

Moreover, as Doyle ends his novel with a "retrospection" chapter in which, on a cold and foggy night at the end of November, two weeks after the events narrated, Watson and Holmes draw out their final implications, the "Last Page" of Adso's memoirs shows him, "years later," as he returns to the scene of the story. Both texts end in the present tense, the time of writing.

What of the hellish hound, Victorian projection of human lust and excess? Eco wouldn't miss him for the world. He is, of course, the Antichrist, the "foul beast" whose imminent arrival is incessantly announced by the blind seer Jorge of Burgos(!) with words of fire and brimstone. But it is the latter, representative of the dark age's darkest dogmatism and religious zeal, who will cause the apocalyptic fire that destroys the library and who will devour (literally) the much-coveted manuscript—that second volume of Aristotle's *Poetics* which the tradition alleged to be a treatise on the comic.

> Fear prophets, Adso [warns Brother William], and those prepared to die for the truth, for as a rule they make many others die with them, often before them, at times instead of them. . . . Jorge feared the second book of Aristotle because it perhaps really did teach how to distort the face of every truth, so that we would not become slaves of our ghosts. Perhaps the mission of those who love mankind is to make people laugh at the truth, *to make truth laugh*, because the only truth lies in learning to free ourselves from insane passion for the truth. (p. 491)

As his first name characteristically suggests, our hero is also modeled on the historical figure of William of Ockham, the empiricist philosopher and Franciscan politician who taught at Oxford and who, having been called to Avignon by John XXII on charges of heresy, sought shelter at the court of Louis the Bavarian and became his supporter. Similarly, the learned *disputationes* on the poverty of Christ, on the allegorical meaning of semi-precious stones, on the properties of herbs, or the political debates among the factions of papal and imperial supporters are all painstakingly derived from actual medieval texts, the transcripts of heretics' trials, and so on.

Eco's particular mix of history and story, of semiotics and fiction, is summarized in the words of Sherlock Holmes: "It is the scientific use of the imagination, but we have always some material basis on which to start our speculations."[7] That is what leads our hero to a perfectly rational explanation of the mystery of the library, and thus to be on the exact spot where the yarn finally unravels. Once there, however, Eco leaves Conan Doyle and steps into the postmodern condition. The crimes, William finds out, were not determined by an individual's scheme or by a single plot—Jorge's, for instance, which William (and the reader, with some degree of smug self-satisfaction) had believed to be patterned on the text of the Apocalypse: seven murders, occurring in seven days, and predictable by the guideline of the revelations of the seven seals. That was not the key to the chain of murders. In fact, there was no key: every crime had a different author or perhaps no author at all; there was no single plan, but rather a multiplicity of causes whose relations depended less on the design of an author than on the project of a reader—in this case, William.

> "There was no plot," William said, "and I discovered it by mistake." . . .
> "Where is all my wisdom, then? I behaved stubbornly, pursuing a semblance of order, when I should have known well that there is no order in the universe."
> "But in imagining an erroneous order you still found something. . . ."
> "What you say is very fine, Adso, and I thank you. The order that our mind imagines is like a net, or like a ladder, built to attain something. But afterward you must throw the ladder away, because you discover that, even if it was useful, it was meaningless. Er muoz gelichesame die leiter abewerfen, sô er an ir ufgestigen. . . . Is that how you say it?"
> "That is how it is said in my language. Who told you that?"
> "A mystic from your land. He wrote it somewhere, I forget where. . . ." (p. 492)

The quote, which Eco retranslates into medieval German, is from Wittgenstein.

Scene iv. The Text

A taste for the apocryphal, the fake, the anachronistic, the pseudo-allegorical, the unwonted analogy, and the parodic employ of hyperbole and baroque imagery as distancing devices are a stylistic constant in Eco's occasional writings since the very popular and funny short pieces of his *Diario minimo*. Sustained through five hundred and some pages, their effect is something of a literary equivalent of pop art, a pop novel. *The Name of the Rose* has no authorial voice, and hence no author-ity of its own, for every scrap of discourse—every description, incident, or character, every turn of phrase, narrative styleme, metaphor, or metonymy—is an *objet trouvé*, whether it has been found in mass culture or high art, in an obscure patristic work or a contemporary text of French theory. One more example will suffice: the description of Adso's dream, which, according to Eco, is practically his translation of the medieval *Coena Cipriani* (and I must take his word for that, since I have never read or seen or heard of it before), but which I read as an imposing pastiche of Voltaire, Brueghel, Buñuel, Lyotard, and who knows who else, seasoned with comic book iconography and the liturgical cadence of litanies. At the end of the ten-page account of the dream or vision he had while the choir chanted the "Dies Irae," Adso says: "My vision, rapid like all visions, if it had not lasted the space of an 'amen,' *as the saying goes,* had lasted almost the length of a 'Dies irae'" (p. 435, my emphasis).

I am reminded of Eco's own response to the film *Casablanca*, which he points out as a modern example of the sublime:

> When all the archetypes erupt indecently and unrestrained, Homeric depths are reached. Two clichés will make us laugh, but one hundred will move us. For one senses somehow that the clichés are speaking among themselves and celebrating their reunion. Just as the acutest pain trespasses into pleasure and perversion can touch the threshold of mystical energy, the utmost banality discloses the possibility of the sublime. Something has spoken [in the film] in the place of the director. This occurrence deserves, if nothing else, our veneration.[8]

In *The Name of the Rose,* too, something speaks in the name of the author. But what? The very term *rose,* as Eco obviously chose it, is so dense with literary allusions, references, and connotations that it no longer has any, and thus appears to refer to what Baudrillard has called the implosion of meaning: a rose is a rose is a rose is a black hole, as it were. The writing itself, in the "Last Page," seems rather to stop than to end.

It is cold in the scriptorium, my thumb aches. I leave this manuscript, I do not know for whom; I no longer know what it is about: stat rosa pristina nomine, nomina nuda tenemus.

However, does the book not aim to be like *Casablanca,* a thrust toward the modern, or perhaps the postmodern, sublime? Despite this ending—as low-key, self-denying, and non-authorial as the Prologue was lofty and resounding with the joint authorities of God and History—narrativity and laughter have been deployed in full force, the pleasure of the text and the "pure love of writing" have been consummated, and there is even some room left for writing a sequel. And is it not true, as Maria Corti observed, that this novel by the major theorist of the open work "is so lucidly constructed and so 'closed' as to respect the Aristotelian unities of time, place, and action in a manner that is nowadays all but exceptional"?[9]

Eco's formulation of the "open work," dating back to the period of his direct involvement with the Italian *neoavanguardia* movement in the years 1958–63, was prompted by the necessity to find a critical language and new aesthetic categories that would account for certain contemporary artistic works produced by the second avant-garde, as it was called—the music of Berio, Boulez, Pousseur, Stockhausen, Calder's mobiles, as well as their precursors, notably Mallarmé, Joyce, and Brecht. He defined these "works in movement," argued that they should be seen as "epistemological metaphors," and related them to Einsteinian physics and the theoretical constructs of Husserl and Merleau-Ponty.[10] The emphasis on indeterminacy, which at the time appeared to be the quintessence of "openness" and the *conditio sine qua non* of a radical avant-garde art, was historically motivated by the specific texts considered and the general intellectual climate. But the concern with form, if not yet structure, was equally strong in Eco, as the subtitle of *Opera aperta: forma e indeterminazione nelle poetiche contemporanee* more than suggests.

The notion of "open work," then, was one that applied equally to *The Divine Comedy* and to *Finnegans Wake,* though yielding different interpretive results, and though only the latter was a "work in movement." When Eco returns to it in *The Role of the Reader* (1979), reformulating it in terms of a pragmatics, rather than an aesthetics, of reception, he also renames it "open text."

An author can foresee an "ideal reader affected by an ideal insomnia" (as happens with *Finnegans Wake),* able to master different codes and eager to deal with the text as with a maze of many issues. But in the last analysis what matters is not the various issues in themselves but the maze-like structure of the text. You cannot use the text as you want, but only as the text wants you to use it. An open text, however "open" it be, cannot afford whatever interpretation.

> An open text outlines a "closed" project of its Model Reader as a component of its structural strategy.[11]

In other words, the Reader's role in interpreting the text is a "collaboration" demanded by the text's "generative structure," for the Reader is already contemplated by the text, and is in fact an element of its interpretation, a set of particular competencies and conditions which must be met if the text is to be "fully actualized" in its potential content. Much like Althusser's account of the subject's relation to ideology, Eco's recent theory of textuality at once invokes a reader who is already "competent," a (reading) subject fully constituted prior to the text and to reading, *and* poses the reader as a term of the text's production of certain meanings, as an effect of its structure.[12] Writer and reader do have interpretive "freedom" (the term is Eco's), but that freedom is conditional and overdetermined: for the writer, by the (historically specified) universe of discourses available, which Eco calls at different times "the world of the encyclopedia" and "the format of the semantic space"; for the reader, it is overdetermined as much by the reader's knowledge of codes and frames as by the text's own project. But, if both reader and author are "textual strategies," pre(in)scribed or "foreseen" in the "maze-like structure of the text," then the question, What speaks in the name of the rose? may indeed have already been answered by Eco against himself.

Scene v. The Name

As Dorothy Sayers could have said, in *The Name of the Rose* Eco wants to "have his carcase"—he wants a mystery both with and without solution, a text both open and closed, an epistemology with and without truth. He wants, that is, to be an author-function (the term is Foucault's), but also and concurrently Rabelais and Descartes. He hints at the implosion of meaning and openly thematizes the abyss, classificatory difference, the "arche-writing," and the originary "violence of the letter"; yet does he not finally side with Lévi-Strauss against Derrida, as William educates Adso in their progress through the babelic labyrinth of the abbey, and as the text takes the reader through the maze of its "writing lesson?"[13]

The labyrinth, like the text, is an abstract model of inference or conjecture. In an essay written after the publication of the novel and in response to its initial reception, Eco states his conviction that the appeal of the detective story lies neither in the representation of murder and guilt nor in the final triumph of justice and order, but in its being an instance of pure conjecture, on a par with "medical detection, scientific research, even metaphysical inquiry."[14] He then describes three types of labyrinth. In the Greek labyrinth, "no one could get lost: you enter, reach the center, and from the center the exit. That's why at the center there is the Minotaur; otherwise the story would make no sense, it would be just a stroll." In the mannerist labyrinth there are a lot of dead ends and only one exit; however, "you can miss it. You need Ariadne's thread in order not to get lost. This is a model of the trial-and-error process." The third type of labyrinth is "the network, or what Deleuze and Guattari call rhizome," built in such a way that every road connects with every other. It has no center, no periphery, and no exit, and is virtually infinite.

> The space of conjecture is a rhizomatous space. The labyrinth of my library is still a mannerist labyrinth, but the world in which William lives, as he realizes, is already structured like a rhizome: that is to say, it is susceptible to being structured but never definitively. (Eco, "Postille," p. 21)

The detective novel, Eco continues, poses and seeks to answer the "basic question of philosophy (as well as of psychoanalysis): whose fault is it?" In order to find out, "one must hypothesize that everything happens according to a logic, a logic imposed by the murderer. . . . Thus my basic story (who is the murderer?) sends out as offshoots many other stories, all of them stories of conjectures and all having to do with the structure of conjecture as such." Now, if Eco is asking the question of philosophy, and if the result of his "inferential walk" through the rhizomatous space of the novel is the discovery of the "truth of nontruth," as Derrida claims for Nietzsche's styles in *Spurs*, are we to understand that writing in the name of the rose is but another form of "the becoming-female" of the idea?[15] In short, is Eco deconstructing here?

In her reading of *Spurs*, Derrida's reading of Nietzsche, Gayatri Spivak suggests that such feminization of philosophy—philosophy as a practice of writing, or "philosophizing"—as serves the male deconstructor "might find its most adequate legend in male homosexuality defined as criminality."[16] In *The Name of the Rose*, a story of books and monks, fathers and sons, the search for the name of the murderer could hardly lead to anything else. The brothers murder one another to secure the father's text, which is at last ingested, incorporated by the oldest of the horde, Jorge of Burgos, he who aspires, but alas all too literally, to be the body of the Word, to be what Derrida might call "the vocative absolute," or Eco the definitive edition of the world encyclopedia. But he will burn, and not in a bush, for his presumption to incarnate the Law, truth, and the phallus; for that would reduce difference and unlimited semiosis to (as one brother would say) a pound of flesh. The blind seer should have known—he, of all people—that the symbolic murder of the father finally cannot be achieved. What can be achieved instead, and with less effort, is the real murder of the mother.

Eco's lie may be premeditated and built in a modern, critical-scientific laboratory that has little to share with Mary Shelley's "workshop of filthy creation." Yet the novel does not escape the supreme law of modern fiction, the ultimate pop scenario in which the work, once created, turns against its creator and runs away with him. Like Pirandello's six characters or Frankenstein's monster, Eco/Adso's manuscript looses itself from its meta-narrative moorings, exceeds the triply embedded constraints of its "gener-ative structure," breaks out of the author's elaborate *mise-en-scène*, and stages its own performance of desire.

It is in the name of the Father that Adso writes his memoirs (entitling us to read it as anamnesis), and Eco rewrites it as "an act of love," actually a falling in love ("un gesto di innamoramento"), a transference ("per liber-armi da numerose e antiche ossessioni"). He rewrites it after having lost it on the same "tragic night" in which he also lost his "beloved" and ended up with "a great emptiness in my heart." More accurately, he rewrites it having lost it *to* that person whose name and, more significantly, whose gender remain unstated.[17] Of that person, however, we will encounter the dis-placed image (*en abîme*, to be sure) in Adso's manuscript: on another "tragic" and gaudy night, in a nameless young woman in whose body Adso experiences the "igneous ardor" and "splendid clarity" of the "vital spurt." Gaudeamus, igitur! Predictably enough, this will be followed, for Adso, by the loss of "all memory in bliss" and the dispersal of identity in the abyss of *jouissance*, as well as *post coitum* depression, giving Eco the opportunity to replay various commonplaces of religious, mystical, and metaphysical erot-ica from the Song of Solomon to Bataille—and making one yearn for the *concinnitas* of a Jerry Lee Lewis. As for the woman, the single female character in this story of monks and men, Adso's "igneus ardor" and "vital spurt" will be followed, just as predictably, by her being burned at the stake.

Scene vi. The Stake

Nameless and speechless body, she (it) stands for *natura naturans*, the pre-symbolic or presemiotic realm of, as Kristeva would call it, the maternal *chora*. Not coincidentally, upon waking, Adso will find her absent and in her place, "dead but still throbbing with gelatinous life of dead viscera, lined by livid nerves: a heart, of great size" (p. 250). So the woman, too, like Jorge and like the faithless and corrupt Mother Church embodied in the Abbey, will burn for all eternity. Less obviously, however, she is also the figure of the abyss. As Adso laments the fate of his only earthly love, and the prohibition that bars him from calling out the beloved's name, he discovers, Eco tells us with another wink toward Derrida, "the power of proper names" (p. 397). Once more, at the end of his years and of his writing, will Adso fantasize her, this time as the mystic body of death: "I shall sink into the divine shadow, in a dumb silence and an ineffable union . . . and all differences will be forgotten. . . . I shall fall into the silent and uninhabited divinity where there is no work and no image" (p. 501). This is the abyss at the end of meaning's infinite regression, the empty (w)hole around which whirl the signifiers, the utterly unsignifiable double of a lost transcendental signified.

The associative chain woman-mother-church-truth-death could not be etched more sharply. But this dead, inert maternal body is not our story's obscure object of desire. Eco is not Poe. Just as with Poe's purloined letter, however, the object of desire is right on the surface of *The Name of the Rose*. It is the text itself, metonymically mirrored in the legendary text of the father of philosophy, all the more desired the more it is unattainable, and in the other texts it *generates:* Adso's manuscript and its various "translations," interpretants which together constitute the palimpsest of the symbolic body of the father, the inscription of the father's code and of the name of the father across the cultural history of Western Europe. For indeed, what sustains the master-disciple dialectic of William and Adso is the latter's desire for the father's knowledge, vision, and power: his learning—so often exhibited; his glasses—the better to decipher signs; his hands—delicate yet powerful to build wondrous machines; in short, his possession of the code, the magical instrument that transforms things into signs, nature into books (*natura naturata*), and books into history—actions, practices, events of the world.

As for William, then, what he desires is Adso's desire, the writing which inscribes it and the manuscript which signi-fies that desire and produces it as meaning. William, as we know, is an ex-inquisitor, a politically powerful man who has sought to give up his power and to devote himself instead to the pleasure of the text, the pleasure of constructing his semiotic machines. Yet, in spite of himself, power and knowledge stick to him and confer upon him a social role, a responsibility which he cannot refuse, being the demo-cratic and progressive man that he is. Thus, in the difficult political con-juncture, he takes on the function of mediator between the various agencies of the left and the reactionary establishment. But his political mission fails, the pope and the emperor are going to end up in a stalemate, and the inquisition will continue to squelch dissension. And his work as cultural mediator would seem perfectly useless, were it not for Adso, to whom he can bequeath his knowledge, his "writing lesson." For each of

them, the possibility of existing in history is founded on the other's desire
and recognition.

In this sense, finally, the name of the rose is the name of the father, and
Eco's *homo semeioticus* may find his most adequate legend in homo-sexuality
defined as pedagogy. In this sense, too, one might append to his work the
words that Barbara Kruger collages over a blown-up detail of the creation
scene from the Sistine Chapel: "You invest in the divinity of the masterpiece."[18] If Adam, semiotic subject of the Edenic language, had succeeded
in turning myth into history by showing God out of the Garden door, his
writing counterpart Adso effectively lets him back in through the open
(window of the) text, by turning history into fiction. For the book written in
the name of the father is always a testament, whether old or new. It is a
book without author, but drenched in an author-ity that comes no less from
the ambiguity of the gospels than from the certainty of the tables of the law,
an author-ity bearing the weight of the obsessions of a great, millenary, and
moribund patriarchal tradition.

If writing is an act of love, it is because it works to disavow that death and
to allay its threat in the imaginary narrative of male self-creation. The stake
of writing, then, is the endless reconstruction of the fetish, and the novel an
ancient labor of love: the reconstruction of something lost (stolen) in a
primal night, on another scene, and forever pursued across countries,
years, and books—and the agony and the ecstasy of that pursuit.

Scene vii. The Question

A propos of contemporary art, Craig Owens writes that the "official"
production (by men) seems "engaged in a collective act of disavowal,"
whether it simulates mastery or it contemplates and advertises the artist's
loss of it. This he attributes to the emergent voices of the conquered
"Third-World nations, the 'revolt of nature' and the women's movement."

> Symptoms of our recent loss of mastery are everywhere apparent in
> cultural activity today—nowhere more so than in the visual arts. The mod-
> ernist project of joining forces with science and technology for the transfor-
> mation of the environment after rational principles of function and utility
> (Productivism, the Bauhaus) has long since been abandoned; what we witness
> in its place is a desperate, often hysterical attempt to recover some sense of
> mastery via the resurrection of heroic large-scale easel painting and monu-
> mental cast-bronze sculpture—mediums themselves identified with the
> cultural hegemony of Western Europe. Yet contemporary artists are able at
> best to *simulate* mastery, to manipulate its signs; since in the modern period
> mastery was invariably associated with human labor, aesthetic production has

degenerated today into a massive deployment of the signs of artistic labor—
violent, "impassioned" brushwork, for example.[19]

A massive deployment of the signs of writing is certainly an apt description
of *The Name of the Rose,* a work which may well be the updated version of the
"master narrative," the patriarchal *grand récit* of all times (look at the sales
on the international market, including the sale of the screenplay rights); yet
it is a remake clever enough to admit that the *récit* has lost credibility, a
masterwork invested in divinity, but clever enough to disguise itself as a
Text.

If that is true of Eco's writing, however, is it less true of those other
writers to whom he constantly alludes, his contemporary intertextual refer-
ees, his brothers of the discursive fellowship? Is the postmodern condition
not reconstructing its own fetishistic economy in *La Condition postmoderne?*[20]
Isn't a metaphysical drive engaged in the critique of metaphysics? Isn't the
discourse of power rhetorically reversible in the power of discourse? Ironically, these questions were once asked by Eco himself in his critique of
structuralism—of Lévi-Strauss's "ontological structuralism" as well as its
opponents and/or epigones, Lacan, Foucault, and Derrida, in *La struttura
assente.* For in denying any origin, presence, or ontological foundation to
the structure(s) of signification, the latter would also constrain the question
of meaning production, and hence the social practices of signs, within a
purely discursive dimension. They would cast the semiotic inquiry in the
terms of a metaphysics of absence.

Their question, Eco charged, is, Who speaks?—the question of philosophy, which has been asked for several thousand years and can be said to
constitute thought itself. However, *who* has been asking that question? "A
category of men who could afford the contemplation of Being because of
the slave labor of others, and who thus held this question as the most urgent
of all."

Let us suppose there is another question, an even more constitutive one,
that is asked not by the free man who can afford "contemplation," but *by the
slave* who cannot; for the slave the question *"Who dies?"* is a more urgent
question than "Who speaks?" . . .

For the slave *the proximity of being* is not the most radical kinship: *the
proximity of his own body and the bodies of others* come first. And in perceiving this
other kinship, the slave does not leave the domain of ontology to regress (or
to remain without consciousness) in the realm of matter: rather, he accedes
to thought from another, equally worthy, pre-categorical situation.

By asking "Who dies?" we have not entered an empirical dimension in
which all philosophies are worthless, but rather we have set out from another
pre-philosophical presupposition in order to found another philosophy.[21]

Eco's proposal thus to reground philosophy was made in 1968. Read in the present context, it may seem either facile or, with regard to his most recent work, to have come to nought. But the sense of his gesture, a rhetorical cutting of the Gordian knot, still retains its polemical charge of negativity and critical productivity. In his own work, these should be looked for rather in the theoretically crucial, but regrettably unrecognized, achievement of *A Theory of Semiotics*, where indeed the question of meaning production is posed not from within the philosophical brotherhood or in the name of the father, but from the field of social practices in their materiality and historicity.

As for the slave's and other bodies burnt at the stake, they do not ask who's dying—that, they know. What they are asking, instead, is Juliet's question, What's in a name? And Eco's answer in *The Name of the Rose*, nothing and everything, is not what they want, is not enough.

Epilogue

Just a few weeks after I completed this paper, the *Boston Globe* reported on Eco's recent visit to Cambridge. "On the first of two lectures Monday and Tuesday, he told 500 people wedged into a Harvard lecture hall that he sees a 'new medieval wave' in America and Europe," wrote Richard Higgins, quoting Eco.

> In the Middle Ages, he said, lie the roots "of all our contemporary 'hot' problems." Both our "so-called post-modern era" and the Middle Ages are periods of political, cultural and technological transformation in which "the whole deck of historical cards is shuffled. . . . All the problems of the Western world come out [then]: modern languages, merchant cities, banks, the prime rate, the rising of modern armies, the national state, as well as the idea of a supranational federation . . . the struggle between the poor and the rich, the concept of ideological deviation . . . the clash between state and church, worker unions, the technological transformation of labor [through such as windmills, horseshoes, oxen collars, more advanced rudders, compasses and stirrups] . . . the rise of modern ways of computing with the acceptance of Arab mathematics . . . even our contemporary notion of love as a devastating unhappy happiness."[22]

Need I point out the one "problem" that is not mentioned? Indeed, the one issue of political, cultural, and technological transformation that did not rise in the Middle Ages—or, if it did, was handled most effectively by burning its proponents at the stake (as shown in *The Name of the Rose*)? The problem, in short, of gender: the issue of a difference that divides the social subjects and imposes the question of the relation of subjectivity and experience to meaning, social formations, and power; a question only implied in Juliet's, but critically and politically articulated by feminism. And hence the "problem" of women, a contradiction in the semiotic universe which metaphysics and poetics can no longer hide, or patriarchal fictions reconcile.

The awareness of that contradiction as well as the improbability of reconciliation is not new to literature or even to the fictional genre chosen by Eco. Although not acknowledged contextually as Conan Doyle is, Dorothy Sayers's classic *Gaudy Night* comes immediately to mind.[23] What is remarkable there is not just the similarity in setting; the extensive, integral use of literary reference; the topos of the investigator being called into a closed, monastic, single-gendered community and finding there her or his own imaginary, and her or his real complicity in its crimes (Oedipus, once again?); or the double point of view and dialogic manner in which conjecture is worked out and the evidence sifted by the couple Harriet Vane and Peter Wimsey, heterosexual version of Adso and William. What is more remarkable in Sayers's novel is that the relationship between Harriet and Peter, explored within the frame of the narrative, is itself explicitly inscribed in theme of the mystery and thus intrinsically compromised, despite the happy ending, by the plot's resolution. For the threat posed by the unknown offender to the college female community is revealed to be exactly reversible in the threat that a community of women scholars poses to the institution of heterosexuality. Conversely, as Eco demonstrates, semiotics poses no threat to the Word.

While Eco's gaudy *Rose* pretends to have no master plot and alleges to be a story of books, a game of conjecture in which the referent, historical reality, is always already infinitely mediated, and truth ultimately beside the point, what the book finally affirms is the truth of discourse, the *Name* of the rose, and thus the continuity of the very institution it seems to challenge: the Name of the Father. Sayers's *Gaudy Night,* on its part, admits to a double plot (with fewer murders) whose narrative resolution exposes the very contradiction constitutive of women as subjects in a social reality instituted in the name of the father and, beyond that, points to the contradiction of plot itself, the compromise of narrative discourse as it exists historically in that reality.

The point of this brief reference to *Gaudy Night* is not the futile one of giving Sayers's novel one label and Eco's another, but modestly to propose that some things have happened in America and Europe, as well as in literature and criticism, since the Middle Ages, and one of them is that one now knows that the "logic" of the murderer or of the writing is not the same when the gender is different. In both novels, the motives of the murderers are the same: a conservative, misconceived, even pathetic, last-ditch attempt to salvage the status quo. Yet the logic is not. For, as I read them, the romance of William and Adso emerges unscathed, comforting, and ever-lasting from their journey through history and murder, whereas the ro-mance of Harriet and Peter ends up on the shore of that contradiction which, the novel has shown, brings a woman to murder. Thus, if the mystery story's true achievement is its successful demonstration that the murderer is the reader, as Eco suggests, that "we are the guilty ones,"[24] then from at least some readers he should expect the question, Who's we, white man?—a question not unbecoming *The Name of the Rose*, after all.

Notes

1. Umberto Eco, *Il nome della rosa* (Milano: Bompiani, 1980), p. 503. All further references to this work, given in parentheses in the text, will be to the English translation, *The Name of the Rose*, trans. William Weaver (New York: Harcourt Brace Jovanovich, 1983).
2. In Umberto Eco, *Le forme del contenuto* (Milano: Bompiani, 1971). The En-glish version of this essay, "On the Possibility of Generating Aesthetic Messages in an Edenic Language," is in Umberto Eco, *The Role of the Reader: Explorations in the Semiotics of Texts* (Bloomington: Indiana University Press, 1979), pp. 90–104.
3. Umberto Eco, *A Theory of Semiotics* (Bloomington: Indiana University Press, 1976), p. 6.
4. Umberto Eco, *Diario minimo* (Milano: Mondadori, 1976 [first published in 1963]), p. 96; translation mine.
5. Elsa Morante, *La storia* (Torino: Einaudi, 1974); *History, A Novel*, trans. William Weaver (New York: Knopf, 1977).
6. See "Pierre Menard, Author of the *Quixote*," in Jorge Luís Borges, *Labyrinths*, ed. Donald A. Yates and James E. Irby (New York: New Directions, 1964).
7. Sir Arthur Conan Doyle, *The Hound of the Baskervilles* (Garden City, N.Y.: Doubleday, 1974), p. 47.
8. Umberto Eco, "Ore 9: Amleto all'assedio di Casablanca," *L'Espresso*, 17 agosto 1975; translation mine. See *"Casablanca:* Cult Movies and Intertextual Collage," *Sub-Stance*, no. 47 (1985): 3–12.
9. Maria Corti, "È un'opera chiusa," *L'Espresso*, 19 ottobre 1980; translation mine.
10. See Umberto Eco, "The Poetics of the Open Work," in Eco, *The Role of the Reader*, pp. 47–66.
11. Eco, *The Role of the Reader*, p. 9.
12. See Louis Althusser, *Lenin and Philosophy*, trans. Ben Brewster (New York and London: Monthly Review Press, 1971), p. 176. I have suggested elsewhere that the circularity of the argumentation and the reappearance of critical imagery and concerns recurrent in structuralist writers such as Lévi-Strauss and Greimas point to a kind of retrenchment, on Eco's part, to the positions which he himself was among the first to criticize in *La struttura assente* and which his *Theory of Semiotics* subse-quently argued to be untenable. I have offered a reading of the possible reasons for such an unhappy return in chapter 6 of my *Alice Doesn't: Feminism, Semiotics, Cinema* (Bloomington: Indiana University Press, 1984).
13. For Derrida's critique of Lévi-Strauss, see *Of Grammatology*, trans. Gayatri Chakravorty Spivak (Baltimore: Johns Hopkins University Press, 1976), pt. 2, chap. 1.
14. Umberto Eco, "Postille a *Il nome della rosa*," *Alfabeta*, no. 49 (giugno 1983): 19–

22; translation mine. This work has been recently published in English by Harcourt Brace Jovanovich.

15. Jacques Derrida, *Eperons: Les styles de Nietzsche,* English trans. by Barbara Harlow (Venezia: Corbo e Fiore, 1976), p. 69.

16. Gayatri Chakravorty Spivak, "Displacement and the Discourse of Woman," in *Displacement: Derrida and After,* ed. Mark Krupnick (Bloomington: Indiana University Press, 1983), p. 177.

17. The significance of the latter can be inferred from the apparent effort made to maintain gender neutrality in a language, Italian, that is strictly two-gendered. In Weaver's excellent translation, the three references to that person are rendered as: "a dear friend," "my beloved," and "the person with whom I was traveling" (*The Name of the Rose,* pp. 1–2). The Italian text is even more controlled in the second reference: "una persona cara," "la persona attesa," and "la persona con cui viaggiavo" (*Il nome della rosa,* p. 11).

18. Cited by Craig Owens, "The Discourse of Others: Feminism and Postmodernism," in *The Anti-Aesthetic: Essays on Postmodern Culture,* ed. Hal Foster (Port Townsend, Wash.: Bay Press, 1983), p. 77.

19. Owens, "The Discourse of Others," p. 67.

20. Jean François Lyotard, *La Condition postmoderne* (Paris: Minuit, 1979). An unusual essay by Lyotard, "One of the Things at Stake in the Women's Struggle," *Sub-Stance,* no. 20 (1978): 9–17, may be usefully considered in this regard. An intervention in the feminist debate, or so it purports, the essay appears to speak for women ("It is a philosopher who is speaking here about relations between men and women. He is trying to escape what is masculine in the very posing of such a question; . . . [he] is tempted to give his pen over to the antonym of the inquisitive adult male, to the little girl"). But the argument is in fact a peroration *pro domo sua,* an effort to build the notion of a generalized libidinal economy on the model of what the philosopher understands as female sexuality: "a puzzle of erotic potentialities (fertility, passivity, sensitivity, jealousy)." The conception of such a different sexual space would put an end to "the signifier's *imperium* over the masculine body," would free "the master-warrior-speaker . . . from his armor of words and death." In short, the women's struggle is reclaimed as a tool for the philospher's discourse, a stake to be driven into the heart of metalanguage and metaphysics.

21. Umberto Eco, *La struttura assente: Introduzione alla ricerca semiologica* (Milano: Bompiani, 1968), pp. 357–58; translation mine.

22. *Boston Globe,* 5 April 1984, p. 2.

23. Dorothy L. Sayers, *Gaudy Night* (New York: Avon Books, 1968 [first published in 1936]).

24. Eco, "Postille a *Il nome della rosa,*" p. 22.

4

CALVINO AND THE AMAZONS
Reading the (Post) Modern Text

> Federico V., who lived in a city in Northern Italy, was in love with Cinzia U., a resident of Rome.

Thus begins the story of the traveler in "L'avventura di un viaggiatore," a short story included in the 1958 volume of Calvino's *Racconti* and later reprinted in a separate collection bearing the title *Gli amori difficili* (Difficult Loves).[1] This opening is also, of course, the beginning of a story—in the current sense of love affair, erotic adventure, or sentimental relationship. The intimate connection of narrative with love, articulated in the necessary link of distance and desire throughout Calvino's fiction, is here inscribed in a late-romantic thematic of travel as quest without attainment. When that connection is remade in *If on a winter's night a traveler,* a novel that obstreperously proclaims its participation in the postmodern aesthetics of simulation, textual spectacle, masquerade, and self-reflexive excess, the result is again a love story.[2] But that love, unlike the earlier ones, is all too easy.

Or so it seems to me, woman reader, who is neither the Woman Reader of the text's fantasy nor one reading "as a woman" in the fantasies of some contemporary male criticism, but rather a woman whose understanding of self and of the world of men and women, whose relations to culture, history, art, language, and especially love have been profoundly transformed by feminism. It is in this perspective that I begin my reading of Calvino's text from one of his earlier and more difficult loves.

Gli amori difficili tells, in thirteen distinct stories, how a couple does not come together, how two people in love do not meet, and shows that it is

---

Written for a seminar I conducted at Mount Holyoke College in 1984, this essay was later revised and titled "Reading the (Post) Modern Text: *If on a winter's night a traveler,*" as a contribution to a forthcoming volume of essays in honor of Italo Calvino edited by Franco Ricci for Dovehouse Press in Ottawa, Ontario. But, to the best of my knowledge, its first appearance in print is in this volume.

precisely in their non-encounter that the couple and the love itself consist. For instance, at the end of an overnight train ride that will take him to his beloved, a man named Federico realizes that the night he has just spent on the train—that very night ride, with its anticipation, memory, desire, and the absence of the beloved one—that was the true erotic encounter, the consummation of his love. The story is titled "The Adventure of a Traveler," and all of the thirteen stories are similarly named, each being the adventure of someone; so that the book appeared in French translation as *Aventures* (1964), and the introductory note, most likely written by Calvino himself, stated: "This definition of 'adventure', which recurs in the title of each story, is ironic. . . . In most cases it indicates only an inner movement, the story of a state of mind or state of being [stato d'animo], an itinerary toward silence."[3]

This core of silence at the bottom of human communication is an area of passivity, a non-disposable residue of negativity that, for Calvino, is the essence of the sexual relationship. Desire is founded in absence, in the tension-toward rather than the attainment of the object of love, in the delays, the displacements, the deferrals. Epistemologically and emotionally, that is, Calvino stands somewhere between later romanticism and (post)modernism, or between Freud and Derrida. The scene of writing is always adjacent, though never collapsible on/to the oedipal scenario, and sexual difference is as much an end result of symbolic castration as it is an effect of writing, of *différance*. That becomes quite clear when one rereads the early "adventures" against the recent ones, especially comparing "The Adventure of a Reader" (in *Gli amori difficili*) with what appears to be its blown-up version or postmodern remake, *If on a winter's night a traveler.*

The reader's adventure takes place on a quasi-deserted beach—and here one cannot help but think of Antonioni's perhaps greatest film, *L'avventura*, released almost contemporaneously in 1960 and also very much centered on desire as absence, negativity, deferment, all of which are exactly inscribed in the form of the film text; a film text, exactly, where the theoretical notion of a filmic writing, of film as *écriture*, might as well have originated, at least insofar as Italian cinema is concerned. Conversely, one is reminded of the increasing effort on Calvino's part to inscribe the visual register, the sensory immediacy of the image, in his own written texts, an effort that reaches its goal of perfect balance in one of his greatest books, *Invisible Cities*, and again returns, for instance, in the more recent *Palomar*.

But back to "L'avventura di un lettore": its protagonist is the young Amedeo, an average reader partial to long, involved, and heavily plotted nineteenth-century novels. He is immersed in one of them, one day, on a solitary beach, when his eye catches the image of a woman sunbathing nearby. Torn between the desire to read, the imaginary of the written page which, Calvino says, "opened up to him a life more exciting, profound and true" than any action or feeling in the real world; torn between the pleasures of the imaginary and the demands of the symbolic (for his socialization as a young male requires him to take an interest in that female body there on the beach), Amedeo resorts to a compromise:

> He lay on his side, holding the book in such a way as to block the sight of her, but it was uncomfortable to keep his arm raised, and he had to lower it. Now the same gaze that ran along the printed lines would meet, at the end of each line, just beyond the margin of the page, the legs of the solitary sunbather.[4]

The two pleasures, looking and reading, are thus for a moment parallel and in perfect equilibrium. But when by sunset Amedeo and the unnamed woman have actually gotten together and are making love, he's thinking of his novel and silently counting in his mind how many pages are left till the end.

The adventure, the frustrations, and the small victories of Amedeo, average reader of the fifties, are nothing when compared to the adventures, the agonies, and the ecstasies of the postmodern reader in *If on a winter's night a traveler.* This is a reader with the capital *R*, whom the text addresses as "you," the Reader as eternal double of the Author, *son semblable, son frère,* or, in Calvino's phrase, the "absolute protagonist." To call him a postmodern reader, however, is not quite correct. It would be better said that "you" is the Reader of the postmodern text—and a Reader of postmodern texts against his will.

But let me first give at least a working definition of *postmodern*, a term employed so often nowadays, and in so many contexts, as to be nearly empty of reference—and thus itself, probably, postmodern. In the preface to *The Anti-Aesthetic*, a widely cited volume of essays on postmodern culture, the editor, Hal Foster, begins by asking:

> Postmodernism: does it exist at all and, if so, what does it mean? Is it a concept or a practice, a matter of local style or a whole new period or economic phase? What are its forms, effects, place? How are we to mark its advent? Are we truly beyond the modern, truly in (say) a postindustrial age?[5]

These questions are then addressed by many in the volume, from many angles. Some critics see postmodernism as a break with the aesthetic field of modernism; others define it as a politics of interpretation. For some it means "the end of ideology," while others see it as an epistemological shift in social consciousness. Others still think of it as an artistic practice that construes its object, the artifact, "less as a *work* in modernist terms—unique, symbolic, visionary—than as a *text* in a postmodernist sense—'already written,' allegorical, contingent" (pp. x–xi). For Rosalind Krauss, the artistic object is no longer "defined in relation to a given medium . . . but rather in relation to the logical operations on a set of cultural terms" (p. x). Similarly, the practice of literary criticism has become a kind of "paraliterary" writing, in Greg Ulmer's word, "which dissolves the line between critical and creative forms" (p. x); and vice versa, literary writing has become a "para-critical" practice, as Ihab Hassan suggests and, I might add, Calvino's text perfectly exemplifies.

Modernism, of course, started out as an oppositional view of art, marking the crisis of nineteenth-century bourgeois culture with its myths of progress, mastery, universality, and what Habermas calls the "false normativity" of its history; but today it has become the official culture. The idea that science, art, language, morality, politics are autonomous spheres possessed of an inner logic, closed systems like the museum, the scientific community (think of the literary topoi of the library, the labyrinth, etc.), is one that was developed by the Enlightenment (it is impossible here not to think of Calvino's often avowed partiality for the eighteenth century). But the idea of art as a separate sphere within society is still very much with us, as is the notion of an opposition, within that sphere, between an artistic establishment which relies on traditional forms, and an experimental, anarchic, or subversive avant-garde.

This duality of stability/subversion—like the other familiar dichotomies of subject and object, self and other—is what contemporary critical thought (poststructuralism) challenges with notions such as heterogeneity, difference, deconstruction, contradiction. But it remains an enduring cognitive paradigm; and even as postmodern writers would wish to do away with it, this binary structure in one way or another informs their very theorizations. Indeed, Foster himself sees a "basic opposition" in cultural politics today between a "postmodernism of resistance . . . which seeks to deconstruct modernism and resist the status quo" and a "postmodernism of reaction" which repudiates modernism only to celebrate the status quo (pp. xi–xii). This latter is evident in the neoconservative return to the verities of tradition in art, religion, the family, and so forth. It is accomplished by declaring modernism passé, reducing it to a style, and then recuperating or resurrecting the old pre-modernist, humanist tradition and proposing it as a new, "affirmative" and pluralistic culture. Anything goes, and all is well. Or, as Ronald Reagan keeps saying, we're all happy again.

The postmodernism of resistance, on the other hand, Foster says, "arises as a counter-practice not only to the official culture of modernism but also to the 'false normativity' of a reactionary postmodernism" or neoconservatism (p. xii). It manifests itself as a textual practice whose strategy is to "rewrite" modernism: not simply to oppose it or to reject it, but to open it up, to deconstruct it, to challenge its assumptions, and to show its historical limit, that is to say, its non-universality, its being located in a precise sociohistorical situation. The question to be asked here, then, is, Where does Calvino's text fit in this model? For I think that the model does fit, perhaps with a few wrinkles here and there.

To say that *If on a winter's night a traveler* is a self-reflexive text would be a gross understatement. It is a novel about novels, a story about storytelling, a book about the reading and the writing of books, whose characters are only readers and writers. To be exact, there is, exceptionally, one Non Reader, whose character status is signaled by the capital *N* and capital *R;* there is as well, though unremarked by the text, a non-writer (I'll let you guess who the non-writer is). In short, this is a text about textuality, a piece of writing about the process of writing; and we are never for a moment allowed to forget that we are, at that very moment, reading it. It tells of other books that we have read and of the other books Calvino has written. It tells us how we read, what we do while reading, what we want as readers, as well as what the writer wants, how he writes, what he does while writing, and so forth. What HE wants, I said: because the writer, there is no doubt, is male. The readers may also be women; in fact, it is necessary for the writer that at least one Reader be female (I will return to this interesting idea later on), but the Writer or the Author is only and always male.

At a certain point, halfway through his journey in pursuit of the elusive book(s) he is dying to read—a pursuit which coincides with his pursuit of the Woman Reader (la Lettrice, or, in Weaver's excellent translation, the Other Reader)—the hero of the story, i.e., the Reader himself, encounters two strange types, who are also pursuing the Woman Reader. As one can easily surmise, these two new characters are figures or representations of the contemporary writer: one is "the famous Irish writer Silas Flannery," a successful author of best-sellers, whose name and works more than suggest Ian Fleming grafted onto Sean Connery (I opt against the other, linguistically possible but otherwise improbable, combination of Silas Marner and Flannery O'Connor). The other is an imposter, a counterfeiter of manuscripts, who under the guise of literary agent and translator of novels from foreign languages fills the literary market with apocrypha and fakes; his name, Ermes Marana, is a wink to his allegorical status as Hermes, the Olympian trickster who deceives even Apollo with his song, Hermes the eternal gambler and the god of travelers, who takes mortals across the last frontier.

This Ermes Marana, the trans-lator (to translate, etymologically, is to carry beyond, to convey, to transport elsewhere), whose letters arrive from the four corners of the world bearing stamps that never correspond to the countries they are mailed from, is supposedly promoting the latest work of

Silas Flannery, the hot author of best-sellers. But in fact he's not. The very soul of mystification, he is intent on falsifying absolutely everything and creating a babelic confusion of titles, names of authors, pseudonyms, translations, original languages and countries, chapters, endings and beginnings. In short, he embodies the author-function, or, better, stands for it, for he never actually appears as a character in the novel but is merely, and constantly, referred to. The Reader never meets him, much as he tries, and thinks of him with burning jealousy because he suspects that the Woman Reader is very much taken by this personage. Marana is, the Reader thinks,

> the invisible rival who came constantly between him and Ludmilla [the Other Reader], the silent voice that speaks to her through books, this ghost with a thousand faces and faceless, all the more elusive since for Ludmilla authors are never incarnated in individuals of flesh and blood, they exist for her only in published pages, the living and the dead both are there always ready to communicate with her, to amaze her, and Ludmilla is always ready to follow them, in the fickle, carefree relations one can have with incorporeal persons. How is it possible to defeat not the authors but the functions of the author? (p. 159)

Always, the Reader thinks, Ermes Marana "dreamed of a literature made entirely of apocrypha, of false attributions, of imitations and counterfeits and pastiches." Briefly, Marana is the genius of simulation, in Baudrillard's terms, the postmodern artist in the age of media implosion, the age of the infinite multiplication of discourses; the writer poised on the rim of the black hole of meaning, as it were.

The other figure of the writer, Silas Flannery, is one generation older and still sits on the late-modernist "abyss" of meaning, so to speak. "How well would I write if I were not here!" he cries out.

> If I were only a hand, a severed hand that grasps a pen and writes . . . . Who would move this hand? The anonymous throng? The spirit of the times? The collective unconscious? I do not know. It is not in order to be the spokesman for something definable that I would like to erase myself. Only to transmit the writable that waits to be written, the tellable that nobody tells. Perhaps the woman I observe with the spyglass knows what I should write [you guessed it again: the woman he's watching is Ludmilla, the Woman Reader]; or, rather, *she does not know it,* because she is in fact waiting for me to write what she *does not know;* but what she knows for certain is her waiting, the void that my words should fill. (p. 171; emphasis in the text)

This vision of woman as passive capacity, receptivity, readiness to receive—a womb waiting to be fecundated by words (*his* words), a void ready to be filled with meanings, or elsewhere a blank page awaiting insemination by the writer's pen—is a notorious cliché of Western literary writing. In its most recent version, it is the hymen, the figure of deconstruction and

Derrida's model of the textual operation: the hymen which represents dissemination, the dispersal of meaning effected by the writer's style or stylus or spur (have it anyway you want it).

This, then, explains the unusual and intriguing fact that for Calvino's Writer it is necessary to have a Woman Reader, a privilege we are unaccustomed to, except in those particular genres of "feminine literature" written specifically for women, such as Harlequin romances or *romanzi rosa*. But Calvino is not Louis L'Amour. So we're at first intrigued, until we realize that in this book reading, like writing, is a function of desire, literally. The pursuit of the book's ending corresponds to the pursuit of the unattainable love object, narrative closure is impeded by *écriture*, the dispersal of meaning, writing as *différance;* and the pleasure of the text is infiltrated or intercut with the *jouissance* of the text. More simply put, as the American critic Robert Scholes once suggested, the archetype of this fiction is the male sexual act.

Thus, like the other privileges granted to women, this one—the essential role that Woman appears to have in men's creative writing—is double-edged. We begin to glimpse it early in the story, when we first meet Lotaria, the bad sister (the "mirror image," Calvino says) of Ludmilla the Woman Reader. Lotaria, as her Teutonic name heavily hints, is the Non-Feminine Woman. Indeed, she is the feminist militant who doesn't read novels simply for the pleasure of reading but cannot help analyzing and debating them. (You begin to see where my identification lies.) In particular, when first introduced, Lotaria is leading a seminar at the University, and discussing a novel (in German translation) entitled *Without Fear of Wind or Vertigo*. She is described thus:

> a girl . . . with a long neck and a bird's face, a steady, bespectacled gaze, a
> great clump of curly hair; she is dressed in a loose tunic and tight pants. . . .
> Crowding behind Lotaria is the vanguard of a phalanx of young girls with
> limpid, serene eyes, slightly alarming eyes, perhaps because they are too
> limpid and serene. (p. 73)

Clearly, Lotaria and her comrades are the Amazons, a recurrent figure in Calvino's fiction. But here, to the threat the narrator reads in their eyes (Why are they *too* limpid? Too serene for what?), another feature is added: a hard, ironic voice. This is a feature that in Italian literature since Pavese (who obsessively attributed it to his harsh, cold, domineering female characters) has come to denote symbolic castration. You might say I'm overreading. I am not. Let me offer two proofs, both textual, that is to say, two pieces of internal evidence.

First, in talking to Lotaria, who in this book represents the Critical (Woman) Reader (she is writing a thesis on Silas Flannery and uses electronic instruments for content analysis), our hero the (male) Reader is addressed by Calvino as follows:

> Again you feel the sensation you felt when the paper knife revealed the facing white pages. . . . You are dazed, contemplating that whiteness cruel as a wound. (pp. 44, 42)

Two paragraphs earlier, the text asserted that

> the pleasures derived from the use of a paper knife are tactile, auditory, visual, and especially mental. Progress in reading is preceded by an act that traverses the material solidity of the book to allow you access to its incorporeal substance. *Penetrating* among the pages from below, *the blade vehemently moves upward,* opening a *vertical cut* in a flowing succession of *slashes* that one by one *strike the fibers* and mow them down. . . . [It goes on, but you get the idea.] (p. 42; emphasis added)

Obviously, when this orgasmic process is abruptly interrupted by a blank page, the Reader, (post)modern Oedipus, is dazzled and blinded by the "whiteness cruel as a wound." It is, recognizably, one of the classic "Psychical Consequences of the Anatomical Distinction between the Sexes" described at length by Freud.

The second piece of internal evidence that Lotaria, the critical feminist reader, is ipso facto non-feminine (that is, masculine or, in harsher words, castrating) is toward the end of the book, when the hero's adventures take him to Ataguitania, a fictional country of Latin America; and there among revolutionaries and counterrevolutionaries, among military dictatorships and censorship experts with electronic reading machines and text processers, he meets her again as Sheila, the computer programmer who, his captors tell him, "will *insert* the program we want" (p. 217; emphasis added). Indeed she does, and as the printout of yet another novel begins to unfurl, this Sheila-Lotaria, the Feminist Revolutionary/Counterrevolutionary, actually attempts . . . to rape him. Fortunately, we're told, they're interrupted by the flash of a bulb and the click of a camera, which, the text remarks, "devour the whiteness of your convulsed, superimposed nudity" (p. 219).

In short, Lotaria, the bad sister and mirror image of Ludmilla, is the negative image of Woman, the *unheimlich* double of a female Dorian Gray. She is the woman reader we shouldn't be. Or so the text tries to convince us. For, whether because of male narcissism, blinding homophobia, or a rather shocking cultural naiveté in a writer so sophisticated otherwise, Calvino seems unaware that there are women readers—let alone the Amazons of old—who simply have no interest in men or men's desire; or who, while sharing Lotaria's militant and critical disposition, would not waste their revolutionary energy on raping or castrating.

But let us turn to the true heroine, Ludmilla, the Woman Reader desired and pursued by Reader and Writer alike, and in the end attained, captured, and safely married off to the hero. Because there is an ending to this story, after all. Whether intentionally or not, I do not know, Calvino appropriates the famous ending of *Jane Eyre,* "Reader, I married him," and rewrites it to fit his plan: "Reader, you married her." Only, in compliance with the current liberal ideology of gender equality, he writes: "Now you are man and wife, Reader and Reader." As if that fooled anyone.

Like her sister, Ludmilla also first appears among the bookshelves, on page 29,

> looking among the Penguin Modern Classics, running a lovely and deter-mined finger over the pale aubergine-colored spines. Huge, swift eyes, com-plexion of good tone and good pigment, a richly waved haze of hair. And so the Other Reader makes her happy entrance into your field of vision, Reader, or rather, into the field of your attention; or, rather, you have entered a magnetic field from whose attraction you cannot escape. (p. 29)

With accurate symmetry, as he devotes chapter 9 to Lotaria (a chapter featuring the one sex scene of the novel), so he devotes chapter 7 to Ludmilla, and for six pages gives the Woman Reader the honor of the second-person pronoun, of being addressed as "you"—of being, that is, the protagonist. Meanwhile, the hero, the male Reader, now referred to as "he," walks around "inspecting" her apartment. The text speaks to the Woman Reader, thus:

> What are you like, Other Reader? It is time for this book in the second person to address itself no longer to a general male you, perhaps brother and double of a hypocrite I, but directly to you who appeared already in the second chapter as the Third Person necessary for the novel to be a novel, for something to happen between that male Second Person and the female Third, for something to take form, develop, or deteriorate according to the phases of human events. . . . Let us see, Other Reader, if the book can succeed in drawing a true portrait of you, beginning with the frame and enclosing you from every side, establishing the outlines of your form. . . . To understand this, our Reader [the male Reader again] knows that the first step is to visit the kitchen. (pp. 141–42)

The text then goes on to comment that "your" relationship with objects is "a relationship with the physicality of things, not with an intellectual or affec-tive idea" (p. 143); it notes "a certain aesthetic tendency" among the uten-sils, and condescends to appreciate the fact that "your" few books do not make up a library: "they are not very numerous," but they are a "living part" of your space, which "you enjoy handling, seeing around you," ready for immediate consumption (p. 146).

By the end of his search of the apartment, the male Reader has become again the "you": "Don't believe that the book is losing sight of you, Reader," Calvino feels the need to reassure him, since the second-person discourse has shifted to the Woman for all of six pages. And, to reimburse him for his temporary loss of narrative status, the text gives him a bonus: when the Other Reader comes home, shortly after, he succeeds in getting her into bed. A lyrical ellipsis follows—similar to the fade to black that in classical cinema conventionally stands for the sexual act, the consummation of love, and occurs immediately after the first serious kiss. In this ellipsis, the equation of reading and lovemaking is played out through the topos of the body as text. It begins:

> Ludmilla, now you are being. read. Your body is being subjected to a sys-
> tematic reading. . . . And you, too, O Reader, are meanwhile an object of
> reading. (p. 155)

The reading of each other's bodies (or, as Calvino wittily says, "of that concentrate of mind and body which lovers use to go to bed together") is an equal opportunity, leading to conjugal harmony: "the fullnesses and the voids compenetrate, the two of you a single subject" (p. 154).

That sounds all very wonderful. But what of the sisterly symmetry, what of Lotaria and the sex scene with her? There, it is clearly a matter of sex—crude, violent, and conventionally "erotic." There are no ellipses or paren-theses. Her body is described as she undresses out of successive sets of clothes in a kind of futuristic striptease, as if she were a simulant, a female android; and the description is in the language of glossy, softcore porn (p. 218). Nothing lyrical or philosophical about it. Why is it so?

Before "you" rush to say that, obviously, it's the old story of wife and mistress, chaste bride versus licentious whore; or that Calvino's allegory of desire merely updates the classical allegory of sacred and profane love, let me caution against too quick an answer. Calvino, as I have already pointed out, is not Louis L'Amour. The stakes of his text are higher, for it does not simply inscribe received popular wisdom but actually engages contempo-rary theories of signification. It may have occurred to you, my readers, that one of the charms of Ludmilla—the book's most original character, accord-ing to several male reviewers—is that, besides not being interested in authors of flesh and blood (what she loves is the Author-function, as you recall), she positively refuses to have anything to do with writing. She won't even go to the publishing company's office in order not to cross the boundary between those who make books and those who read them. She wants to remain a reader, "on principle." Thus, she takes no part in her sister's critical or intellectual activities and does not like the "feminist" novel discussed in the women's seminar. Her notion of the ideal novel is, naturally enough, an organic one:

> The novel I would most like to read . . . should have as its driving force only
> the desire to narrate, to pile stories upon stories, without trying to impose a
> philosophy of life on you, simply allowing you to observe its own growth, like
> a tree, an entangling, as if of branches and leaves. (p. 92)

Now, we know from Lacan as well as Calvino that writing is the masculine activity par excellence, because it exists in the order of the symbolic where language, the circulation of signifiers, and signification itself are subject to the name of the Father, to the structure of symbolic castration in which the phallus is the signifier of desire. Writing thus presupposes possession of the phallus—symbolically speaking, of course; and for a woman to write is to usurp a place, a discursive position, she does not have by nature or by culture. Hence, in our allegory, Lotaria's "masculinity," which the attempted rape is there to signify beyond a doubt.

Calvino then seems to side with Lacan, abandoning Freud, who—let it be said to his credit—did entertain the possibility of symbolic bisexuality, of an ambiguity in the female subject that would mean that women are not just the Other, the complementary opposite of man, voids and fullnesses compenetrating, but in effect different, heterogeneous, not quite comparable. And that implies a concept of gender asymmetry, a possible new way of understanding social relations, on which only feminist theorists are currently working (and only a small number of feminist theorists, at that).

If Calvino is no longer with Freud, neither is he quite with Derrida, whose "affirmative woman" is rather more like Lotaria, one who masquerades, simulates, pretends to be what she is not, and is only what she pretends. But alas, Lotaria is also masculine, castrating, and so she falls short of Derrida's Ideal Woman. The character in this book who comes closest to that, actually, is Ermes Marana; in fact, Derrida's "woman" is not a woman but a figure of writing, a question not of gender but of genre, style, not difference but *différance*. However, Marana doesn't make it either, for as it turns out, all of his masquerades and machinations, deconstructions and simulations had one very old-fashioned purpose: they were all for the love of Ludmilla.

Finally, therefore, one is tempted to read this text "aberrantly," as another author of postmodern fiction, Umberto Eco, would say. One is tempted to read Lotaria as the true postmodern writer/reader, the representative of a postmodernism of resistance who successfully escapes not only capture by the narrative (she vanishes from the text after the sex scene) but also, and more important, captivity in the conjugal bed. To read Lotaria so, however, one would have—precisely—to "rewrite" her, which in a sense is what I've done, with a bona fide postmodern gesture. And so it is time to come back to the question of postmodernism.

In another essay of the volume *The Anti-Aesthetic,* an essay on postmodern art, Craig Owens discusses the work of Mary Kelly, Laurie Anderson, Martha Rosler, Barbara Kruger, and others. These artists are engaged, he argues, in the double process of "deconstructing femininity" (deconstructing the received notions and images of Woman), and "investigating" not only the representation of Woman but "what representation *does* to women" (p. 71). However, he laments, in most critical discussions of their work, the issue of gender is carefully avoided; and, needless to say, these artists are considered rather marginal. On the other hand, he states, the "official" artistic production (by men, that is) seems "engaged in a collective act of disavowal," whether it simulates mastery or it contemplates and advertises the artist's loss of it. And this Owens attributes to the emergent voices of the conquered, "Third-World nations, the 'revolt of nature' and the women's movement."

> Symptoms of our recent loss of mastery are everywhere apparent in cultural activity today—nowhere more so than in the visual arts. The modernist project of joining forces with science and technology for the transformation of the environment after rational principles of function and utility (Productivism, the Bauhaus) has long since been abandoned; what we witness in its place is a desperate, often hysterical attempt to recover some sense of mastery via the resurrection of heroic large-scale easel painting and monumental cast-bronze sculpture—mediums themselves identified with the cultural hegemony of Western Europe. Yet contemporary artists are able at best to *simulate* mastery, to manipulate its signs; since in the modern period mastery was invariably associated with human labor, aesthetic production has degenerated today into a massive deployment of the signs of artistic labor—violent, "impassioned" brushwork, for example. (p. 67)

A massive deployment of the signs of writing is certainly an apt description of Calvino's book. All the elements of fiction are there: the nuts and bolts of storytelling; the chassis and the engine, narrative frame and driving force of narrative; down to the rear-view mirror and vinyl seat covers of the novel as desiring machine. They are all there, if a bit scrambled, superimposed onto the story and placed in evidence on the surface of the text; a "rhetoric of fiction" added on to the fiction.

A massive deployment of the signs of writing, then, rather than "an intinerary toward silence" in the manner of a Beckett, is what constitutes this text: not the impossibility of expression, the absence, the traces, the shredding and dissolution of language into silence, but instead the massive presence, the concrete materiality, the pressure, the multiplication of words and meanings. Unless this is, in fact, that "implosion" prophesied by

Baudrillard, the mad rush of both modernism and postmodernism together into the black hole.

Yet, it is this very display of the signs of writing, the signs of the labor of
writing which, Calvino has said over and over, is a labor of love—it is this
labor of love that seduces us and draws us to him even as he will not grant
us equal access to writing; even as he waves the specter of Lotaria the
android before us, women who read *and* write, and who love to write as
much as he did.

Why is that necessary? Why has the women's movement of the seventies,
which after all demanded little more than equal access to cultural production and self-determination, engendered the neoconservative reaction that
we see all around us, and that leads so many writers, artists, and theorists to
employ their labor and their talent in order to re-contain women in male-
centered systems? Just as the female reader here is finally re-contained
within the frame of the book as merely a character in a man's fiction,
reduced to a portrait, an image, a figure of the male imaginary? Because, I
suggest, Woman is still the ground of representation, even in postmodern
times. Paradoxically, for all the efforts spent to re-contain real women in
the social, whether by economic or ideological means, by threats or by
seduction, it is the absent Woman, the one pursued in dreams and found
only in memory or in fiction, that serves as the guarantee of masculinity,
anchoring male identity and supporting man's creativity and self-representation. Just as it was with Flaubert, Madame Bovary *c'est lui.*

So here is the modernist Calvino emerging in the palimpsest of the
postmodern text, reappearing in the rewriting of his own modernist works,
those works where the love adventure was "an inner movement, a state of
mind, an itinerary toward silence." I want to conclude by referring back to
another story of *Gli amori difficili* entitled "L'avventura di due sposi" (The
Adventure of a Young Married Couple). Again, the comparison with the
two Readers of *If on a winter's night a traveler* suggests to me that Owens may
be right; and that if Calvino, in rewriting his own texts, feels the necessity
on the one hand to engage or deal with feminism, and on the other to put
us in our place, that may mean that "the discourse of the others" is indeed
challenging, disturbing, or threatening the status quo.

In "L'avventura di due sposi," two young married factory workers have
very little time to spend together. He works the night shift, she the daytime
shift. When he comes home at seven in the morning, her alarm clock has
just gone off, and by the time she gets home in the evening with the
shopping and they've eaten dinner, he's off to work. Coming home to a cold
house in the morning, he gets into her side of the bed, still unmade and still
warm. When she goes to sleep at night, lying on the bed he's just pulled up,
she stretches a leg toward her husband's side feeling for his warmth. But

every time, Calvino wrote, "she realized that her own side was warmer; so evidently Arturo too had slept there, and she felt a great love for him."[6]

This, I would say, rather than Lotaria's matter-of-fact sexual aggressiveness or Ludmilla's unenthusiastic acquiescence, is an insightful rendering of the sexual relation between a woman and a man who love each other.

Notes

1. Italo Calvino, *Gli amori difficili* (Torino: Einaudi, 1970), p. 47. This and all subsequent quotations from this work are in my translation. It may be noted that *Difficult Loves* is the title of a recently published selection of Calvino's short stories. Eight of the thirteen stories originally included by Calvino in *Gli amori difficili* are now in *Difficult Loves* (San Diego: Harcourt, Brace, Jovanovich, 1984), in William Weaver's translation, grouped in a section under the subheading of "Stories of Love and Loneliness."

2. Italo Calvino, *If on a winter's night a traveler,* trans. William Weaver (San Diego: Harcourt Brace Jovanovich, 1981), from the original *Se una notte d'inverno un viaggiatore* (Torino: Einaudi, 1979).

3. Calvino, *Gli amori difficili,* p. ix.

4. Ibid., p. 63.

5. Hal Foster, "Postmodernism: A Preface," in *The Anti-Aesthetic: Essays on Postmodern Culture* (Port Townsend, Wash.: Bay Press, 1983), p. ix. All further references to this work are given in the text.

6. *Gli amori difficili,* p. 90. This story is not included in *Difficult Loves.*

5

GRAMSCI NOTWITHSTANDING, OR, THE LEFT HAND OF HISTORY

What is the place of textuality in feminist criticism? (I mean criticism both in the narrow sense of literary criticism and in the broad sense of sociocultural critique.) Since textual analysis has a fundamental place in any theory of culture, how should the feminist critic approach her work with texts? What should her purpose be? I am not sure that a theory of women's writing is useful or even desirable at this point. Because women have been a colonized population for so long, I fear that any critical category we may find applicable today is likely to be derived from or imbued with male ideologies. As writers, critics, teachers, we know that from our daily experiences. I am not suggesting that we ought to clean the slate of history and start anew, because I am enough of a historical materialist and semiotician that I cannot conceive of a totally new world rising out of, and in no way connected with, the past or the present. I believe neither in utopias nor in the myth of Paradise Now, or ever. What I am suggesting is that theory is dialectically built on, checked against, modified by, transformed along with, practice—that is to say, with what women do, invent, perform, produce, concretely and not "for all time" but within specific historical and cultural conditions.

In the summer of 1975, I was in the small town of Sant' Arcangelo di Romagna (near Bologna, Italy), where an open-air theater festival sponsored performances by militant and experimental groups in the town square and courtyards of two medieval castles. One of these performances attracted my attention by its title, *Nonostante Gramsci* (Despite Gramsci or

Written in 1976–77 as a contribution to the Heresies Collective's project on "Women's Traditional Arts and the Politics of Aesthetics." Presented at the symposium "Women/Texts" organized by Marilyn Schneider at the University of Minnesota in 1977. First published in *Heresies: A Feminist Publication on Art and Politics,* no. 4 (Winter 1978), with the title "The Left Hand of History." Reprinted here with minor changes in editorial style and format.

Gramsci Notwithstanding). It was performed by a militant feminist collective, La Maddalena, based in Rome. Antonio Gramsci was founder of the Italian Communist Party and one of the major European Marxist thinkers. He was the most important influence on the Italian left in general and on the politics of the Italian Communist Party (PCI) in particular. His historical analyses and theoretical foundations for Italian Communism continue to be effective today.

Gramsci was imprisoned in 1926 by the newly consolidated Fascist dictatorship. He received a mock trial, was given a life sentence, and died in 1937 of illness and abuse suffered in Mussolini's prisons. The circumstances of his death and his extraordinary intellectual and moral stature have made him perhaps the greatest hero and martyr of the Italian resistance. That is why the play's title, *Despite Gramsci*, surprised and intrigued me, since I knew that Italian feminist groups consisted almost exclusively of women with a record of militancy in the left. They couldn't be "against" Gramsci. Therefore, what did they mean by "despite"?

The background of the production reveals the group's ideological stance. Both the text of the theatrical production and the underlying research on original documents were published together the following year under the editorship of Adele Cambria, a feminist writer and one of the editors of the major Italian feminist monthly *EFFE*.[1] Cambria formulated and conducted the research, but the theatrical work was performed, directed, and written collectively. The published volume, entitled *Amore come rivoluzione* (Love as Revolution), contains, I believe, not two texts—one creative/artistic and one historical/biographical—but rather a single text. It self-consciously attempts to be at once historical and artistic, and deliberately presents itself as tendentious and critical. It is a text with its ideology clearly stated and with a basis of original research behind its fiction. This text is posited as a set of questions dealing with love and revolution—a complex problem that emerged in the late 1960s and was pushed to the foreground of political consciousness by radical feminism.

During the last eleven years of his life, the imprisoned Gramsci wrote the bulk of his theoretical work, now published as *Quaderni dal carcere* (Prison Notebooks).[2] In 1922 Gramsci spent several months in the Soviet Union as Italian envoy to the Executive Committee of the Communist International. While hospitalized in a sanatorium outside Moscow, he met Eugenia Schucht, also a patient in the hospital, and her sister Giulia. Giulia and Antonio fell in love. After Gramsci had returned to Western Europe, recalled by his political duties, their son Delio was born in 1924. The couple were together only once again, the following year, when Giulia, the baby, and Eugenia spent a few months in Rome with Gramsci, who by then had been elected to the Italian parliament. When she returned to the Soviet

Union, Giulia was pregnant with their second son, Giuliano, whom Gramsci
never saw. History records that during his long years in prison, the only
link between Gramsci and his family was Giulia's other sister, Tatiana
Schucht, who lived in Italy and followed Gramsci as he was sent from one
jail to another. She supported him materially and spiritually, assisting him
through his long agony. It was Tatiana who rescued Gramsci's *Prison Notebooks* after his death. But, history being the history of men, only Gramsci's
letters were deemed important historical documents.[3] The letters he received from Giulia and Tatiana were not published, although they existed,
lying in a file at the Gramsci Institute in Rome. Official historiography
scorned them. They were women's letters, dealing "only with children and
marmalade," banal, insignificant. Little information could be found about
these mute women, whose complex relationships to Gramsci and to one
another constituted the most intense private aspect of Gramsci's life as a
revolutionary. Biographers record that Giulia grew more and more alien-
ated from her husband as a result of mental illness. In his letters he
lamented and grieved over her silence. Tatiana acted as a sister of mercy,
visiting Gramsci in jail, sending him socks and medicines, relaying letters
between him, Giulia, and the children. Here ends their official history. Yet,
if we read Gramsci's letters, many of the questions posed in them remain
unanswered: What exactly was the nature of Giulia's "illness"? Why did
Tatiana and not she stay in Italy to assist him in jail? What moved Tatiana to
literally devote her life to him? What was Eugenia's role? There is no doubt
that Gramsci's thoughts were directed to these private concerns as much as
to political problems and theory—his letters prove it despite the self-
restraint imposed by personal ethics and prison censorship. Some of his
most moving letters to Giulia deal with the education of their children and
with the problems posed by his responsibilities to the revolution and to
their love relationship—he even suggested a formal separation that would
allow Giulia to remarry, if that would restore her well-being.

Who were these women outside of the pale, pathetic hagiography constructed by Gramsci's biographers? That is what Adele Cambria set out to
investigate. She carefully read all of the women's letters in conjunction with
Gramsci's, interviewed people who had been close friends of the sisters,
studied Eugenia's letters to a friend in Rome and the notebooks in which
Giulia had practiced composition as an adolescent. Cambria's purpose
throughout was to reconstruct an "affective biography" of the Schuchts and
to discover the sources and modes of that "emotional energy" Shulamith
Firestone identifies as the essential female contribution to male thought.[4]
Cambria's project was a political one: to rewrite history, inscribing in it the
missing voices of women, and therefore to examine the relationships between the private and the public, love and revolution, personal/sexual/

emotional needs and political militancy—relations which she sees as the moving forces of all revolutionary struggle. In restoring to Gramsci's epistolary monologue its real nature as dialogue, Cambria adds depth to the cultural image of a person whose complex humanity has been expediently stereotyped.

In a letter to Giulia in 1924, before his imprisonment and at the height of his revolutionary activities, Gramsci himself posed the problem. He wrote:

> *How many times have I asked myself whether it was possible to tie oneself to a mass without ever having loved anyone . . . whether one could love a collectivity if one hadn't deeply loved some single human beings. . . . Wouldn't that have made barren my qualities as a revolutionary, wouldn't it have reduced them to a pure intellectual fact, a pure mathematical calculation?*[5]

Gramsci's question unwinds the ideological thread that runs through Cambria's work and the collective theater production, both of which focus on the "private" aspect of Gramsci's life. Thus, an understanding of the Schucht family is essential, in the context of the turn-of-the-century cultural values and of the changes brought by the October Revolution, by Lenin, and later by Stalinism and Fascism.

Apollo Schucht, father of the three sisters, was an exile from czarist Russia who had settled in Rome in 1908. Born into the upper bourgeoisie, he had belonged to the Russian populist social reform movement (*narodvol'stvo*) in the mid-nineteenth century. Deported with Lenin to Siberia, where his third daughter, Eugenia, was born, he asked his friend Lenin to be her "godfather." The family lived in Rome from 1908 to 1917. After the October Revolution, they all returned to the Soviet Union and worked in the CPSU, except Tatiana, who stayed at her teaching position in Rome. Significantly, nothing much is known of Apollo's wife, Lula, except that she was an excellent cook and housewife. It was Apollo's strong influence that shaped the lives of his daughters. His world view, in matters of sex roles, was all but revolutionary. His daughters completed their higher education in Rome in the arts and natural sciences, areas that clearly trained women for the only careers suitable for them—marriage and teaching. The early writings of Giulia and Eugenia reveal how deeply they had absorbed their father's late-romantic humanitarian values: a sense of duty toward the poor and dispossessed; contact with nature as a source of happiness, goodness, and personal fulfillment; the love of children idealized as a pure unspoiled manifestation of Good Nature; a sentimental attachment to Family as nest and shelter from the disorder and potential danger of the outside world. None of that prepared them for the violent realities in which they were to live. In the turmoil after the revolution, there came into their lives the man who, like their father before him, was to magnetize their existence. Gramsci became, for all three women, the center of their emotional world, the unwitting protagonist of romantic mystification, the pivot of a patriarchal model they had deeply internalized. They all were in love with Antonio.

Eugenia met him first, but he fell in love with Giulia, the youngest, most beautiful, and most "feminine" of them. Cambria documents, fairly convincingly, that Eugenia's espousal of the Communist cause—her "wedding" to the Party—came right after Antonio and Giulia met. The sisters' close mother-daughter relationship had made Giulia emotionally and intellectually dependent on her older sister. Eugenia later exploited this dependence by making herself indispensable, supporting Giulia financially, taking care of her children, and living with her before and during Gramsci's imprisonment, thus reinforcing Giulia's feelings of personal inadequacy in the roles of mother and wife. In Cambria's interpretation, Eugenia was mainly responsible for keeping Giulia away from Gramsci. Her reasons were consistent with the prevailing values of the time: Giulia must stay in the Soviet Union to care for the children, who would be in great danger in Fascist Italy; Giulia was "sickly and subject to depressions"; Giulia was a Soviet Communist, and the Party needed her. Eradicating from her life the possibility of a "private" relationship with any man, Eugenia played the male role as political activist and head of the household. While praising and mythicizing Gramsci as a revolutionary leader (she translated his writings for the Soviet workers), Eugenia increased the human distance between him and Giulia.

Tatiana met Antonio after his return to Rome, already "married" to Giulia (the marriage was officially recorded after the first child was born). Tatiana's love for Gramsci, avowed as sisterly love, developed over the twelve years during which she performed for him the duties of the prisoner's wife. A close reading of their letters shows the ambivalence of their relationship, which, considering their strong ethical sense and material and social constraints, was perhaps the most fulfilling, if deformed, love relationship of any of the Schucht sisters. In defining herself as Giulia's representative, she slowly made herself indispensable to the man she loved. She maintained contact with underground left leaders outside Italy in hopeless attempts to free Gramsci through prisoner exchanges. As the only correspondent authorized by jail officials, she copied and relayed his letters to Giulia and the children and theirs to him. By this "charitable sacrifice" and sisterly devotion, and by never allowing her own needs to surface (but they are there, between the lines of the letters), Tatiana gradually acquired a wife's right to husbandly gratitude, a wifely possessiveness, and the subtle power gained by female self-denial.

Of the three stories, unrecorded by history, Giulia's is the most lonely. She is still alive, as far as we know, in some psychiatric hospital, where she has spent most of her life, imprisoned in her "mental illness" as Antonio was in his cell. He burned in the hell of pain, captivity, and death, but he won— he is a protagonist of history. Giulia is still burning, quietly, bothering no one, unnoticed, useless. One of Cambria's most significant contributions to feminist analysis is her effort to understand Giulia's personal world with love and generosity, outside of myth and without mystification. She sees Giulia as a sensitive, intelligent, gifted woman in whom the traditional female socialization, with its emphasis on dependence, frailty, and childlike trust, found a most receptive terrain. Giulia did not relate intellectually to others or to her own experience. Women of her time were not supposed to. She needed direct sensuous contact with reality, her children, her man. She gave up her violin for her children and the Party. The distance between her and Antonio was caused not only by circumstances but also by decisions made for her by Eugenia, to which Gramsci acquiesced. Her response to the distance was expressed by a sense of personal inadequacy, increasing depression, surrendering her will to others and to the mechanical details of daily existence. The notion that absence makes the heart grow fonder did not work for her: she blamed herself for not being able to feel, for losing contact with Antonio, who was becoming a mere abstraction—The Father of Her Children, The Revolutionary Hero—no longer her lover whom she could touch or her friend whom she could see and hear and speak to. She felt guilty about that, and when she finally dared to write to him about her illness, he did not answer, could not accept the idea of *mental* illness, spoke harshly of psychoanalysis as a crutch, and like the rest of the family recommended iron, vitamins, and will power. No one ever seriously considered the possibility that Giulia move to Italy to assist Antonio, and she herself believed that she could never do for him what Tatiana did. In short, Eugenia and Tatiana usurped her roles as mother, housekeeper, and wife and effectively deprived her of meaningful emotional relationships and intensified her sense of powerlessness. At last, Cambria maintains, Giulia's inability to define herself conceptually or through any type of personal power, and the unreality of her existence that could not function within any socially accepted mode of female behavior, pushed Giulia to live her rebellion inwardly, in total passivity. That is precisely what is often diagnosed as madness in women.[6]

In a sense, the personalities and social roles assumed by the three Schucht sisters sketch almost to a *T* the only choices allowed women in most Western cultures: service functions within male structures, adherence to the feminine mystique of charity, sacrifice, and self-denial, and madness.

The textual strategies of *Amore come rivoluzione* are the result of ideological choices. The materials being mainly letters, there were three obvious genre possibilities: (1) publishing the letters, with some editing (as was

done with Gramsci's letters); (2) putting together a sort of three-way epistolary novel of Giulia's, Tatiana's, and Gramsci's letters; or (3) giving the
materials a narrative form, i.e., writing a biography of the Schucht sisters.
Cambria discarded all three alternatives. Her decision to avoid a "novelistic"
organization was a political as well as aesthetic choice: as recent critical
theory in literature and film argues, narrative form is the primary aesthetic
code developed to convey bourgeois and counter-revolutionary values.[7]
Simply printing the letters without attempting to reproduce such "physical"
qualities as handwriting, or the context in which they were written and
discovered, would have erased altogether the function of the subject
(Cambria herself), as both writer and narrator of her book and at the same
time reader of the Schucht letters.

Cambria chose to print portions of the original documents in italics
interspersed with passages from Gramsci's letters, quotations, statements by
friends or others involved in the events, while her own comments link,
interpret, and contextualize each passage. The rigorous separation, by
different typefaces, between the women's letters and her own commentary
explicitly manifests the interpretive nature of the commentary, its tenden-
tiousness, its having a viewpoint, its being "sectarian" rather than an innocent or "objective" explanation. In this manner, a twofold process is set in
motion in the text: the release of affective energies contained in the first-
hand documents, which were personal writings aimed at a real person
(Gramsci), not a literary readership; and the release of a corresponding
emotional response in the modern woman reading the letters and mediat-
ing them for us through her personal and ideological, affective and conceptual codes. In many passages, Cambria shares her emotion at
discovering the letters, looking at the faded colors of the paper, the elegant
old-fashioned handwriting of Tatiana, the broken sentences and pencil
scrawls of an already ill Giulia. Cambria also describes her feelings as she
approached the Moscow house where Giulia lived and where Cambria
interviewed her son Giuliano.[8]

Cambria conveys to the readers how she absorbed Giulia, Tatiana, and
Eugenia as fragments of her own self, how their experiences can act as
reactor to other women's understanding of themselves; she also conveys
her elation in discovering and unearthing a writing which is the testimony
of unknown women. She reaches into an immense reservoir of women's
folklore, millions of letters in which women have spent their imagination
and creativity writing to those they loved, all lost, but for the few who made
literary history by loving a male protagonist.

The performance I saw was in an open courtyard and used the Brechtian
concept of epic theater. In the theatrical text, the double function of the
subject as writer and as reader is dramatized in the character of The Girl,

epic narrator and didactic commentator, who circulates among the four characters (the three sisters and Gramsci), each of whom is confined to an assigned scenic space. The Girl has a double function: as narrator and commentator, she provides the historical background and the feminist interpretation of the performed action. As character, she voices the lyrical consciousness of the play, Woman-Orpheus. A contemporary woman, she is a barometer for the audience, reacting with pity and anger to the events enacted around her. The fact that she also acts *visibly* as a stage hand (she projects the slides, moves the structures, dresses the actors) is a brilliant theatrical idea, for she is perceived by the audience as a performer, i.e., as a real person participating in the entire fictional creation and not simply acting out a memorized part in somebody else's play. Furthermore, since she models audience response, it is very important that she does not remain emotionally detached or objective in relation to the characters; at the same time, her involvement must never become total. For, in the intentions of the epic theater, the audience and the performers must not identify totally with the characters, must not be drawn into the story forgetting that it is a fiction, must not experience catharsis at the conclusion of the play. Rather, they must remain conscious of the problems raised by the play and seek their solution outside, after the play, in the real world. One example: in "dressing" Giulia, revealing her to us, The Girl is a woman of today discovering her roots in a woman of the past and reenacting herself in a fictional character. But when The Girl acts out the pain of pregnancy and childbirth, shouting her rejection of motherhood as a physical violence done to her body, as an emotionally traumatic infringement on her total person, at this moment The Girl *is* Giulia; she expresses the feeling that Giulia could never express, the repression of which was one of the forms of her "insanity."

Certain aspects of this production—the use of voices on tape, slides, lighting, the designed structures, objects of personal "ritual" created by the performers—are discussed in the direction notes and contributions by performers and designers printed in the appendix to the volume. These provide an integral, essential part of the text, outlining the difficult but rewarding practice of the performance, collective in every aspect from writing to staging to each performer's self-direction.

The historical text and the theatrical text were conceived interdependently. Although they are addressed to different, if overlapping, audiences and make different assumptions as textual mechanisms, they are not two distinct texts as would be, say, a biography and a play based on it. They are, rather, one set of raw materials examined with an identical ideological perspective and presented differently to achieve a double impact by juxtaposition; when we experience them together, the historical text has a distancing effect from the highly emotional impact of the dramatic text. The first is rational, documented, footnoted; the second is lyrical and intensely charged with emotion. The verbal material in the play is almost entirely from the original letters, with the addition of some contemporary poems and other quotations, which serve as intertextual links to expand the historical resonance of the themes.

The characteristic features of Cambria's entire work point to a new practice and vision of the relation between subject and modes of textual production.[9] As for the *form of content:* historical, not mythical, materials are chosen from a concrete situation and real events. These are not necessarily contemporary but always refer to the current concerns of the audience.[10] The historical events are examined in their sociocultural complexity from the ideological and emotional viewpoints of contemporary feminism. The human sources of these views—writers, performers, *and* the specific audience addressed (this is a play for women)—are clearly identified to avoid mystification and mythologizing. As for the *form of expression:* the rejection of the novelistic as the single organizing principle of classical narrative forms such as biography, novelistic romance, or the "realist" novel must be seen in the light of current theories of the plurality of the text, in which the rejection of the novelistic emphasizes the process of reading as a constitutive act of the subject. In this new textual form, where the rational historical inquiry is continually intersected by the lyrical and the personal, the subject is at once writer and reader, performer and audience. The resonance of the (documented) historical events in the subject is made possible by the "private" dimension and in turn makes possible the emergence of pathos as a creative critical process. The text is produced and meant to be received as the intersecting of the personal and the social, a process articulated dialectically on subjective codes and on objective realities.

Working along these lines, we can perhaps develop a *feminist theory of textual production* which is neither a *theory of women's writing* nor just a theory of textuality. In other words, it is not a matter of finding common elements among the texts written or produced by women and defining them in terms of a presumed femaleness or femininity, which, to my mind, is highly suspect of sexual metaphysics; rather, it is our task to envision a feminist theory of the process of textual production and consumption, which is of course inseparable from a theory of culture. In a recently translated article entitled "Is There a Feminine Aesthetic?" Silvia Bovenschen argues that there is no such thing as an ever-present female counterculture as such, or a "female nature" outside of historical development; and that to insist on such notions as irrational perception, cosmic powers, or archetypal forms as categories for femaleness is at best playing men's games, and at worst indulging in reactionary ideologies.[11] Since it is the specifics of feminine experience and perception that determine the form the work takes, we must not accept a priori categories and should look for evidence of feminine sensitivity in concrete tests. It is good, Bovenschen claims, that no formal criteria for "feminine art" can be definitively laid down. That enables us to reject the notion of artistic norms and facile labeling, and prevents cooptation and further exploitation of women's creativity. So it is not a question of what or how women write, but of how women produce (as makers) and reproduce (as receivers) the aesthetic object, the text; in other words, we need a theory of culture with women as subjects—not commodities but social beings producing and reproducing cultural products, transmitting and transforming cultural values.[12]

In this sense, and so that we can take possession of our cultural (re)production, I think we should assert that women's work is never done.

Notes

I am grateful o the Center for 20th Century Studies of the University of Wisconsin-Milwaukee for the 1976–1977 Fellowship that has made possible the research and the writing of this paper. I must also thank my friends Renny Harrigan, Andreas Huyssen, Judith Mayne, Sheila Radford-Hill, Sylvie Romanowski, and Marcella Tarozzi, who helped me greatly by lending me books, arguing against me, and sharing their knowledge and insights.

1. Adele Cambria, *A' .ore come rivoluzione* (Milano: Sugar Co., 1976). The volume includes the script and production notes for *Nonostante Gramsci*.

2. The complete Italian edition, in four volumes, is Antonio Gramsci, *Quaderni dal carcere*, a cura di Valentino Gerratana (Torino: Einaudi, 1975). In English see *Selections from the Prison Notebooks of Antonio Gramsci*, ed. and trans. Quintin Hoare and Geoffrey Nowell-Smith (New York: International Publishers, 1971).

3. Antonio Gramsci, *Lettere dal carcere*, a cura di S. Caprioglio e E. Fubini (Torino: Einaudi, 1973). In English see Antonio Gramsci, *Letters from Prison*, selected and translated by Lynne Lawner (New York: Harper & Row, 1973). See also Guiseppe Fiori, *Antonio Gramsci: Life of a Revolutionary* (New York: Schocken Books, 1973).

4. *The Dialectic of Sex: The Case for Feminist Revolution* (New York: Bantam Books, 1970), pp. 126–27.

5. Quoted by Cambria, p. 9, from *Duemila pagine di Gramsci* (Milano: Il Saggiatore), vol. 2, p. 23, letter of June 9, 1924; my translation.

6. Cf. Phyllis Chesler, *Women and Madness* (Garden City, N.Y.: Doubleday, 1972).

7. From Umberto Eco, *Opera aperta* (Milano: Bompiani, 1967), to Stephen Heath, "Narrative Space," *Screen* (Autumn 1976): 68–112.

8. On the conditions of women in the Soviet Union since the revolution, see Sheila Rowbotham, "If You Like Tobogganing," in her *Women, Resistance, and Revolution* (New York: Vintage Books, 1974), pp. 134–69. Also very important to this topic is the work of Alexandra Kollontai, *The Autobiography of a Sexually Emancipated Communist Woman* (New York: Schocken Books, 1975), *Women Workers Struggle for Their Rights* (Bristol: Falling Wall Press, 1971), and *Sexual Relations and the Class Struggle/Love and the New Morality* (Bristol: Falling Wall Press, 1972).

9. For the notion of modes of sign production, see Umberto Eco, *A Theory of Semiotics* (Bloomington: Indiana University Press, 1976), and Gianfranco Bettetini, *Produzione del senso e messa in scena* (Milano: Bompiani, 1975).

10. In the words of Dacia Maraini, who reviewed *Amore come rivoluzione,* "books like this should be written by the hundreds. There are hundreds of extraordinary women who have so much to teach us (even if often they only speak of failures and defeat), women still buried under the barren, impious ashes of patriarchal history." (*Tuttolibri*, 17 aprile 1976, p. 4; my translation). The terms *form of content* and *form of expression* come from Louis Hjelmslev, *Prolegomena to a Theory of Language* (Madison: University of Wisconsin Press, 1961).

11. Silvia Bovenschen, "Is There a Feminine Aesthetic?" *New German Critique*, no. 10 (Winter 1977): 111–137, and *Heresies*, no. 4: 10–12. Altman's recent film *Three Women* seems to me to come close to the latter group.

12. For a good analysis of women's position as objects of exchange in Lévi-Strauss and Freud/Lacan, see Gayle Rubin, "The Traffic in Women: Notes on the Political Economy of Sex," in Rayna R. Reiter, ed., *Toward an Anthropology of Women* (New York: Monthly Review Press, 1975), pp. 157–210.

6

FELLINI'S 9½

The title of Fellini's film *Giulietta degli spiriti/Juliet of the Spirits* (1964) is a richly suggestive verbal image of woman, evoking youth, love and death, desire and loss—the love of Shakespeare's Juliet doomed forever, recast in modern times and so enduring—an image of femininity eternal. It is also, of course, a shrewd commercial move to enhance box-office returns by casting toward its audience hints of two or three things about her we want to know more of. The "spirits" that beset her, that haunt or accompany this woman, allude to her secret, innermost being (in Italian the word *spiriti* means "spirits," in all the English acceptations, but also ghosts, phantasms, fantasies, and thus points to the supernatural and to the realm of the psyche as much as it suggests spirituality, if not more); and if those "spirits" can be given representation, her mystery can be probed and known via their representation in the film.

On the one hand, then, the film promises, (this) woman is a mystery, but her secret will be told. On the other hand, however, as any filmgoer knows, this "Juliet" is also the star of the film, Giulietta Masina, wife of the director, Federico Fellini, the film thus being her film, in a sense, as much as his. Will the film reflect Masina's real life, her relationship with Fellini? Are those her own "spirits"? Is the film (auto)biographical? This woman, then, is a well-known personality of the entertainment world, but she too has a secret (a "real life") that may be told. And I, spectator, am solicited by this title; I am incited to want to know more; I become involved with this Juliet; I am implicated, whether as a woman or as a man, in this woman's story—this narrative image—because the image in the title already contains or intimates at least one story.

The narrative image of Giulietta/Juliet produced for the film by its title—

Written as an informal talk to introduce Fellini's film *Juliet of the Spirits* at the Mount Holyoke Giamatti Festival of Italian Culture in October 1984. Later revised as a contribution to a forthcoming volume, *Gender: Literary and Cinematic Representation*, edited by Jeanne Ruppert for the Florida State University Press from the 1986 Florida State University Conference on Literature and Film. To the best of my knowledge, this essay first appears in print in this volume.

an image of Woman as unique individual and eternal feminine at once—
functions very much in the manner of a trailer, a preview of coming
attractions, a come-on. In so doing it sets in motion certain narrative
patterns, not only expectations or suspense but also projection and identification, which position the spectator, long before the film begins, in a
specific relation of meaning to gender: the spectator's own gender is implicated and constructed (as self-representation) in relation to the representation of gender produced by cinema in each single film. As this simple
reading of just the title of one film suggests, the cinematic contract that
binds each individual spectator to the social technology of cinema is more
complex than an exchange of money for pleasure or entertainment. For it
produces, as a surplus, certain effects of meaning which are central to the
construction of gender and subjectivity.

The spectator's gendered subjectivity is both implicated and constructed
(as self-representation) in cinematic representation. That must be stressed
again, since gender is not a fact, a datum, but is itself a representation,
whose status (truth value, epistemological or moral weight, etc.) and degree
of "reality" (objective to subjective) vary according to the social hierarchy of
discourses and representations.[1] Thus, one's gendered subjectivity is not
only implicated, such as it is, in the spectator's encounter with each film, but
also constructed, reaffirmed or challenged, displaced or shifted, in each
film-viewing process.

If gender is a representation subject to social and ideological coding,
there can be no simple one-to-one relationship between the image of
woman inscribed in a film and its female spectator. On the contrary, the
spectator's reading of the film (including interpretive and affective responses, cognitive and emotional strategies) is mediated by her existence in,
and experience of, a particular universe of social discourses and practices in
daily life. Thus, for instance, feminist criticism has shown that readings
emerging out of a politically radical or oppositional consciousness can
significantly alter the interpretation and the effects of filmic representation,
as well as the spectator's self-representation, and may contribute to changing the social meanings and finally the codes of representation themselves.
This essay is intended as one such reading, a small contribution to the
feminist project of social change.

The question of how women read or see images, and how the many
images of Woman continuously circulating in the culture affect women's
self-image (as it is called) or sense of self, is not a question we can reason-
ably expect Fellini to have asked himself in 1964. But it has been a recurrent
question and a primary concern of feminist criticism, writing, and filmmak-

ing, starting with the famous passage in Virginia Woolf's *A Room of One's Own* that reads:

> Indeed, if woman had no existence save in the fiction written by men, one would imagine her a person of the utmost importance; very various; heroic and mean; splendid and sordid; infinitely beautiful and hideous in the extreme; as great as a man, some think even greater. But this is woman in fiction. In fact . . . she was locked up, beaten and flung about the room. . . .[2]

Woolf's point here is that the representation of Woman has served a specific social purpose. "Women," she added, and note the plural form, "have served all these centuries as looking-glasses possessing the magic and delicious power of reflecting the figure of man at twice his natural size." This metaphor of Woman as the looking-glass held up to Man is particularly relevant to cinema, where, as I have suggested elsewhere and as current film theory has argued most convincingly, the screen functions very much like a mirror. A corollary, and even more interesting, question is the one that some feminist theorists are now asking: What happens when Woman serves as the looking-glass held up to women?[3]

In psychoanalytic terms, the cinema screen acts like a dream screen for the spectator-subject, a screen at once bearing and hiding, displaying and displacing, unconscious images and "thoughts." One can speak, in other words, of the "film-work"—the working of the film on or for the spectator—in a manner rather similar to what Freud called the dream-work *(Traumarbeit)*. Christian Metz has used the expression "imaginary signifier" to speak of the cinema, meaning that the way in which film signifies (or produces meaning for the spectator) links it with the psychic order which Jacques Lacan designated "the imaginary": the imaginary is a modality of subject processes, a dimension of subjectivity, very much dependent on vision, seeing, on the scopic drive, and has its inception at a very early age, before the oedipal stage and even prior to the acquisition of language, at a stage of psychic development which Lacan actually calls "the mirror stage."[4]

In her book *The Subject of Semiotics*, Kaja Silverman undertakes to combine, or rather to read together, semiotic and psychoanalytic theories in order to sketch out a theory of signification that takes into account subjective processes. Remarking on the affinity between the views of Freud and of C. S. Peirce on the relationship of word and image, or verbal and visual signs, Silverman argues that Peirce's definition of the sign as icon (the pictorial aspect of a sign) also relates to Lacan's notion of the imaginary as "a spectrum of visual images which precedes the acquisition of language in the experience of the child, and which continues to coexist with it afterwards."[5] Like Metz, Silverman accepts the analogy between film-work and dream-work, though unlike him, she's not concerned solely with cinematic signification, or with filmic texts, but draws insights and examples from literary texts, as well. Film, however, she observes, gets closer to the primary process "because one of the registers of its inscription [the image-track] is that used by the unconscious in the production of dreams"; and therefore, "the totality of image and sound tracks permits [film] to engage simultaneously in the discourses of the unconscious and the pre-conscious."[6]

This twin hold of cinema on the spectator has been one of the most insistent concerns of contemporary critical work with film (I say with film, rather than on film, because I mean to include the work of filmmakers as well as critics), and has been especially important in the feminist analysis of cinema. A justly famous text of feminist film theory, Laura Mulvey's essay "Visual Pleasure and Narrative Cinema," precisely identifies the "system of the look" as the foremost semiotic mechanism that operates in classical cinema to produce the representation of woman.[7]

Everyone looks, in the cinema. The characters within the film look at each other, at objects, landscapes, and so on; the spectators look at the film projected on the screen; and for all of these looks to be possible, another look must have preceded them—the look of the camera at the actors, sets, locations, and so forth. However, the conventions of narrative cinema deny the last two looks: the spectators are not aware of their own look, of themselves as looking on, as being voyeuristically complicit in the pleasures built into the image; second, they are not aware of the look of the camera, so that they have the impression that the events, people, and places figured on the screen exist somewhere, in an objective—if fictional—world created by the filmmaker, the director, the artist. Thus, having no say and no control over the film's world or its images, the spectators feel exempt of any responsibility, are not personally or individually implicated in the fiction, and are therefore free to enjoy it. Classical cinema, in short, seems to offer the spectator a safe fantasy. But is that fantasy really safe? Or, rather, is it safe for everyone?

Juliet of the Spirits is a film about fantasies, figures both real and imagined by their viewer, the character Juliet. Made immediately after *8½*, Fellini's auteurial feat of self-reflexive cinema, obsessively turned upon itself and its maker in a fantastic meditation on cinema as expressive medium, *Juliet of the Spirits* is also, inevitably, a film about the cinema as spectacle, about looking, about images and mirrors. From the point of view of Juliet, the film makes us see what she sees, except that we spectators are given privileged knowledge, "we" know which figures are "real" in the film and which are imaginary, hallucinatory, figments of her imagination. *She* is not always sure. In other words, Juliet is both our guide, our mediator, the representative of the spectator inside the fiction of the film, and at the same time the object of our gaze and of our knowledge, because at all times throughout the film "we" are supposed to know, at least to know better than Juliet. But what do we actually know? Or, rather, *what* are we supposed to know? And who is "we"?

Let me go back for a moment to Mulvey's essay. The possibility of shifting, varying, and exposing the look, she argues, is what distinguishes cinema from other visual arts (painting, sculpture, or theatre) and governs its representation of woman. Typically, she writes, a classical narrative film

> opens with the woman as object of the combined gaze of spectator and all the male protagonists in the film. She is isolated, glamorous, on display, sexualised. But as the narrative progresses she falls in love with the main male protagonist and becomes his property, losing her outward glamorous characteristics, her generalised sexuality, her show-girl connotations; her eroticism is subjected to the male star alone.[8]

The apparatus of looks converging on the female figure integrates voyeurism into the conventions of storytelling, combining a direct solicitation of the scopic drive with the demands of plot, conflict, climax, and resolution. The woman is framed by the look of the camera as an icon, an image, the object of the gaze, and thus, precisely, spectacle: that is to say, an image made to be looked at by the spectators(s) as well as the male character(s), whose look most often relays the look of the audience. But it is the male protagonist, the "bearer" of the spectator's look, who also controls the events of the narrative, moving the plot forward. The male protagonist, Mulvey writes, is "a figure in a landscape," "free to command the stage . . . of spatial illusion in which he articulates the look and creates the action." In this manner, both visually and narratively, cinema defines woman as image: as spectacle to be looked at and object to be desired, investigated, pursued, controlled, and ultimately possessed by a subject who is masculine, that is, symbolically male. For the system of the look, the fundamental semiotic structure of cinematic narrative, attributes the power of the gaze to the man, be he the male protagonist, the director (or, more properly, the camera, as the function of enunciation), or the spectator.

If this analysis is correct (and everyone seems to agree it is, feminists and non-feminists), then one may say that classical cinema endlessly replays the oedipal fantasy of pursuit and capture, distance and desire, memory and loss. The analogy of cinema and dream is reconfirmed. Only, cinema does something more: it grants the fantasy. For a two-hour period and the relatively small price of the ticket, it actually performs the capture in behalf of the spectators.

Two questions then arise. First, what happens to female spectators? Do women see films the same way as men do? Are women constituted as masculine subjects of vision by the apparatus of cinema, or are they lured by narcissistic identification to the side of the image, to the position of object of the gaze?[9] In either case, it is still necessary to ask, Is such a fantasy really safe, for women? Second, what happens when the protagonist of the film is female? Is the model still valid if the film narrative has a heroine rather than a hero?

Both of these questions are directly pertinent to *Juliet of the Spirits*, not because Fellini was concerned with the possible responses of female spectators, which is rather doubtful, but because his film has a female protagonist, purports to tell a woman's story, and is, as Molly Haskell used the phrase, "a woman's film." Moreover, it specifically poses the question of women's relation to the image of Woman, defining it exactly as a question of "self-image."

The film thematizes the relation of one woman—an individual, historically specified, though fictional woman—to Woman as cultural representation, to the multiple and often conflicting images of Woman that are incessantly held up, suggested, or exhibited to her by her culture, her family, her religion, and her own fantasies. Juliet is a thirtyish, well-to-do housewife who lives in a beautiful home in Fregene, a rich suburb near Rome. She has a dapper husband, Giorgio, who is vaguely in "public relations" and has no interest in her; and no children. But she has servants, a large family, and a host of social acquaintances constantly dropping in. As usual with Fellini's films, the latter represent in caricature various types of the Italian bourgeoisie as the director sees it: a hefty doctor, an aging lawyer, a homosexual spiritualist, a muscular young gigolo—the men; the women, besides several nondescript wives, include a vapid socialite infatuated with astrology, another who sculpts male nudes, and an American waspish psychoanalyst. In addition to her two young maids, Juliet's immediate family consists of her mother, a very beautiful and equally vain woman, and two glamorous sisters: one an aspiring actress, the other a happy young mother of twins. And then there is Susy, her next-door neighbor, a high-class prostitute with the proverbial heart of gold.

Susy is a central character in the film, because she is the counterpart, the double, of Juliet. Susy is as beautiful and sexually aggressive as Juliet is plain, modest, and "repressed" (or so the film argues). And although Susy is a real person in the diegesis (in the fictional world of the film), she is also, for Juliet, the embodiment of the image of Woman. That is made visually explicit by the fact that two other imaginary figures, the two most significant "spirits" that surround Juliet, share her image (literally, as they are played by the same actress, Sandra Milo): the spirit Iris, who speaks to

Juliet during a seance and appears to her high on a swing, and Fanny, the circus ballerina who eloped with Juliet's grandfather many years before.

This doubling of the images and the pairing of all the characters either by similarity or by contrast is a pervasive strategy of the text. It creates an effect of endless duplication, the sense of being trapped inside a house of mirrors—which is, of course, where Juliet is. The initial sequence makes that clear. The film opens with a shot of leaves, in a garden. Then the camera travels rapidly through the boughs and cranes to reveal a house. Inside, it frames hands holding a red candle and the back of a woman seated at a mirror, suggesting a ritual. The woman is trying on wigs, attended by two maids in white uniforms. We don't see her face. The entire scene is shot with mirrors as background. Having finally dressed, discarding the wigs, the woman lights the candles on a table set for two and turns off the overhead lights. She is still seen from behind. Her husband's arrival home is announced. He stands at the front door, center-framed in long shot, and looks toward her. Then—cut to the woman—we finally see her, in the reverse shot, from his point of view (i.e., as he sees her). Her face is framed in a medium shot (from the waist up), softened by the penumbra of the room and glowing, because the light source is behind her (a technique called backlighting and used regularly in classical cinema, mainly for the female star). Thus filmed in the style of the 1940s films, Juliet is as beautiful as she could ever be—all for her husband, who doesn't notice any of it and has totally forgotten the day's special occasion, their anniversary.

From this point on, we know that Juliet has a problem, and it is one of self-image. The mirror, like her husband, sends back negative messages to her: she is not glamorous or desirable. She doesn't fit the image of Woman that she sees posted all around her. Her mother tells her to wear makeup; her husband's mistress is a fashion model. The clairvoyant suggests she doesn't please her husband because she's not sexy enough; the paragon of sexiness is Susy, a whore. And her Catholic upbringing gives her yet another image of Woman, the martyred saint who preferred death to losing her virginity—a common myth imparted to all Catholic girls in Italy (as if one could suppose that early Christian women were given the choice by the Roman soldiers about to rape them), a myth still popular and daily reproduced by images, pictures and paintings of such martyr-saints disseminated in all the churches, museums, and prayer books of Italy. It is no wonder that Juliet, caught in this barrage of conflicting representations, is more than slightly schizoid and has a problem of narcissism, which the theme of the mirror insistently remarks. But there is more.

She is surrounded by twins or twinlike pairs, and all are female: her twin little nieces, the two maids, and her two glamorous sisters next to whom she is like a midget Cinderella, in her ridiculous outfits and pagoda hats. Her spirits, voices, and apparitions take the form of doubles, uncanny figures of her self or selves, all referring back to the primary dichotomy of virgin-saint and whore, Juliet and Susy. In short, what poor Juliet is stuck with is all of Fellini's own obsessive images, which recur in all of his films: twins, horses, the circus, huge women, rows of identical figures in religious habit (here they are nuns), and the most idiosyncratic of all, the androgyne—who in this film looks very much like Gertrude Stein—a testimonial to the director's monumental homophobia.

Is it any wonder, given all that, that Juliet lacks a positive self-image? Where would she get on in a world made up of Fellinesque imagery? And here is where I put again my first question: Where does the woman spectator stand, or who are "we," vis-à-vis such a film? Can this fantasy be safe for us, when it is clearly not safe for Juliet? Could we possibly see it as men do, with the same detached enjoyment or the same erotic participation? What happens to us as we watch it? Leaving these questions dangling, for the time being, I will nevertheless observe that Mulvey's model of the representation of Woman in narrative cinema does in fact apply to this film. For even though the protagonist is a woman, even though there is no male protagonist, as Giorgio, the husband, clearly does not deserve the status, nevertheless it is not Juliet who controls the images and events of the film and moves the plot forward.

On the contrary, things happen to her: people drop in, spirits come and go, Giorgio takes off with his mistress without even saying goodbye. Admittedly, the plot is not Hitchcock, and the suspense is provided by the fast crescendo of Juliet's "hallucinations," and the increasingly bizarre surrealistic imagery (imagery which, by the way, watching the film again after many years, makes one realize how much Kubrick's *The Shining* owes to Fellini's film). But still there is a plot, an arrangement of shots and sequences that constructs a narrative space in which Juliet is caught and moved along by a design, a scenario, not her own. In other words, she is definitely not "free to command the stage of spatial illusion" in which someone (not she) controls the look and promotes the action.

Someone else—but who? As I was pondering this very serious problem, another critic came to my help. In her reading of *Juliet of the Spirits*, an interpretation in Jungian key which I find rather objectionable in itself because it accepts the film's message at face value, Carolyn Geduld makes a very acute observation. Juliet, she says, is "Guido's anima." That is the paradoxical subtitle of her essay, for Guido is a character in another film. He is, of course, the protagonist-director of *8½*, played by Marcello Mastroianni as Fellini's flattering ego-ideal (whereby, incidentally, one could note that Fellini does not have any problems with mirrors, self-image, or insufficient narcissism). Geduld's point is so well taken that her argument deserves a hearing.

> *Juliet of the Spirits* is frequently interpreted as *8½* from a female viewpoint. The character of Juliet seems to correspond closely with that of Luisa, Guido's wife in *8½*, and this correspondence is particularly compelling if *8½* is viewed as an autobiographical film. Guido is, like Fellini, a director directing a film called "8½." Mario Pisu, Guido's alter ego who deserts his wife for a younger woman, physically resembles Fellini, which is possibly why he was cast as the husband of Fellini's real wife, Giulietta Masina, in *Juliet*. Together, *Juliet* and *8½* seem to be a composite of the Fellini marriage, with *Juliet* representing Giulietta Masina's or Mrs. Fellini's side of the story. Rumors about the director's marital difficulties at the time of the filming of *Juliet* lend support to this assumption.[10]

However many things Juliet-Luisa and Guido-Giorgio may have in common, and however closely they may reflect "the nature of the Fellini marriage," Geduld continues, the most striking correspondence in the two films is the one between Guido and Juliet. Thus, "*Juliet of the Spirits* is not simply *8½* from Luisa's point of view, although the female viewpoint is what is represented" (p. 139). This reasoning is not easy to follow, so I must interject a question: If *Juliet of the Spirits* is not Luisa's or Mrs. Fellini's side of the story, whose side or what female viewpoint is being represented? It is, Geduld explains, the point of view of Juliet, who is Guido's anima. (Or, Woolf would say, his delicious looking-glass.)

> According to Jung the conscious extravert is an unconscious introvert and the conscious introvert is an unconscious extravert. Similarly, every male has an unconscious female identity (anima) and every female an unconscious male identity (animus). In marriage, a man will tend to choose a woman who resembles his anima, and a woman will choose a man who resembles her animus. Thus, Juliet is both an individual woman and the unconscious feminine side of Guido-Giorgio. (p. 139)

If I translate Geduld's brilliant insight into the terms of my argument, I can now answer my own question as to who articulates the look and creates the action of the film *Juliet of the Spirits*. It is indeed Guido, or, better, Fellini's persona, the representative of the artist-director, the enunciator of the film text's discourse, who asks himself: What would my eighth-and-a-half film be like if I explored my (unconscious) femininity? And, having been in therapy with a Jungian psychoanalyst during the filming of *8½* (as reported by Geduld), he now makes his ninth-and-a-half film about his anima, in the persona of his wife.

In fact, Geduld's comparative analysis of the two films' major narrative/thematic sequences makes a fully convincing case that *8½* and *Juliet of the*

104   Technologies of Gender

Spirits have an identical plot structure: the events, encounters, conflicts, and climactic scenes are all the same, changing the costumes; and even the main antagonist, the arch-villian, is one and the same, namely, the Mother figure ("Juliet's splitting of the mother archetype into whore-nun is perhaps the strongest evidence of her correspondence with Guido," remarks Geduld, who then, understandably, has the impossible and fruitless task of explaining Juliet's sexual inhibitions as stemming from the repression of *female* sexuality).

Now, then, it becomes apparent why the same actors are cast in very similar roles, in relation to the protagonist; why the famous "harem" scene in *8½* has an equivalent scene here in the party at Susy's bordello (a bordello with one male inmate, and Juliet as his most improbable client); or again why the child-Guido, at the end of *8½*, is the magic pied-piper who leads the parade, the symbol of creativity (the artist-as-a-young-boy, as it were), while the child-Juliet, in the corresponding scene, is just a girl. But most of all, for those spectators who wondered and tried in vain to identify with her, we can now finally understand why it is that Juliet's overtly sexual fantasies are centered on female bodies, with a few exotic men acting as props. For it is not a question of Juliet's being a lesbian—a possibility that this film obviously could not have entertained at all—but rather that she looks at women with male eyes, the eyes of Guido, and that her phantasms, Juliet's "spirits," are in fact Guido's and Fellini's fantasies.

In this film, too, as in *8½*, the whole sphere of sexuality, from conjugal love to carnal lust, the lure of the body with its costumes and decorations, sensuality, subjectivity, and even the unconscious are represented in the image of Woman. Woman is the origin and the aim of desire, the object and the locus of sexuality as defined by man, from his point of view, through his look, his cinema, his institutions. Therefore, indeed, the solutions offered in both films to the protagonist's problems are one and the same, as Geduld puts it: "For Guido as well, the final answer does not come from giving up *one of his women or images of Woman.* . . . The final answer for Juliet and Guido [alike] is to assimilate the two female images" (p. 147; emphasis added).

Here is the reason why I find this Jungian reading inadequate—not only inadequate to answer the question of female spectatorship, but inadequate as well to the requirement of minimal self-consistency: it does not account for, or even wonder about, the rather obvious fact that if both Juliet and Guido have "images of Woman" (to give up or not), it is only Guido who "has" women. Juliet does not (and in the universe of the film she *could not*). That means that in Fellini's films, as in all patriarchal representations of gender in Western culture, sexuality is located in Woman, but, like desire and meaning, it is the property and the prerogative of man. All of sexuality, that is, refers to man, is an "economy of the same," in effect a "hom(m)osexuality," as Luce Irigaray remarks in her writing: "Female homosexuality represented for Freud a phenomenon so alien to his imaginary economy that it could only be 'neglected by psycho-analytic research', and even neglected in the therapy of the homosexual woman patient."[11] The attitude Irigaray describes is Freud's, not Jung's, but it is perfectly applicable to Fellini's film as well. As for Geduld's "Jungian perspective," it too fails to account for the social reality and the political consequences of gender asymmetry, whose underlying symbolic structure Adrienne Rich has designated with the term *compulsory heterosexuality.*[12]

In this sense, then, I would revise the definition of the cinematic contract given earlier to say that it is a heterosexual contract designed to bind or "entertain" spectators, especially female spectators, within the male-designed social technology of gender that is cinema. And again I cannot refrain from making a brief comment on the titles of Fellini's films, which seem chosen to confirm the male design and ownership of that technology: *8½*, the story of man, refers to the professional, public achievement of the filmmaker, author and subject of the discourse produced through it (not coincidentally, the English title is actually *Fellini's 8½*); while *Juliet of the Spirits,* the story of woman, is given the lyrical but intimate and real-life name of (we might say) just a woman, one the filmmaker knows, has the right to represent, and, by another social contract, indeed owns (Giulietta Masina, as Geduld correctly notes, is "Mrs. Fellini"). The cinematic contract, in short, is not unlike the marriage contract; and he wouldn't have it otherwise. Whether she would or not (the film's ending is predictably fuzzy on this point) can be known only if and when she, too, begins to make movies. Her first film, we would like to anticipate, might be entitled *The Man Who Envied Women.*

Yvonne Rainer's film *The Man Who Envied Women* (1985) is precisely, among other things, a cinematic critique of the kind of "woman's film" exemplified by *Juliet of the Spirits.* It does, moreover, address many of the questions of female spectatorship that I have raised in the course of this reading of Fellini's film but necessarily, in such a con-text, left unanswered. For further discussion and possible answers to those questions—How do women see, read, or make films? How is female subjectivity implicated and constructed in cinematic representation? What forms of narrative coherence may be developed by a feminist cinema?—I refer the (female) readers to Rainer's film and my own reading of it, and to the other issues in women's filmmaking addressed in the essays that follow.

Notes

1. See Sandra Harding, *The Science Question in Feminism* (Ithaca, N.Y.: Cornell University Press, 1986).

2. Virginia Woolf, *A Room of One's Own* (New York and London: Harcourt Brace Jovanovich, 1957), p. 45.

3. The distinction between Woman and women, as well as other theoretical terms and concepts summarily presented or drawn upon in this essay, is more fully elaborated in my book *Alice Doesn't: Feminism, Semiotics, Cinema* (Bloomington: Indiana University Press, 1984).

4. See Jacques Lacan, *Ecrits: A Selection*, trans. Alan Sheridan (New York: W. W. Norton, 1977), pp. 1–7; and Christian Metz, *The Imaginary Signifier: Psychoanalysis and the Cinema*, trans. Celia Britton, Annwyl Williams, Ben Brewster, and Alfred Guzzetti (Bloomington: Indiana University Press, 1982).

5. Kaja Silverman, *The Subject of Semiotics* (New York: Oxford University Press, 1983), p. 21.

6. Ibid., p. 85.

7. Laura Mulvey, "Visual Pleasure and Narrative Cinema," *Screen* 16, no. 3 (Autumn 1975): 6–18.

8. Ibid., p. 13.

9. Several attempts to answer or to reformulate these questions have been made in the context of the debate instigated by Mulvey's essay and still continuing. See, for example, Mulvey's own "Afterthoughts on 'Visual Pleasure and Narrative Cinema' Inspired by *Duel in the Sun*," *Framework*, nos. 15/16/17 (1981): 12–15; Mary Ann Doane, "Film and the Masquerade: Theorising the Female Spectator," *Screen* 23, nos. 3–4 (September–October 1982): 74–87; Tania Modleski, "Never to Be Thirty-six Years Old: *Rebecca* as Female Oedipal Drama," *Wide Angle* 5, no. 1 (1982): 34–41; and Linda Williams, "When the Woman Looks," in *Re-vision: Essays in Feminist Film Criticism*, ed. Mary Ann Doane, Patricia Mellencamp, and Linda Williams (Frederick, Md.: University Publications of America, 1984), pp. 83–99.

10. Carolyn Geduld, "*Juliet of the Spirits:* Guido's Anima," in *Federico Fellini: Essays in Criticism*, ed. Peter Bondanella (New York: Oxford University Press, 1978), p. 137. Subsequent references to this work are given in the text.

11. Luce Irigaray, *Speculum of the Other Woman*, trans. Gillian C. Gill (Ithaca, N.Y.: Cornell University Press, 1985), p. 101.

12. Adrienne Rich, "Compulsory Heterosexuality and Lesbian Existence," *Signs* 5, no. 4 (Summer 1980): 631–60. Rich's term *compulsory heterosexuality* is quite compatible with Irigaray's *hom(m)osexuality*, despite their apparent morphological discrepancy, for what they both imply is the repression of female sexuality and its elision in discourse.

7

STRATEGIES OF COHERENCE
Narrative Cinema, Feminist
Poetics, and Yvonne Rainer

> Words are uttered but not possessed by my
> performers as they operate within the filmic
> frame but do not propel a filmic plot.
> —YVONNE RAINER

In the early years of the present decade, speculating upon her own development as an artist and filmmaker, Yvonne Rainer saw herself moving,
almost against her will, toward narrative film:

> From description of individual feminine experience floating free of both
> social context and narrative hierarchy, to descriptions of individual feminine
> experience placed in radical juxtaposition against historical events, to ex-
> plicitly feminist speculations about feminine experience, I have just formu-
> lated an evolution which in becoming more explicitly feminist seems to
> demand a more solid anchoring in narrative conventions. (I am not sure of
> the reasons, but I suspect the worst.)[1]

Why this suspicion? Remember Joan Fontaine's suspicion, in Hitchcock's
film (*Suspicion*, 1941), about her husband's (Cary Grant's) plot to kill her?
Or Mimi's suspicion that she has been murdered by the plot of Puccini's
opera *Bohème* in Sally Potter's *Thriller* (1979)? Or Dora's suspicion of Freud's
plotting of her case history? Is this suspicion of narrativity on the part of
women simply a particular case of paranoia, or is it somehow justified? In
other words, are we right in suspecting the worst? And if we are, then how
do we account for women's apparently irresistible attraction to narrative,

Written as an address to the Sixth Annual Conference in the Humanities organized by
James Phelan at the Ohio State University in April 1986 on the theme "Narrative Poetics."
Revised and entitled "Strategies of Coherence: The Poetics of Film Narrative" for inclusion in
the forthcoming volume *Reading Narrative: Form, Ethics, Ideology*, edited by James Phelan from
that conference. But again, it is most likely that the essay may first appear in print in this book.

from Anne Radcliffe to Alice Walker, from Germaine Dulac to Yvonne Rainer? Is it simply, again, a case of masochism, of victimism, a gender-specific pathological condition, or is there something else, or something more, at stake?

In a chapter of *Alice Doesn't* entitled "Desire in Narrative," I have argued that desire is inscribed as well as contained "in the very *movement* of narrative, the unfolding of the Oedipal scenario as *drama*";[2] and however problematic—doubled and contradictory—the position of a female spectator or reader may be in relation to (pre)oedipal desire, it is nevertheless from there that any possibility of reading, any process of identification or effect of meaning must proceed.

Therefore, contrary to what was perceived to be the common project of radical, independent, or avant-garde cinema in the sixties and seventies—namely, the destruction of narrative and visual pleasure (a project in which feminist filmmakers and critics participated enthusiastically, producing both film texts and textual readings which, together, articulated the feminist critique of representation that was to shape most of film theory as we now have it); contrary to that stoic prescription to destroy all pleasure in the text, I proposed, feminist work in film should be not anti-narrative or anti-oedipal but quite the opposite. It should be narrative and oedipal with a vengeance, working, as it were, with and against narrative in order to represent not just a female desire which Hollywood, in the best tradition of Western literature and iconography, has classically represented as the doomed power of the fetish (a fetish empowered for the benefit of men and doomed to disempower women); but working, instead, to represent the duplicity of the oedipal scenario itself and the specific contradiction of the female subject in it.

I now want to suggest that plot, narrative (i.e., the growth and flowing of plot into story across the narrative layering of events, actantial functions, and discursive registers), and narrativity (the effective functioning of narrative on and with the reader/spectator to produce a subject of reading or a subject of vision)—in short, all the ingredients of the pleasure of the text—are mechanisms of coherence. Which is not to say solely mechanisms of closure, traps in which the subject is totally and necessarily contained, for closure is only an effect of particular narrative strategies (those of the so-called classical cinema, for example, or of Barthes's "readerly text," a notion which his own reading, however, has belied); and particular narrative strategies, moreover, whose effectivity in producing closure is not universal or atemporal but historically and semiotically specific—I mean specific with regard to the history of cultural forms, media, genres, and spectatorship or context of reception.

Thus, to our contemporary eyes, even the texts of classical narrative cinema display, as feminist critics have repeatedly shown, the very gaps and paradoxes that the operation of narrative is meant to cover up; paradoxes which now can be seen to be at once the figure of repression and "of the repression of the very functioning of repression," as Shoshana Felman pointed out of a non-filmic classic text, a Balzac novella, in her well-known essay "Rereading Femininity" quite some time ago.[3] If it now can be said, not only of Balzac but also of the classical narrative text *tout court*, that the text "opens up an ironic space which articulates the force of the question of femininity," it is because of Felman's rereading, Barthes's rereading, and the feminist rereadings and rewritings (I would like to say, remakes) of classical narrative films.

Here, then, I want to explore how narrative and narrativity, because of their capacity to inscribe desire and to direct, sustain, or undercut identification (in all the senses of the term), are mechanisms to be employed strategically and tactically in the effort to construct other forms of coherence, to shift the terms of representation, to produce the conditions of representability of another—and gendered—social subject. Obviously, therefore, much is at stake in narrative, in a poetics of narrative. Our suspicion is more than justified, but so is our attraction.

The terms *narrative* and *poetics,* especially when juxtaposed in "narrative poetics," evoke the presence or the phantom of an "anterior discourse," as Todorov used the phrase, à propos of Bakhtin's notion of intertextual polyvalence as a characteristic register of poetic (or literary) discourse.[4] They evoke the phantom of, precisely, *that* discourse: structuralist poetics, the systematic study of literary language in its most intimate quality—literaturnost, literariness—and specificity, the totality of its verbal structures; and hence, as concerns narrative, the vicissitudes of that basic model of structural analysis developed in the sixties, out of Propp and Lévi-Strauss, by the contributors to the now legendary issue of *Communications* 8, and its further adventures in the somewhat narrower straits of contemporary narratology. (As you see, I can't resist the temptation to make a story. The attraction is evident. But . . . is the suspicion also justified?)

The program of structuralist poetics, with its detailed discussion of narrative syntax, as Peter Brooks remarks in his introduction to the Minnesota English edition of Todorov's *Poetics,* aims "to *decompose* literary discourse into its component parts, and to study the *logic* of the possible significant combinations of parts."[5] Brooks is very careful in choosing that word *decompose,* careful lest it should bear any resemblance to another word, which a less astute writer might have let slip incautiously in the sentence: the word *deconstruct.* For *deconstruct* is indeed a word "already inhabited," as Bakhtin would say, by the thought of others—others not wholly sympathetic to the project of structural poetics.

I am referring to Paul de Man's critique of literary semiotics and its "use of grammatical (especially syntactical) structures conjointly with rhetorical structures, without apparent awareness of a possible discrepancy between them."[6] "Todorov, who calls one of his books a *Grammar of the Decameron*," wrote de Man with just a touch of sarcasm, may rightly think of his work as "the elaboration of a systematic grammar of literary modes, genres, and also of literary figures" (pp. 6–7). However, if the relationship of grammar and logic is one of mutual and "unsubverted" support, de Man argued, it is not so of the relationship between grammar and rhetoric. To study tropes and figures as a mere subset of syntactical relations is to assume a continuity between grammar and rhetoric which is in fact a discontinuity, a tension, even a contradiction.

He illustrated this point by analyzing a glaring case of what seems to be convergence, but is actually discontinuity, between grammatical and rhetorical structures: the rhetorical question, the very instance of a figure that is conveyed by means of a syntactical device. The contradiction there, de Man observed, is that "grammar allows us to ask the question, but the sentence by means of which we ask it may deny the very possibility of asking" (p. 10). Thus, in effect, barring the intervention of an extratextual intention (which neither de Man nor Todorov would consider germane to his own enterprise), "rhetoric radically suspends logic and opens up vertiginous possibilities of referential aberration."[7]

But de Man's project for rhetorical deconstruction (the deconstructive reading of rhetorical figures and patterns in search of a negative truth) is also, in its way, constructive. The "vertiginous possibilities of referential aberrations" must not be yielded to (again I cannot help hearing a loud intertextual intrusion: Hitchcock's film *Vertigo*, with its entirely made-up, constructed, filmic, illusionistic, non-referential image of the stairwell);[8] nor, on the other hand, will indetermination, absolute undecidability among readings, serve literature any better. A certain kind of coherence will be necessary, to replace the structural coherence of grammatical models and narrative logic, and one perhaps that will stand to logic and grammar in a relationship of "subverted" support. De Man would find that in the notion of an "allegory of reading," a coherence as formal and as internal to the text as is the linguistic-semiological notion of poetics, a coherence by which not only can the extratextual, "the authority of the reference," be kept at a distance, but "the entire question of meaning can be bracketed" (p. 5). Now, this bracketing of the question of meaning, which deconstruction and narratology have in common as a shared methodological, nay, epistemological, presupposition, is not yet altogether a moot or uncontested claim. Fredric Jameson, for one, arguing for narrative and, beyond that, for literature as "a socially symbolic act," is not averse to calling his own readings of texts "so many *interpretations*" and to defining the critical project of his *Political Unconscious* as "the construction of a new *hermeneutics*."[9] All that, of course, by way of taking a position, announcing a polemic, against precisely the poststructuralist program and its misconceived critique of all interpretive activity as necessarily totalizing, teleological, or historicist.

Meaning, for Jameson, does exist and constitutes a perfectly legitimate object of study on our part; all the more so, in fact, since it informs the operations of the political unconscious as they construct the master narratives, the political allegories, of both literature *and* criticism in any historical period. "Master narratives," he writes, "have inscribed themselves in the texts as well as in our thinking about them; such *allegorical narrative signifieds* are a persistent dimension of literary and cultural texts precisely because they reflect a fundamental dimension of our collective thinking and our collective fantasies about history and reality" (p. 34; emphasis added).

Once meaning is posed as a pertinent question (the "allegorical narrative *signifieds*," he stresses; and note, too, if you will, the interesting intertextual return of the term *allegory* here), the relation of meaning to the referent need be addressed; and Jameson does, acknowledging his debt to Althusser, in a statement which strongly resonates in my mind, with the Eco of *A Theory of Semiotics*, where Eco's own debt to Peirce is also properly acknowledged. Jameson writes:

> History is *not* a text, not a narrative, master or otherwise, but . . . , as an absent cause, it is inaccessible to us except in textual form, and . . . our approach to it and to the Real itself [capital *R* in *Real*, signaling that this is Lacan's term] necessarily passes through its prior textualization, its narrativization in the political unconscious.[10]

In this sense, then, interpretation can be seen as a rewriting of the text intended to show how the text itself is "the rewriting or restructuration of a prior historical or ideological *subtext*," which the process of interpretation (re)constructs as the symbolic resolution of determinate contradictions in the Real. In such a way, for Jameson, the critical or aesthetic act "always entertains some active relationship with the Real . . . draw[ing] the Real into its own texture" (p. 81).

The Peircean cast of this definition is apparent. A rewriting of a rewriting of a prior subtext that can be reconstructed only after the fact is a generational series very similar to Peirce's series: interpretant, sign, object, and ground.[11] And, interestingly enough, it is to Peirce that de Man appeals to provide, jointly with Nietzsche and Saussure, the philosophical foundation of semiotics as rhetoric (rather than grammar or logic); notably, Peirce's definition of "pure rhetoric" (elsewhere called semiosis) as the process by which the interpretant of a sign produces not meaning but another sign, another interpretant, "and so on, *ad infinitum.*"[12] Therefore, were it not for the important emphasis on the connection, however mediated, between text and world—an emphasis also definitely present in Peirce's notion of semiosis, as remarked by Eco, and apparently retained by Jameson—it might be tempting to see the latter's project of an "immanent hermeneutics" as an allegory of writing, a theory of the practice of ideological deconstruction.

But another, somewhat unexpected, factor precludes such a reading: the coherence of Jameson's model is to be found less in deconstructive negativity than in the thick of the enemy camp, so to speak: in the structural logic of Greimas's semiotic rectangle, which Jameson reappropriates for dialectical negation as the "locus and model of ideological closure": "Seen in this way, the semiotic rectangle becomes a vital instrument for exploring the semantic and ideological intricacies of the text . . . because it maps the limits of a specific ideological consciousness and marks the conceptual points beyond which that consciousness cannot go" (p. 47). In other words, the structured semantic investments of a given text, which may be schematized by Greimas's rectangle, are taken by Jameson as symptomatic of the terms of an ideological system implicit in the logic of the narrative but "unrealized" in the surface of the text, and so can be used to render manifest what the text does not say, hides, or "represses."

If proof be wanted that the rectangle doesn't lie, one could interrogate it, as does Christine Brooke-Rose in the lead essay of a recent issue of *Poetics Today,* on a matter of general competence: sexual relations. The rectangle, in its wisdom, provides three answers, i.e., conjures up three models or sets of oppositions, contraries, permutations, etc.: a social model, an economic model, and a "personal" one. In all three cases the ideological system implicit in the logic of the narratives considered is one so familiar that it makes Brooke-Rose "laugh out loud": for it is none other than "the old double standard," which, she puns, "lingua in sheer semiotic cheek, is made explicit as an 'elementary structure of significance'."[13]

For some of us, that is too obvious to be funny. But I have wanted to cite the incident as an nth version of the story of a woman who, innocent of the past ten years of feminist critique around the notion of woman as sign, and quite on her own, venturing into the wilds of semiotics, discovers an inconsistence in Lévi-Strauss and begins to suspect that semiotics is "a peculiarly reactionary discipline."[14] Which, of course, it isn't—peculiarly, that is. But this nth version of the story shows that the suspicion (of semiotics, of narrative, and of the wisdom of the rectangle) *was* justified. As for the attraction. . . .

Let me propose quite plainly (I am aware of the risk) that the attraction is in the possibility, glimpsed if not assured, to make up one's story, the possibility to speak as subject of discourse, which also means to be listened to, to be granted authorship and author-ity over the story. Not that women have not been writing stories for several hundred years, or telling stories for much longer than that, but they have done so with little or no authority, with severe constraints as to genre, medium, and address, and mostly, in someone else's phrase, after great pain. Yet, Yvonne Rainer suggests, the urgency of narrative may even increase with one's work becoming more consciously and explicitly feminist.

But why would feminists, even more than women (the distinction is not easy to make but perhaps all the more important), want author-ity and authorship when those notions are admittedly outmoded, patriarchal, and ethically compromised? Exactly. That is the cause of the suspicion. What we have for an answer to this question, then, is a paradox which is not one— that is to say, we have a contradiction. Of that contradiction, only feminism provides a critical understanding: not femaleness (the *fact* of being female), not femininity (as a positionality of desire, a narrative trope, a figure of style), but feminism, which is a critical reading of culture, a political inter-pretation of the social text and of the social subject, and a rewriting of our culture's "master narratives."

It is feminism that has, first, articulated the paradox of woman as both object and sign, at once captive and absent on the scene of Western repre-sentation; and it is feminism that now proposes—although, it must be said, there is more controversy on this issue than consensus—that what we thought to be a paradox, a seeming contradiction, is in effect a real contradiction, and, I will go so far as to say, an irreconcilable one. What that means is that I may speak, to be sure, but insofar as I speak I don't speak as a woman, but rather as a speaker (and when I do, I naturally take advan-tage of the podium). I also may read and write, but not as a woman, for men too have written "as woman"—Nietzsche, Artaud, Lautréamont, even Joyce apparently did—and others nowadays, all honorable men, are "read-ing as a woman."

Then, when I look at the movies, film theorists try to tell me that the gaze is male, the camera eye is masculine, and so my look is also not a woman's. But I don't believe them anymore, because now I think I know what it is to look at a film as a woman. I do because certain films, by Yvonne Rainer, Chantal Akerman, Lizzie Borden, Sally Potter, and others, have shown it to

me; they have somehow managed to inscribe in the film my woman's look—
next to, side by side, together with, my other (cinematic) look. I shall come
back to that. For now, let me rephrase the notion of contradiction, again
quite plainly.

Feminism has produced, at least for feminists, a political-personal consciousness of gender as an ideological construct which defines the social
subject; in thus en-gendering the subject, and in en-gendering the subject
as political, feminism understands the female subject as one that, unlike
Althusser's or Jameson's or Eco's, is not either "in ideology" or outside
ideology (e.g., in science), but rather is at once inside and outside the
ideology of gender, or, as I have used the terms, is at once woman and
women. In other words, woman is inside the rectangle, women are outside;
the female subject of feminism is in both places at once. *That* is the contradiction.

Prompted by the feminist discourse on gender and representation, and
by their own commitment to feminism (a discourse and a commitment
which do not always go hand in hand), some contemporary filmmakers
have begun a project to develop the means, conceptual and formal, to
represent that contradiction itself, the contradiction which I see as constitutive of the female subject of feminism: to speak, like Cassandra, a
discourse that elides woman as speaker-subject, and hence will not be heard
by most; to tell stories resisting the drift of narrativization (the operation of
narrative closure, or the "family plot," as Hitchcock had occasion to call it);
to make films against the plot that frames woman as narrative image, object,
and ground of cinematic representation. In short, to reread, rewrite, remake all cultural narratives striving to construct another form of coherence, one that is, alas, founded on contradiction.

To that end, the mere reversal of the terms of narrative—heroine instead
of hero, but they get married in the end anyway—will not do, although, as
Charlotte Brontë more than intimates and as Jake says to Brett at the close
of Hemingway's *The Sun Also Rises*," "Isn't it pretty to think so?" But the
other, if more sophisticated, kind of reversal will also not do; I am referring
to anti-narrative programs promoting notions of *jouissance* (Kristeva,
Barthes), libidinal dispersal (Lyotard), unbounded *différance* (Derrida), or
the undifferentiated affectivity of a subject free of identification and
(self-)representation (Deleuze).

What has come to mind, as I try to put into words something that will not
fit, like the sense of a double, self-contradictory coherence, is the figure that
I teased out a while ago from de Man's discussion of the relation between
grammar and rhetoric: the oxymoron of a "subverted support." The relation of women to woman, as well as the female subject's relation to narrative
(cinema), seems to me to be graspable in that contradictory, mutually

subversive, and yet necessary or coexisting relationship of grammar and rhetoric in the figure of the rhetorical question, whereby one instigates the question, but the terms (the sentence) in which we ask the question may deny, as de Man wrote, "the very possibility of asking." For this reason I have dwelt at some length on the notions of rereading and rewriting in de Man and Jameson respectively: they may serve to convey, in terms already known and by analogy, if you will, my effort to articulate the form of a particular coherence which I see delineated in feminist critical writing and in feminist cinema. I hasten to specify that the phrase "feminist cinema" is a notation for a process rather than an aesthetic or typological category: the notation for a process of reinterpretation and retextualization of cultural images and narratives whose strategies of coherence engage the spectator's identification through narrative and visual pleasure and yet succeed in drawing "the Real" into the film's texture.

Having addressed thus far more general questions of narrative poetics, I must now sketch out something of the context in which the film-theoretical concern with narrative has developed, less in the direction of a narratology than toward a more ambitious or far-reaching theory of cultural process, linking social technologies (such as cinema) to the production of subjectivity in spectatorship. In this sense, the question of a poetics of film narrative splits into two intersecting lines of inquiry. On the one hand, there is the theoretical hypothesis of narrativity in cinema as a twofold operation, a production of meaning effects which work, I suggest, both in the manner of a grammar and in the manner of a rhetoric; a hypothesis cast widely across contemporary critical discourses from semiotics to feminism and from psychoanalysis to the theory of ideology.

On the other hand, a poetics of film narrative comprises the analysis of the film text and an account of the specific formal and generic problems addressed by filmmakers and critics as they grapple with expressive strategies ranging from the anti-narrative, abstract, or structural-materialist films of the fifties and sixties to the metanarrative experiments of the past decade (just in the United States, films such as *Blood Simple, Eating Raoul, Stranger Than Paradise, Variety, The Purple Rose of Cairo*—films that confront or engage narrative, unlike those of a De Palma, whose metanarrativity is unabashedly a box-office gimmick, an advertisement for itself). To the metanarrative category may be allocated, as well, those independent films that in shop talk are called theoretical films—films made explicitly to illustrate, reflect on, or re-present (I'm thinking here of Michael Snow) issues and terms of the theoretical discourse on cinema; and finally, the films to which I alluded earlier with the phrase "feminist cinema," suggesting that in their work with and against narrative, such films employ strategies of what I call a double or self-subverting coherence.

Eventually, my own narrative will rejoin, coming full circle, the statement by Yvonne Rainer I quoted at the beginning of this essay—a statement of poetics, in fact: an individual artist's view of her own artistic process and concern with aesthetic form. I will suggest that this notion of poetics, discredited in formalist and functionalist days but perhaps on its way to renewed appreciation in these postmodern times, may offer artists and theorists something more interesting than the intentional fallacy of phallo-centric criticism.

Now, then, to provide something of a context, one should say that the nexus of cinema, narrative, and semiotics may be initially located, like the broader question of cinematic signification—cinema as a system of signs and codes—in the early years of semiotics (or semiology, as it was then called) in the mid-sixties. Thereafter, with the shifting emphasis on cinema as a signifying practice and cinema as semiotic production or productivity, the issue of narrative, or, better, narrativity, would also be reformulated.

The European debate around cinematic articulation, which developed in the context of the Mostra del Nuovo Cinema in Pesaro (Italy), and the various stances taken by Eco, Pasolini, Metz, and Barthes on the question "Is cinema a language?", are by now part of the legend of the semiotics of the cinema—a legend I need not retell in this setting.[15] Peter Wollen's influential book *Signs and Meanings in the Cinema*, which introduced semi-ology into Anglo-American film studies in 1969, did not yet single out the issue of narrative as one especially important or troublesome to cinema, although it was a central one in semiology—and had been so since Lévi-Strauss's arguments for the structural analysis of myth and the English translation of Propp's *Morphology of the Folktale* in 1958. The latter was a veritable milestone, a seminal work that prompted a flurry of research culminating in the 1966 issue of *Communications* devoted to "The Structural Analysis of Narrative," edited by Roland Barthes, and including practically all the subgenres and prominent figures of narratology—people such as Greimas, Todorov, Bremond, Genette, Eco, and Metz.

Metz's contribution to this volume, a paper he first presented at the Pesaro film festival the same year, proposed the notion of a cinematic syntax ("la grande syntagmatique du film narratif") made up of six types of larger units or syntagms (e.g., the scene, the shot, parallel montage, "auton-omous" shots such as inserts, etc.).[16] It was this kind of inquiry into the ways of narrative organization specific to the medium that, some ten years later, captured the attention of film scholars in North America and caused them to become interested in semiology and structuralism, and thus to begin to follow the work of the film journal *Screen*, which by the mid-seventies was performing the role of mediator between French thought and British film culture.

But something had happened to semiology and structuralism in those ten years, which, as you have surely reckoned, included 1968 and 1970. What had happened to semiology and structuralism on their way across the Channel and the Atlantic is that they ran into psychoanalysis and feminism; and much as it was for Oedipus after the encounter with the Sphinx, this encounter forever changed the story of cinema. Thus, the next major step in the theory of narrative cinema after "la grande syntagmatique" occurred in 1975–76 with the publication of three essays in *Screen:* a partial translation of Metz's *The Imaginary Signifier,* Laura Mulvey's "Visual Pleasure and Narrative Cinema," and Stephen Heath's "Narrative Space." At this time, both the feminist critique of representation and psychoanalysis, or certain epistemological assumptions derived thereof, became established at the center of film narrative theory.

As Judith Mayne states in her rich and illuminating review of feminist film theory and criticism since the late sixties, women's cinema has been shaped by the conjuncture of three major forces: the women's movement, independent filmmaking, and academic film studies. "It is only a slight exaggeration to say that most feminist film theory . . . of the last decade has been a response, implicit or explicit, to the issues raised in Laura Mulvey's article: the centrality of the look, cinema as spectacle and narrative, psychoanalysis as a critical tool."[17] The year 1966, besides the *Communications* issue on the structural analysis of narrative, had also seen the publication of Jacques Lacan's *Écrits*. Thus, it was hardly coincidental, though not a little surprising at the time, that Barthes's introduction to a volume concerned with the logic of narrative possibilities ended with the now-famous statement: "It may be significant that it is at the same moment (around the age of three) that the little human 'invents' at once sentence, narrative, and the Oedipus."[18]

Once suggested, the connection between narrative and the Oedipus, or desire and narrative, appeared to be incontestable and opened up the likelihood that such relationship might be akin to that of desire and language. And that evoked, on the scene of narrative and film theory, the uncanny presence of the subject: its constitution and ideological interpellation (as Althusser had called it) in the relations of meaning, in the symbolic and the imaginary, in cinema and in the film text. The nexus narrative/subjectivity thus came to the forefront of film theory, displacing the problematic of a cinematic language or narrative syntax. Two quotes from the essays by Mulvey and Heath referred to earlier, published in 1975 and 1976 respectively, will give an idea of the new cast of the film-theoretical question. Of cinematic codes, Mulvey writes:

> Playing on the tension between film as controlling the dimension of time
> (editing, narrative) and film as controlling the dimension of space (changes in
> distance, editing), cinematic codes create a gaze, a world, and an object,
> thereby producing an illusion cut to the measure of desire. . . . Going far
> beyond highlighting a woman's to-be-looked-at-ness, cinema builds the way
> she is to be looked at into the spectacle itself.[19]

And Heath:

> The film poses an image, not immediate or neutral, but posed, framed and
> centered. Perspective-system images bind the spectator in place, the suturing
> central position that is the sense of the image, that sets its scene (in place, the
> spectator completes the image as its subject). Film too, but it also moves in all
> sorts of ways and directions, flows with energies, is potentially a veritable
> festival of affects. Placed, that movement is all the value of film in its
> development and exploitation: reproduction of life and the engagement of
> the spectator in the process of that reproduction as articulation of coherence.
> What moves in film, finally, is the spectator, immobile in front of the screen.
> Film is the regulation of that movement, the individual as subject held in a
> shifting and placing of desire, energy, contradiction, in a perpetual re-
> totalization of the imaginary.[20]

Even beyond cinema, in the mainstream of semiotic studies since the mid-
seventies, especially thanks to Umberto Eco's reading of Peirce, semiotic
theory has favored a dynamic, processual view of signification as a working
of the codes, a production of meaning which involves a subject in a social
field. The object of narrative and of film-narrative theory, redefined ac-
cordingly, would be not narrative but narrativity, not so much the structure
of narrative (its component units and their relations) as its work and effects;
it would be less the formulation of a logic, a grammar, or a rhetoric of
narrative per se—fundamental as the latter has been to our knowledge of
cinema and to the establishment of film criticism as a humanistic discipline
on a par with literary criticism, the obvious references here being Seymour
Chatman's *Story and Discourse* and its literary antecedent, Wayne Booth's *The
Rhetoric of Fiction;* and it would be less the description of a rhetoric of film
narrative than the understanding of narrativity as the structuring and
destructuring, even destructive, processes at work in the textual and semiotic relations of spectatorship.

   The notion of spectatorship is most important at the present stage of film
theory in its questioning of cinema as a social technology, a system of
representation massively involved in the (re)production of social subjects.
The notion of spectatorship, which seeks to define and to articulate that
productive relation of the technology to the spectator-subject, is also pivotal
to my discussion of the poetics of film narrative, to which I now turn in the
next and last section of this essay. One, and not the least, reason why

spectatorship is pivotal to what I have called a feminist cinema is that its concern with address (whom the film addresses, to whom it speaks, what and for whom it seeks to represent, whom it represents) translates into a conscious effort to address the spectator as female, regardless of the gender of the viewers; and that is what allows the film to draw into its discursive texture something of that "Real" which is the untheorized experience of women.

In her statement of poetics, Yvonne Rainer outlines three phases or moments of a process of filmic inscription of "feminine experience," a process which she calls an "evolution"; but I would underplay the strictly chronological connotation of the word *evolution* and stress instead the sense of a dialectical developmental relationship between those three moments, as it indeed appears to be the case in Rainer's own work. Significantly, the three phases go from "description" to "speculation."

The first is the "description of individual feminine experience floating free of both social context and narrative hierarchy." This, I would gloss, is the early and more formally experimental phase of a cinema of women which was aesthetically connected to avant-garde film and to performance art. Rainer herself came to film as a choreographer-performer, and her first film in 1972 was entitled *Lives of Performers*. But one also thinks of Sally Potter and Valie Export, for example, performance artists whose first films, *Thriller* and *Invisible Adversaries* respectively, clearly show that connection; while the relation to the Anglo-American avant-garde and, in Europe, to Godard is also apparent in Laura Mulvey and Peter Wollen's early films *Penthesilea* and *Riddles of the Sphinx*, or Chantal Akerman's *Je Tu Il Elle* and *News from Home*, Bette Gordon's *Empty Suitcases*, Marjorie Keller's *Misconception*, and of course Rainer's own *Film about a Woman Who* (1974), which had as counterpart a live performance entitled *This Is the Story of a Woman Who* (staged in 1973).

Writing about this film in 1977, Ruby Rich observed that "while Rainer does not consider herself a feminist, while feminism is never the central issue in one of her films, her work is central to feminism."[21] That is so, Rich stated, arguing against the accusation of formalism that was leveled at Rainer's film from the antiformalist and antitheoretical component of the women's movement, because "Rainer's work on the frontier of form" helps women in the struggle against the oppressive mythology of romantic humanism by exposing its hidden agendas in cinematic representation. The two projects of early feminist filmmaking were, on one front, the formal-theoretical experimentation with cinematic codes, narrative frames, point of view and image construction, sound-image displacements, etc., in an attempt to alter or invent new terms of vision; and, on the other front, what

Rich called the educational function of agitational or autobiographical filmmaking, which made women visible on the screen by documenting political demonstrations or portraying women's daily, real-life activities in the "pre-aesthetic" sphere, as Silvia Bovenschen called it, of domestic life. In retrospect, both of these projects were equally important, and mutually supportive, in the development of feminism and feminist cinema. But at that time, up to the mid-seventies, they were seen in opposition to each other: the aesthetically radical, anti-narrative, and usually, if not necessarily, anti-feminist, vs. the politically radical, this latter, usually narrative (biographical or documentary) and, yes, definitely feminist.[22]

Something of this dichotomy is suggested in Rainer's own view of the second phase of women's cinema, characterized by "descriptions of individual feminine experience placed in radical juxtaposition against historical events." That is certainly the case of her *Journeys from Berlin/1971,* as well as Helke Sander's *Redupers* (The All-Around Reduced Personality), the collectively made *Sigmund Freud's Dora* and *Song of the Shirt,* or even *Thriller* and *Riddles of the Sphinx* if among the radically juxtaposed historical events we can include, as I would, the experience of European Maoism as represented by the *Tel Quel* group or, in the Anglo-American context, the beginning of a sociopolitical discourse on pornography, and the coming of age of independent cinema's reflection on its own practices and political effectivity.

Yet again, speaking of *Journeys from Berlin* (1980), Kaja Silverman emphasizes how the formal originality of Rainer's experimentation with the disjunction of image and sound, and in particular the detachment or "disembodiment" of the female voice on the soundtrack from the image of the female body on the screen, has not only aesthetic but also strong political implications:

> *Journeys from Berlin/71* makes clearer than any of the other films precisely what is at stake in this disassociation of sound and image: the freeing-up of the female voice from its obsessive and indeed exclusive reference to the female body, a reference which turns woman—in representation *and in fact*— back upon herself, in a negative and finally self-consuming narcissism.[23]

However, in spite of the critical insight, or foresight, of feminists such as Rich and Silverman, and certainly others as well, the two projects of early feminist cinema were thought to be mutually incompatible, as I said: the political demands of a consciousness-raising or educational cinema and the need to document women's lives in the private and public spheres appeared to be at odds with an individual artist's concern with aesthetic process and the formal or theoretical project to construct a new cinematic language and a new poetics of film.[24] These two film practices continued side by side but remained as radically distinct in feminist politics as the personal and the political stood in radical juxtaposition up there on the screen.

But now we come to the third phase of "explicitly feminist speculations about feminine experience," the phase that Rainer sees characterized by an overt and even programmatic return to narrative, and which in her own work corresponds to *The Man Who Envied Women* (1985). Although the elements of narrative, however threadbare or in skeletal form, were present all along throughout the three phases (and not mistakenly Ruby Rich already noted a "serious revitalization of melodrama" in *Film about a Woman Who*),[25] the emphasis on narrativity with regard to the more recent film is correlated to the words *explicitly feminist speculations*.

I said earlier that I intend to bring back and reappropriate the older notion of poetics as an artist's own articulation of her or his artistic project and process. I believe, and have argued elsewhere, that this notion is especially relevant to the understanding of feminist cinema because its project is by definition critical and self-critical, since feminist cinema has developed in a constant and unavoidable connection with feminist theory and practice, or criticism and politics, if you prefer, where the distinctive trait, the specificity, of feminism as a political-personal interpretation of the social text consists in what we call the practice of self-consciousness, that particular kind of ideological analysis which begins from and always refers back to the experience of gender and its construction of subjectivity. Moreover, the older notion of poetics seems especially relevant to the work of a "writerly" filmmaker such as Rainer, who *writes* her films much in the sense in which a critic such as Roland Barthes or Virginia Woolf, or a philosopher such as Irigaray or Derrida, might be said to *write* an essay.

In a recent article in the *Independent*, Rainer makes several observations about TMWEW (*The Man Who Envied Women*) which I would like to quote and comment on:

> In many ways, TMWEW lies outside traditional narrative cinema. There is no plot, for instance, and although the voice of the (absent) female protagonist can be construed as a narrator, this voice departs from convention by refusing to push a story forward or . . . tie up the various strands. In the struggle for the film's truth this equivocal, invisible heroine is not always the victor. Consequently, in relation to the social issues broached within the film, the question of an externally imposed, predetermined and determining coherence looms very large for some. If the process of identification with the trajectory of fictional characters is thwarted, we look for opportunities to identify with an extra-diegetic author or ultimate voice "behind" the film, if not the camera. . . . Rather than repositioning ourselves as spectators in response to cues that indicate we are being multivocally *addressed* and not just worked on by the filmic text, we still attempt to locate a singular author or

wait for a conclusive outcome. The Master's Voice Syndrome all over again. And why not? Why else do we go to see narrative cinema than to be confirmed and reinforced in our most atavistic and oedipal mind-sets?[26]

Having first located the spectator (whom she specifies as gendered) in the clutches of narrativity, a prey to the oedipal logic of desire, to the pull of identification, to the attempt, even though thwarted, to find a coherence and a truth, Rainer then recalls an instance of her own spectatorship, as a ten-year old girl watching a Hollywood film, and her intense response of pleasure and anger, identification and subsequent secondarization (in Freud's term): in short, the making of a coherence for the self which is not only imaginary but profoundly cleft, inherently contradictory.

While this childhood movie-going memory had already surfaced many years earlier in the text of *Film about a Woman Who*, it had remained unanalyzed, simply recorded in the text, and its subjective effects only obscurely felt, until the writing of this essay where, not coincidentally, Rainer discusses the narrative strategies consciously deployed in her latest, "explicitly feminist," film. These are precisely strategies of coherence, but based on contradiction and "poetic ambiguity," formally complex strategies such as: have two actors play the male protagonist, represent the female protagonist not as narrative image but as the narrating voice; disrupt the glossy surface and homogeneous look of "professional cinematography by means of optically degenerated shots," refilming, blown-up super 8 and video transfers; play off and contrast different authorial voices; play on "incongruous juxtapositions of modes of address: recitation, reading, 'real' or spontaneous speech, printed text, quoted texts, *et al.*, all in the same film." If narrativity is disrupted, yet narrative is present and its seduction thematized in several seduction scenes which, again not coincidentally, are to do with theory and a dream sequence which Rainer calls an "oedipal extravaganza." Or, as she says, "if I'm going to make a movie about Oedipus, i.e., Eddy and Edy Pussy Foot, I'm going to have to subject him to some calculated narrative screw-ups. It's elementary, dear Eddy: play with signifiers of desire."[27]

However, you may object, this formal disruption of narrative is hardly news in avant-garde cinema for at least the past ten years. Please explain more fully the connection between these not uncommon narrative strategies and feminist cinema. Okay. Let me point out, first, that the usual view of the political or aesthetic import of subverting narrative, that is to say, of anti-narrative or abstract film practices, is to decenter the individualist or bourgeois subject, to work against or to destroy the coherence of narrativity which both constructs and confirms the coherence of that subject in its imaginary unity. This project does not usually include the questioning of sexual difference or the decentering of the masculinity, and even less the whiteness of the bourgeois subject. Second, if the Western bourgeois spectator-subject is understood, in keeping with the ideology of humanism, as simply human, that is to say, male and white, no less so are both the spectator addressed by radical (non-feminist) avant-garde film practices, and the deluded, divided, or diffuse subject of poststructuralist and anti-humanist discourse. For this latter subject is envisioned as non-gendered— gender being precisely an effect of delusion, an imaginary construct, nothing to do with the Real; which is to say, once again, that the subject is still (usually) white, and male in the last instance.

Feminist cinema, on the contrary, unlike other contemporary avant-garde, poststructuralist, or anti-humanist practices, begins from an under-standing of spectatorship as gendered (as distinguishable, at the very least, in relation to sexual difference and its experience of gender), and then essays to fashion narrative strategies, points of identification, and places of the look that may address, engage, and construct the spectator as gendered subject; and most recently, as in Lizzie Borden's *Born in Flames*, as a subject constructed across racial as well as sexual differences. Hence the effort to devise strategies of a subverted coherence which, in the representation of women, are necessarily also self-subverting. For example, the reversal of penis envy in Rainer's film, ostensibly about a man who envied women but actually another "film about a woman who," is a grammatical kind of reversal, a strategy of subversion of narrative syntax. But that is concurrent with another strategy, this time a rhetorical strategy, which questions or undermines the terms of the prior reversal, for in the end this is a film about *a-woman* who. . . . As Trisha's voice-over says toward the end of the film, opening up a whole new phase of women's cinema,

> I can't live without men, but I can live without a man. I've had this thought before, but this time the idea is not colored by stigma or despair or finality. I know there will sometimes be excruciating sadness. But I also know some-thing is different now. Something in the direction of unwomanliness. Not a new woman, not non-woman or misanthropist or anti-woman, and not non-practicing lesbian. Maybe unwoman is also the wrong term. A-woman is closer. A-womanly. A-womanliness.[28]

To conclude, this is a film that problematizes woman's representability, both her representability as image and her status as narrator and as subject. She cannot be seen, her speech is not authorized or self-consistent, it is embodied in different voices; her narration is not authoritative, it doesn't reach climax or resolution, it doesn't produce a true confession or even a story. And yet, at the same time, the film insists that she is there, her presence inscribed figurally through metonymic effects of voice, other images (film images, video images, photographic images, dream images), and discourses (domestic, public, agitational, sexual, and theoretical). In other words, grammatically or logically, "she" is not there, but rhetorically *she is* there: the absent Trisha's femaleness is clearly foregrounded, as is the maleness of Jack Deller, husband and theorist, for gender is very much at issue and not only overlays the personal and the political, the sexual and the social, but also specifically grounds the very possibility of meaning, of constructing an interpretation of the various cultural texts displayed in the film, and of producing an understanding of the determinate contradictions that the film concurrently locates in the real and in the text of cinema.

It is precisely in that space of contradiction, in the double and self-subverting coherence of its narrative grammar and figural ambiguities, that the film addresses me, spectator, *as a(-)woman;* that it solicits and inscribes my (un)womanly look and gendered subjectivity in what I might call *a recognition of misrecognition;* that is to say, in the personal-political contradictions of my own history of a-womanness.

This film does not move me along, bound in the regulated coherence of a master plot, to the closure of a framed narrative image of Woman as spectacle and object of a controlling gaze—my (master's) gaze. Nor does it, however, repel my woman's gaze, such as it is, or my feminist understanding of the female subject's history of a-womanness, contradiction, and self-subverting coherence. Instead, the film constructs the filmic terms, the filmic conditions of possibility, for women spectators to be asking the question, even as it denies the certainty of an answer. In deconstructing narrative space, the film constructs a critical space in which I am addressed, precisely, as a woman and a-woman.

The fact that, if I speak these words, *a woman* and *a-woman*, those who hear them cannot tell the difference (just as Archie Bunker couldn't in de Man's example of the rhetorical question), may perhaps convey two points I've tried to make: first, the potential of employing grammar and rhetoric in mutually subverting support, in support of subversive narrative practices; and second, the contradiction in which I find myself, as I speak, and which I am at pains to articulate here in writing.

Notes

1. Yvonne Rainer, "More Kicking and Screaming from the Narrative Front/Backwater," *Wide Angle* 7, nos. 1–2 (1985): 8.

2. Teresa de Lauretis, *Alice Doesn't: Feminism, Semiotics, Cinema* (Bloomington: Indiana University Press, 1984), p. 79.

3. Shoshana Felman, "Rereading Femininity," *Yale French Studies*, no. 62 (1981): 44.

4. Tzvetan Todorov, *Introduction to Poetics*, trans. Richard Howard (Minneapolis: University of Minnesota Press, 1981), p. 23

5. Ibid., p. xiv; emphasis added.

6. Paul de Man, "Semiology and Rhetoric," in *Allegories of Reading* (New Haven and London: Yale University Press, 1979), p. 6.

7. Ibid., p. 10.

8. Hitchcock recounts with relish how that image came to be: "I always remember one night at the Chelsea Arts Ball at Albert Hall in London when I got terribly drunk and I had the sensation that everything was going far away from me. I tried to get that into *Rebecca*, but they couldn't do it. The viewpoint must be fixed, you see, while the perspective is changed as it stretches lengthwise. I thought about the problem for fifteen years. By the time we got to *Vertigo*, we solved it by using the dolly and zoom simultaneously. I asked how much it would cost, and they told me it would cost fifty thousand dollars. When I asked why, they said, 'Because to put the camera at the top of the stairs we have to have a big apparatus to lift it, counterweight it, and hold it up in space'. I said, 'There are no characters in this scene; it's simply a viewpoint. Why can't we make a miniature of the stairway and lay it on its side, then take our shot by pulling away from it? We can use a tracking shot and a zoom flat on the ground.' So that's the way we did it, and it only cost us nineteen thousand dollars" (Francois Truffaut, *Hitchcock* [New York: Simon & Schuster, 1967], p. 187).

9. Fredric Jameson, *The Political Unconscious: Narrative as a Socially Symbolic Act* (Ithaca, N.Y.: Cornell University Press, 1981), p. 21.

10. Ibid., p. 35. On the relation of textuality to "the Real," Eco writes: "There is sign production because there are empirical subjects which display labor in order to physically produce expressions, to correlate them to content, to segment content, and so on. But semiotics is entitled to recognize these subjects only insofar as they manifest themselves through sign-functions, producing sign-functions, criticizing other sign-functions and restructuring the pre-existing sign-functions. By accepting this limit, semiotics fully avoids any risk of idealism. On the contrary semiotics recognizes as the only testable subject matter of its discourse the social existence of the universe of signification, as it was revealed by the physical testability of interpretants—which are, to reinforce this point for the last time, *material expressions*" (Umberto Eco, *A Theory of Semiotics* [Bloomington: Indiana University Press, 1976], p. 317).

11. See my reading of Peirce through Eco in *Alice Doesn't*, pp. 172–75.

12. De Man, *Allegories of Reading*, p. 9. The words *ad infinitum*, emphasized by de Man, mark the exact point where his interpretation of Peirce and of semiosis differs from Eco's. See note 11 above.

13. Christine Brooke-Rose, "Woman as a Semiotic Object," *Poetics Today* 6, nos. 1–2 (1985): 10.

14. Ibid., p. 19. Brooke-Rose seems unaware of the extensive work done in this area by feminist critics such as Elizabeth Cowie, "Woman as Sign," *m/f*, no. 1 (1978); Gayle Rubin, "The Traffic in Women: Notes on the 'Political Economy' of Sex," in *Toward an Anthropology of Women*, ed. Rayna R. Reiter (New York: Monthly Review Press, 1975); and my own critique of semiotics in *Alice Doesn't*, to name but a few.

15. An account may be found in *Alice Doesn't*, pp. 40–44.

16. Christian Metz, "La grande syntagmatique du film narratif," *Communications*, no. 8 (1966): 120–24.

17. Judith Mayne, "Feminist Film Theory and Criticism," *Signs* 11, no. 1 (Autumn 1985): 83.

18. Roland Barthes, "Introduction to the Structural Analysis of Narratives," in *Image-Music-Text,* trans. Stephen Heath (New York: Hill and Wang, 1977), p. 124.

19. Laura Mulvey, "Visual Pleasure and Narrative Cinema," *Screen* 16, no. 3 (Autumn 1975): 17.

20. Stephen Heath, "Narrative Space," now in *Questions of Cinema* (Bloomington: Indiana University Press, 1981), p. 53.

21. B. Ruby Rich, "The Films of Yvonne Rainer," *Chrysalis,* no. 2 (1977): 126.

22. The placing of radical feminist artistic practice in opposition to aesthetically radical or avant-garde practices was (and to some extent still is) more marked in the Anglo-American context than, say, in France or Italy; yet the other opposition, the perception of female experience and subjectivity as incommensurable with the discourse of history, was (and to some extent still is) common to Western feminism. For a comprehensive overview of these and other issues, see "Feminist Film Criticism: An Introduction," in *Re-vision: Essays in Feminist Film Criticism,* ed. Mary Ann Doane, Patricia Mellencamp, and Linda Williams (Frederick, Md.: University Publications of America and the American Film Institute, 1984), pp. 1–17; and Mayne, "Feminist Film Theory and Criticism," pp. 81–100. On Silvia Bovenschen, see note 1 of Chapter 8 below.

23. Kaja Silverman, "Dis-embodying the Female Voice," in Doane, Mellencamp, and Williams, *Re-vision: Essays in Feminist Film Criticism,* p. 137; emphasis added.

24. See Laura Mulvey, "Feminism, Film, and the Avant-Garde," *Framework,* no. 10 (Spring 1979): 3–10, and Chapter 8 of this book.

25. Rich, "The Films of Yvonne Rainer," p. 119.

26. Yvonne Rainer, "Some Ruminations around Cinematic Antidotes to the Oedipal Net(les) while Playing with De Lauraedipus Mulvey, or, He May Be Off Screen, but. . . .," *Independent* (April 1986), p. 22.

27. Ibid., p. 25.

28. Yvonne Rainer, *The Man Who Envied Women,* Filmscript, p. 58; also cited in Helen Demichiel, "Rainer's Manhattan," *Afterimage* (December 1985), p. 19. There is a sense in which Trisha's contorted and painful effort to express a female identity for which no current word or established visual form will do goes cautiously in the direction of Monique Wittig's much blunter statement, "Lesbians are not women" ("The Straight Mind," *Feminist Issues,* no. 1 [Summer 1980]: 110). But the feeling that such is "the direction of unwomanliness" where feminism at its best does take one is my own personal feeling, not, obviously, Yvonne Rainer's—or at least not yet.

8

RETHINKING WOMEN'S CINEMA
Aesthetics and Feminist Theory

When Silvia Bovenschen in 1976 posed the question "Is there a feminine aesthetic?" the only answer she could give was, yes and no: "Certainly there is, if one is talking about aesthetic awareness and modes of sensory perception. Certainly not, if one is talking about an unusual variant of artistic production or about a painstakingly constructed theory of art."[1] If this contradiction seems familiar to anyone even vaguely acquainted with the development of feminist thought over the past fifteen years, it is because it echoes a contradiction specific to, and perhaps even constitutive of, the women's movement itself: a twofold pressure, a simultaneous pull in opposite directions, a tension toward the positivity of politics, or affirmative action in behalf of women as social subjects, on one front, and the negativity inherent in the radical critique of patriarchal, bourgeois culture, on the other. It is also the contradiction of women in language, as we attempt to speak as subjects of discourses which negate or objectify us through their representations. As Bovenschen put it, "We are in a terrible bind. How do we speak? In what categories do we think? Is even logic a bit of virile trickery? . . . Are our desires and notions of happiness so far removed from cultural traditions and models?" (p. 119)

Not surprisingly, therefore, a similar contradiction was also central to the debate on women's cinema, its politics and its language, as it was articulated within Anglo-American film theory in the early 1970s in relation to feminist politics and the women's movement, on the one hand, and to artistic

Written initially as a contribution to the catalogue of *Kunst mit Eigen-Sinn* (edited by Silvia Eiblmayr, Valie Export, and Monika Prischl-Meier [Vienna and Munich: Locker, 1985]), an international exhibition of contemporary women's art held at the Museum des 20. Jahrhunderts in Vienna, 1985. First published in the present expanded version, and with the title "Aesthetic and Feminist Theory: Rethinking Women's Cinema," in *New German Critique*, no. 34 (Winter 1985). Reprinted here with minor changes in editorial style and format.

avant-garde practices and women's filmmaking, on the other. There, too, the accounts of feminist film culture produced in the mid- to late seventies tended to emphasize a dichotomy between two concerns of the women's movement and two types of film work that seemed to be at odds with each other: one called for immediate documentation for purposes of political activism, consciousness raising, self-expression, or the search for "positive images" of woman; the other insisted on rigorous, formal work on the medium—or, better, the cinematic apparatus, understood as a social technology—in order to analyze and disengage the ideological codes embedded in representation.

Thus, as Bovenschen deplores the "opposition between feminist demands and artistic production" (p. 131), the tug of war in which women artists were caught between the movement's demands that women's art portray women's activities, document demonstrations, etc., and the formal demands of "artistic activity and its concrete work with material and media"; so does Laura Mulvey set out two successive moments of feminist film culture. First, she states, there was a period marked by the effort to change the *content* of cinematic representation (to present realistic images of women, to record women talking about their real-life experiences), a period "characterized by a mixture of consciousness-raising and propaganda."[2] It was followed by a second moment, in which the concern with the language of representation as such became predominant, and the "fascination with the cinematic process" led filmmakers and critics to the "use of and interest in the aesthetic principles and terms of reference provided by the avant-garde tradition" (p. 7).

In this latter period, the common interest of both avant-garde cinema and feminism in the politics of images, or the political dimension of aesthetic expression, made them turn to the theoretical debates on language and imaging that were going on outside of cinema, in semiotics, psychoanalysis, critical theory, and the theory of ideology. Thus, it was argued that, in order to counter the aesthetic of realism, which was hopelessly compromised with bourgeois ideology, as well as Hollywood cinema, avant-garde and feminist filmmakers must take an oppositional stance against narrative "illusionism" and in favor of formalism. The assumption was that "foregrounding the process itself, privileging the signifier, necessarily disrupts aesthetic unity and forces the spectator's attention on the means of production of meaning" (p. 7).

While Bovenschen and Mulvey would not relinquish the political commitment of the movement and the need to construct other representations of woman, the way in which they posed the question of expression (a "feminine aesthetic," a "new language of desire") was couched in the terms of a traditional notion of art, specifically the one propounded by modernist aesthetics. Bovenschen's insight that what is being expressed in the decoration of the household and the body, or in letters and other private forms of writing, is in fact women's aesthetic needs and impulses, is a crucial one. But the importance of that insight is undercut by the very terms that define it: the "*pre*-aesthetic realms." After quoting a passage from Sylvia Plath's *The Bell Jar,* Bovenschen comments:

> Here the ambivalence once again: on the one hand we see aesthetic activity deformed, atrophied, but on the other we find, even within this restricted scope, socially creative impulses which, however, have no outlet for aesthetic development, no opportunities for growth. . . . [These activities] remained bound to everyday life, feeble attempts to make this sphere more aesthetically pleasing. But the price for this was narrowmindedness. The object could never leave the realm in which it came into being, it remained tied to the household, it could never break loose and initiate communication. (pp. 132–33)

Just as Plath laments that Mrs. Willard's beautiful home-braided rug is not hung on the wall but put to the use for which it was made, and thus quickly spoiled of its beauty, so would Bovenschen have "the object" of artistic creation leave its context of production and use value in order to enter the "artistic realm" and so to "initiate communication"; that is to say, to enter the museum, the art gallery, the market. In other words, art is what is enjoyed publicly rather than privately, has an exchange value rather than a use value, and that value is conferred by socially established aesthetic canons.

Mulvey, too, in proposing the destruction of narrative and visual pleasure as the foremost objective of women's cinema, hails an established tradition, albeit a radical one: the historic left avant-garde tradition that goes back to Eisenstein and Vertov (if not Méliès) and through Brecht reaches its peak of influence in Godard, and on the other side of the Atlantic, the tradition of American avant-garde cinema.

> The first blow against the monolithic accumulation of traditional film conventions (already undertaken by radical film-makers) is to free the look of the camera into its materiality in time and space and the look of the audience into dialectics, passionate detachment.[3]

But much as Mulvey and other avant-garde filmmakers insisted that women's cinema ought to avoid a politics of emotions and seek to problematize the female spectator's identification with the on-screen image of woman, the response to her theoretical writings, like the reception of her films (codirected with Peter Wollen), showed no consensus. Feminist critics, spectators, and filmmakers remained doubtful. For example, Ruby Rich:

According to Mulvey, the woman is not visible in the audience which is perceived as male; according to Johnston, the woman is not visible on the screen. . . . How does one formulate an understanding of a structure that insists on our absence even in the face of our presence? What is there in a film with which a woman viewer identifies? How can the contradictions be used as a critique? And how do all these factors influence what one makes as a woman filmmaker, or specifically as a feminist filmmaker?[4]

The questions of identification, self-definition, the modes or the very possibility of envisaging oneself as subject—which the male avant-garde artists and theorists have also been asking, on their part, for almost one hundred years, even as they work to subvert the dominant representations or to challenge their hegemony—are fundamental questions for feminism. If identification is "not simply one psychical mechanism among others, but the operation itself whereby the human subject is constituted," as Laplanche and Pontalis describe it, then it must be all the more important, theoretically and politically, for women who have never before represented ourselves as subjects, and whose images and subjectivities—until very recently, if at all—have not been ours to shape, to portray, or to create.[5]

There is indeed reason to question the theoretical paradigm of a subject-object dialectic, whether Hegelian or Lacanian, that subtends both the aesthetic and the scientific discourses of Western culture; for what that paradigm contains, what those discourses rest on, is the unacknowledged assumption of sexual difference: that the human subject, Man, is the male. As in the originary distinction of classical myth reaching us through the Platonic tradition, human creation and all that is human—mind, spirit, history, language, art, or symbolic capacity—is defined in contradistinction to formless chaos, *phusis* or nature, to something that is female, matrix and matter; and on this primary binary opposition, all the others are modeled. As Lea Melandri states,

Idealism, the oppositions of mind to body, of rationality to matter, originate in a twofold concealment: of the woman's body and of labor power. Chronologically, however, even prior to the commodity and the labor power that has produced it, the matter which was negated in its concreteness and particularity, in its "relative plural form," is the woman's body. Woman enters history having already lost concreteness and singularity: she is the economic machine that reproduces the human species, and she is the Mother, an equivalent more universal than money, the most abstract measure ever invented by patriarchal ideology.[6]

That this proposition remains true when tested on the aesthetic of modernism or the major trends in avant-garde cinema from visionary to structural-materialist film, on the films of Stan Brakhage, Michael Snow, or Jean-Luc Godard, but is not true of the films of Yvonne Rainer, Valie Export,

Chantal Akerman, or Marguerite Duras, for example; that it remains valid for the films of Fassbinder but not those of Ottinger, the films of Pasolini and Bertolucci but not Cavani's, and so on, suggests to me that it is perhaps time to shift the terms of the question altogether.

To ask of these women's films: What formal, stylistic, or thematic markers point to a female presence behind the camera? and hence to generalize and universalize, to say: This is the look and sound of women's cinema, this is its language—finally only means complying, accepting a certain definition of art, cinema, and culture, and obligingly showing how women can and do "contribute," pay their tribute, to "society." Put another way, to ask whether there is a feminine or female aesthetic, or a specific language of women's cinema, is to remain caught in the master's house and there, as Audre Lorde's suggestive metaphor warns us, to legitimate the hidden agendas of a culture we badly need to change. Cosmetic changes, she is telling us, won't be enough for the majority of women—women of color, black women, and white women as well; or, in her own words, "assimilation within a solely western-european herstory is not acceptable."[7]

It is time we listened. Which is not to say that we should dispense with rigorous analysis and experimentation on the formal processes of meaning production, including the production of narrative, visual pleasure, and subject positions, but rather that feminist theory should now engage precisely in the redefinition of aesthetic and formal knowledges, much as women's cinema has been engaged in the transformation of vision.

Take Akerman's *Jeanne Dielman* (1975), a film about the routine daily activities of a Belgian middle-class and middle-aged housewife, and a film where the pre-aesthetic is already fully aesthetic. That is not so, however, because of the beauty of its images, the balanced composition of its frames, the absence of the reverse shot, or the perfectly calculated editing of its still-camera shots into a continuous, logical, and obsessive narrative space; it is so because it is a woman's actions, gestures, body, and look that define the space of our vision, the temporality and rhythms of perception, the horizon of meaning available to the spectator. So that narrative suspense is not built on the expectation of a "significant event," a socially momentous act (which actually occurs, though unexpectedly and almost incidentally, one feels, toward the end of the film), but is produced by the tiny slips in Jeanne's routine, the small forgettings, the hesitations between real-time gestures as common and "insignificant" as peeling potatoes, washing dishes, or making coffee—and then not drinking it. What the film constructs—formally and artfully, to be sure—is a picture of female experience, of duration, perception, events, relationships, and silences, which feels immediately and unquestionably true. And in this sense the "pre-aesthetic" is *aesthetic* rather than *aestheticized*, as it is in films such as Godard's *Two or Three Things I Know about Her,* Polanski's *Repulsion,* or Antonioni's *Eclipse.* To say the same thing in another way, Akerman's film addresses the spectator as female.

The effort, on the part of the filmmaker, to render a presence in the feeling of a gesture, to convey the sense of an experience that is subjective yet socially coded (and therefore recognizable), and to do so formally, working through her conceptual (one could say, theoretical) knowledge of film form, is averred by Chantal Akerman in an interview on the making of *Jeanne Dielman:*

> I *do* think it's a feminist film because I give space to things which were never, almost never, shown in that way, like the daily gestures of a woman. They are the lowest in the hierarchy of film images. . . . But more than the content, it's because of the style. If you choose to show a woman's gestures so precisely, it's because you love them. In some way you recognize those gestures that have always been denied and ignored. I think that the real problem with women's films usually has nothing to do with the content. It's that hardly any women really have confidence enough to carry through on their feelings. Instead the content is the most simple and obvious thing. They deal with that and forget to look for formal ways to express what they are and what they want, their own rhythms, their own way of looking at things. A lot of women have unconscious contempt for their feelings. But I don't think I do. I have enough confidence in myself. So that's the other reason why I think it's a feminist film—not just what it says but *what* is shown and *how* it's shown.[8]

This lucid statement of poetics resonates with my own response as a viewer and gives me something of an explanation as to why I recognize in those unusual film images, in those movements, those silences, and those looks, the ways of an experience all but unrepresented, previously unseen in film, though lucidly and unmistakably apprehended here. And so the statement cannot be dismissed with commonplaces such as authorial intention or intentional fallacy. As another critic and spectator points out, there are "two logics" at work in this film, "two modes of the feminine": character and director, image and camera, remain distinct yet interacting and mutually interdependent positions. Call them femininity and feminism; the one is made representable by the critical work of the other; the one is kept at a distance, constructed, "framed," to be sure, and yet "respected," "loved," "given space" by the other.[9] The two "logics" remain separate:

> The camera look can't be construed as the view of any character. Its interest extends beyond the fiction. The camera presents itself, in its evenness and predictability, as equal to Jeanne's precision. Yet the camera continues its logic throughout; Jeanne's order is disrupted, and with the murder the text comes to its logical end since Jeanne then stops altogether. If Jeanne has, symbolically, destroyed the phallus, its order still remains visible all around her.[10]

Finally, then, the space constructed by the film is not only a textual or filmic space of vision, in frame and off—for an off-screen space is still inscribed in the images, although not sutured narratively by the reverse shot but effectively reaching toward the historical and social determinants which define Jeanne's life and place her in her frame. But beyond that, the film's space is also a critical space of analysis, a horizon of possible meanings which includes or extends to the spectator ("extends beyond the fiction") insofar as the spectator is led to occupy at once the two positions, to follow the two "logics," and to perceive them as equally and concurrently true.

In saying that a film whose visual and symbolic space is organized in this manner *addresses its spectator as a woman,* regardless of the gender of the viewers, I mean that the film defines all points of identification (with character, image, camera) as female, feminine, or feminist. However, this is not as simple or self-evident a notion as the established film-theoretical view of cinematic identification, namely, that identification with the look is masculine, and identification with the image is feminine. It is not self-evident precisely because such a view—which indeed correctly explains the working of dominant cinema—is now accepted: that the camera (technology), the look (voyeurism), and the scopic drive itself partake of the phallic and thus somehow are entities or figures of a masculine nature.

How difficult it is to "prove" that a film addresses its spectator as female is brought home time and again in conversations or discussions between audiences and filmmakers. After a screening of *Redupers* in Milwaukee (in January 1985), Helke Sander answered a question about the function of the Berlin wall in her film and concluded by saying, if I may paraphrase: "but of course the wall also represents another division that is specific to women." She did not elaborate, but again, I felt that what she meant was clear and unmistakable. And so does at least one other critic and spectator, Kaja Silverman, who sees the wall as a division other in kind from what the wall would divide—and can't, for things do "flow through the Berlin wall (TV and radio waves, germs, the writings of Christa Wolf)," and Edda's photographs show the two Berlins in "their quotidian similarities rather than their ideological divergences."

All three projects are motivated by the desire to tear down the wall, or at least to prevent it from functioning as the dividing line between two irreducible opposites. . . . *Redupers* makes the wall a signifier for psychic as well as ideological, political, and geographical boundaries. It functions there as a metaphor for sexual difference, for the subjective limits articulated by the existing symbolic order both in East and West. The wall thus designates the discursive boundaries which separate residents not only of the same country and language, but of the same partitioned space.[11]

Those of us who share Silverman's perception must wonder whether in fact the sense of that other, specific division represented by the wall in *Redupers* (sexual difference, a discursive boundary, a subjective limit) is in the film or in our viewers' eyes. Is it actually there on screen, in the film, inscribed in its slow montage of long takes and in the stillness of the images in their silent frames; or is it, rather, in our perception, our insight, as—precisely—a subjective limit and discursive boundary (gender), a horizon of meaning (feminism) which is projected into the images, onto the screen, around the text?

I think it is this other kind of division that is acknowledged in Christa Wolf's figure of "the divided heaven," for example, or in Virginia Woolf's "room of one's own": the feeling of an internal distance, a contradiction, a space of silence, which is there alongside the imaginary pull of cultural and ideological representations without denying or obliterating them. Women artists, filmmakers, and writers acknowledge this division or difference by attempting to express it in their works. Spectators and readers think we find it in those texts. Nevertheless, even today, most of us would still agree with Silvia Bovenschen.

"For the time being," writes Gertrud Koch, "the issue remains whether films by women actually succeed in subverting this basic model of the camera's construction of the gaze, whether the female look through the camera at the world, at men, women and objects will be an essentially different one."[12] Posed in these terms, however, the issue will remain fundamentally a rhetorical question. I have suggested that the emphasis must be shifted away from the artist behind the camera, the gaze, or the text as origin and determination of meaning, toward the wider public sphere of cinema as a social technology: we must develop our understanding of cinema's implication in other modes of cultural representation, and its possibilities of both production and counterproduction of social vision. I further suggest that, even as filmmakers are confronting the problems of transforming vision by engaging all of the codes of cinema, specific and non-specific, against the dominance of that "basic model," our task as theorists is to articulate the conditions and forms of vision for another social subject, and so to venture into the highly risky business of redefining aesthetic and formal knowledge.

Such a project evidently entails reconsidering and reassessing the early feminist formulations or, as Sheila Rowbotham summed it up, "look[ing] back at ourselves through our own cultural creations, our actions, our ideas, our pamphlets, our organization, our history, our theory."[13] And if we now can add "our films," perhaps the time has come to re-think women's cinema as the production of a feminist social vision. As a form of political critique or critical politics, and through the specific consciousness that women have developed to analyze the subject's relation to sociohistorical reality, feminism not only has invented new strategies or created new texts, but, more important, it has conceived a new social subject, women: as speakers, writers, readers, spectators, users, and makers of cultural forms, shapers of cultural processes. The project of women's cinema, therefore, is no longer that of destroying or disrupting man-centered vision by representing its blind spots, its gaps, or its repressed. The effort and challenge now are how to effect another vision: to construct other objects and subjects of vision, and to formulate the conditions of representability of another social subject. For the time being, then, feminist work in film seems necessarily focused on those subjective limits and discursive boundaries that mark women's division as gender-specific, a division more elusive, complex, and contradictory than can be conveyed in the notion of sexual difference as it is currently used.

The idea that *a film may address the spectator as female*, rather than portray women positively or negatively, seems very important to me in the critical endeavor to characterize women's cinema as a cinema for, not only by, women. It is an idea not found in the critical writings I mentioned earlier, which are focused on the film, the object, the text. But rereading those essays today, one can see, and it is important to stress it, that the question of a filmic language or a feminine aesthetic has been articulated from the beginning in relation to the women's movement: "the new grows only out of the work of confrontation" (Mulvey, p. 4); women's "imagination constitutes the movement itself" (Bovenschen, p. 136); and in Claire Johnston's non-formalist view of women's cinema as counter-cinema, a feminist political strategy should reclaim, rather than shun, the use of film as a form of mass culture: "In order to counter our objectification in the cinema, our collective fantasies must be released: women's cinema must embody the working through of desire: such an objective demands the use of the entertainment film."[14]

Since the first women's film festivals in 1972 (New York, Edinburgh) and the first journal of feminist film criticism (*Women and Film,* published in Berkeley from 1972 to 1975), the question of women's expression has been one of both self-expression and communication with other women, a question at once of the creation/invention of new images and of the creation/ imaging of new forms of community. If we rethink the problem of a specificity of women's cinema and aesthetic forms in this manner, in terms of address—who is making films for whom, who is looking and speaking, how, where, and to whom—then what has been seen as a rift, a division, an ideological split within feminist film culture between theory and practice, or between formalism and activism, may appear to be the very strength, the drive and productive heterogeneity of feminism. In their introduction to the recent collection *Re-vision: Essays in Feminist Film Criticism,* Mary Ann Doane, Patricia Mellencamp, and Linda Williams point out:

> If feminist work on film has grown increasingly theoretical, less oriented towards political action, this does not necessarily mean that theory itself is counter-productive to the cause of feminism, nor that the institutional form of the debates within feminism have simply reproduced a male model of academic competition. . . . Feminists sharing similar concerns collaborate in joint authorship and editorships, cooperative filmmaking and distribution arrangements. Thus, many of the political aspirations of the women's movement form an integral part of the very structure of feminist work in and on film.[15]

The "re-vision" of their title, borrowed from Adrienne Rich ("Re-vision— the act of looking back, of seeing with fresh eyes," writes Rich, is for women "an act of survival"), refers to the project of reclaiming vision, of "seeing difference differently," of displacing the critical emphasis from "images of" women "to the axis of vision itself—to the modes of organizing vision and hearing which result in the production of that 'image'."[16]

I agree with the *Re-vision* editors when they say that over the past decade, feminist theory has moved "from an analysis of difference as oppressive to a delineation and specification of difference as liberating, as offering the only possibility of radical change" (p. 12). But I believe that radical change requires that such specification not be limited to "sexual difference," that is to say, a difference of women from men, female from male, or Woman from Man. Radical change requires a delineation and a better understanding of the difference of women from Woman, and that is to say as well, *the differences among women.* For there are, after all, different histories of women. There are women who masquerade and women who wear the veil; women invisible to men, in their society, but also women who are invisible to other women, in our society.[17]

The invisibility of black women in white women's films, for instance, or of lesbianism in mainstream feminist criticism, is what Lizzie Borden's *Born in Flames* (1983) most forcefully represents, while at the same time constructing the terms of their visibility as subjects and objects of vision. Set in a hypothetical near-future time and in a place very much like lower Manhattan, with the look of a documentary (after Chris Marker) and the feel of contemporary science-fiction writing (the post-new-wave s-f of Samuel Delany, Joanna Russ, Alice Sheldon, or Thomas Disch), *Born in Flames* shows how a "successful" social democratic cultural revolution, now into its tenth year, slowly but surely reverts to the old patterns of male dominance, politics as usual, and the traditional Left disregard for "women's issues." It is around this specific gender oppression, in its various forms, that several groups of women (black women, Latinas, lesbians, single mothers, intellectuals, political activists, spiritual and punk performers, and a Women's Army) succeed in mobilizing and joining together not by ignoring but, paradoxically, by acknowledging their differences.

Like *Redupers* and *Jeanne Dielman*, Borden's film addresses the spectator as female, but it does not do so by portraying an experience which feels immediately one's own. On the contrary, its barely coherent narrative, its quick-paced shots and sound montage, the counterpoint of image and word, the diversity of voices and languages, and the self-conscious science-fictional frame of the story hold the spectator across a distance, projecting toward her its fiction like a bridge of difference. In short, what *Born in Flames* does for me, woman spectator, is exactly to allow me "to see difference differently," to look at women with eyes I've never had before and yet my own; for, as it remarks the emphasis (the words are Audre Lorde's) on the "interdependency of different strengths" in feminism, the film also inscribes the differences among women as *differences within women*.

Born in Flames addresses me as a woman and a feminist living in a particular moment of women's history, the United States today. The film's events and images take place in what science fiction calls a parallel universe, a time and a place elsewhere that look and feel like here and now, yet are not, just as I (and all women) live in a culture that is and is not our own. In that unlikely, but not impossible, universe of the film's fiction, the women come together in the very struggle that divides and differentiates them. Thus, what it portrays for me, what elicits my identification with the film and gives me, spectator, a place in it, is the contradiction of my own history and the personal/political difference that is also within myself.

"The relationship between history and so-called subjective processes," says Helen Fehervary in a recent discussion of women's film in Germany, "is not a matter of grasping the truth in history as some objective entity, but in finding the truth of the experience. Evidently, this kind of experiential immediacy has to do with women's own history and self-consciousness."[18] That, how, and why our histories and our consciousness are different, divided, even conflicting, is what women's cinema can analyze, articulate, reformulate. And, in so doing, it can help us create something else to be, as Toni Morrison says of her two heroines:

> Because each had discovered years before that they were neither white nor male, and that all freedom and triumph was forbidden to them, they had set about creating something else to be.[19]

In the following pages I will refer often to *Born in Flames*, discussing some of the issues it has raised, but it will not be with the aim of a textual analysis. Rather, I will take it as the starting point, as indeed it was for me, of a series of reflections on the topic of this essay.

Again it is a film, and a filmmaker's project, that bring home to me with greater clarity the question of difference, this time in relation to factors other than gender, notably race and class—a question endlessly debated within Marxist feminism and recently rearticulated by women of color in feminist presses and publications. That this question should reemerge urgently and irrevocably now is not surprising, at a time when severe social regression and economic pressures (the so-called "feminization of poverty") belie the self-complacency of a liberal feminism enjoying its modest allotment of institutional legitimation. A sign of the times, the recent crop of commercial, man-made "woman's films" (*Lianna, Personal Best, Silkwood, Frances, Places of the Heart,* etc.) is undoubtedly "authorized," and made financially viable, by that legitimation. But the success, however modest, of this liberal feminism has been bought at the price of reducing the contradictory complexity—and the theoretical productivity—of concepts such as sexual difference, the personal is political, and feminism itself to simpler and more acceptable ideas already existing in the dominant culture. Thus, to many today, "sexual difference" is hardly more than sex (biology) or gender (in the simplest sense of female socialization) or the basis for certain private "life styles" (homosexual and other nonorthodox relationships); "the personal is political" all too often translates into "the personal instead of the political"; and "feminism" is unhesitatingly appropriated, by the academy as well as the media, as a discourse—a variety of social criticism, a method of aesthetic or literary analysis among others, and more or less worth attention according to the degree of its market appeal to students, readers, or viewers. And, yes, a discourse perfectly accessible to all men of good will. In this context, issues of race or class must continue to be thought of as mainly sociological or economic, and hence parallel to but not dependent on gender, implicated with but not determining of subjectivity, and of little relevance to this "feminist discourse" which, as such, would have no competence in the matter but only, and at best, a humane or "progressive" concern with the disadvantaged.

The relevance of feminism (without quotation marks) to race and class, however, is very explicitly stated by those women of color, black, and white who are not the recipients but rather the "targets" of equal opportunity, who are outside or not fooled by liberal "feminism," or who understand that feminism is nothing if it is not at once political and personal, with all the contradictions and difficulties that entails. To such feminists it is clear that the social construction of gender, subjectivity, and the relations of representation to experience do occur within race and class as much as they occur in language and culture, often indeed across languages, cultures, and sociocultural apparati. Thus, not only is it the case that the notion of gender, or "sexual difference," cannot be simply accommodated into the preexisting, ungendered (or male-gendered) categories by which the official discourses on race and class have been elaborated; but it is equally the case that the issues of race and class cannot be simply subsumed under some larger category labeled femaleness, femininity, womanhood, or, in the final instance, Woman. What is becoming more and more clear, instead, is that all the categories of our social science stand to be reformulated *starting from* the notion of gendered social subjects. And something of this process of reformulation—re-vision, rewriting, rereading, rethinking, "looking back at *ourselves*"—is what I see inscribed in the texts of women's cinema but not yet sufficiently focused on in feminist film theory or feminist critical practice in general. This point, like the relation of feminist writing to the women's movement, demands a much lengthier discussion than can be undertaken here. I can do no more than sketch the problem as it strikes me with unusual intensity in the reception of Lizzie Borden's film and my own response to it.

What *Born in Flames* succeeds in representing is this feminist understanding: that the female subject is en-gendered, constructed and defined in gender across multiple representations of class, race, language, and social relations; and that, therefore, differences among women are differences *within* women, which is why feminism can exist despite those differences and, as we are just beginning to understand, cannot continue to exist without them. The originality of this film's project is its representation of woman as a social subject and a site of differences; differences which are not purely sexual or merely racial, economic, or (sub)cultural, but all of these together and often enough in conflict with one another. What one takes away after seeing this film is the image of a heterogeneity in the female social subject, the sense of a distance from dominant cultural models and of an internal division within women that remain, not in spite of but concurrently with the provisional unity of any concerted political action. Just as the film's narrative remains unresolved, fragmented, and difficult to follow, heterogeneity and difference within women remain in our memory as the film's narrative image, its work of representing, which cannot be collapsed into a fixed identity, a sameness of all women as Woman, or a representation of Feminism as a coherent and available image.

Other films, in addition to the ones already mentioned, have effectively represented that internal division or distance from language, culture, and self that I see recur, figuratively and thematically, in recent women's cinema (it is also represented, for example, in Gabriella Rosaleva's *Processo a Caterina Ross* and in Lynne Tillman and Sheila McLaughlin's *Committed*). But *Born in Flames* projects that division on a larger social and cultural scale, taking up nearly all of the issues and putting them all at stake. As we read on the side of the (stolen) U-Haul trucks which carry the free women's new

mobile radio transmitter, reborn as Phoenix-Regazza (girl phoenix) from
the flames that destroyed the two separate stations, the film is "an adventure in moving." As one reviewer saw it,

> An action pic, a sci-fi fantasy, a political thriller, a collage film, a snatch of the
> underground: *Born in Flames* is all and none of these. . . . Edited in 15-
> second bursts and spiked with yards of flickering video transfers . . . *Born in
> Flames* stands head and shoulders above such Hollywood reflections on the
> media as *Absence of Malice, Network,* or *Under Fire.* This is less a matter of its
> substance (the plot centers on the suspicious prison "suicide," à la Ulrike
> Meinhoff, of Women's Army leader Adelaide Norris) than of its form, seizing
> on a dozen facets of our daily media surroundings.[20]

The words of the last sentence, echoing Akerman's emphasis on form
rather than content, are in turn echoed by Borden in several printed
statements. She, too, is keenly concerned with her own relation as filmmaker to filmic representation ("Two things I was committed to with the
film were questioning the nature of narrative . . . and creating a process
whereby I could release myself from my own bondage in terms of class and
race").[21] And she, too, like Akerman, is confident that vision can be transformed because hers has been: "Whatever discomfort I might have felt as a
white filmmaker working with black women has been over for so long. It
was exorcized by the process of making the film." Thus, in response to the
interviewer's (Anne Friedberg) suggestion that the film is "progressive"
precisely because it "demands a certain discomfort for the audience, and
forces the viewer to confront his or her own political position(s) (or lack of
political position)," Borden flatly rejects the interviewer's implicit assumption.

> I don't think the audience is solely a white middle-class audience. What was
> important for me was creating a film in which that was *not* the only audience.
> The problem with much of the critical material on the film is that it assumes a
> white middle-class reading public for articles written about a film that they
> assume has only a white middle-class audience. I'm very confused about the
> discomfort that reviewers feel. What I was trying to do (and using humor as a
> way to try to do it) was to have various positions in which everyone had a
> place on some level. Every woman—with men it is a whole different ques-
> tion—would have some level of identification with a position within the film.
> Some reviewers over-identified with something as a privileged position.
> Basically, none of the positioning of black characters was *against* any of the
> white viewers but more of an invitation: come and work with us. Instead of
> telling the viewer that he or she could *not* belong, the viewer was supposed to
> be a repository for all these different points of view and all these different
> styles of rhetoric. Hopefully, one would be able to identify with one position
> but be able to evaluate all of the various positions presented in the film.

> Basically, I feel this discomfort only from people who are deeply resistant to it.[22]

This response is one that, to my mind, sharply outlines a shift in women's cinema from a modernist or avant-garde aesthetic of subversion to an emerging set of questions about filmic representation to which the term *aesthetic* may or may not apply, depending on one's definition of art, one's definition of cinema, and the relationship between the two. Similarly, whether or not the terms *postmodern* or *postmodernist aesthetic* would be preferable or more applicable in this context, as Craig Owens has suggested of the work of other women artists, is too large a topic to be discussed here.[23]

At any rate, as I see it, there has been a shift in women's cinema from an aesthetic centered on the text and *its* effects on the viewing or reading subject—whose certain, if imaginary, self-coherence is to be fractured by the text's own disruption of linguistic, visual, and/or narrative coherence—to what may be called an aesthetic of reception, where the spectator is the film's primary concern—primary in the sense that it is there from the beginning, inscribed in the filmmaker's project and even in the very making of the film.[24] An explicit concern with the audience is of course not new either in art or in cinema, since Pirandello and Brecht in the former, and it is always conspicuously present in Hollywood and TV. What is new here, however, is the particular conception of the audience, which now is envisaged in its heterogeneity and otherness from the text.

That the audience is conceived as a heterogeneous community is made apparent, in Borden's film, by its unusual handling of the function of address. The use of music and beat in conjunction with spoken language, from rap singing to a variety of subcultural lingos and nonstandard speech, serves less the purposes of documentation or cinema vérité than those of what in another context might be called characterization: they are there to provide a means of identification of and with the characters, though not the kind of psychological identification usually accorded to main characters or privileged "protagonists." "I wanted to make a film that different audiences could relate to on different levels—if they wanted to ignore the language they could," Borden told another interviewer, "but not to make a film that was anti-language."[25] The importance of "language" and its constitutive presence in both the public and the private spheres is underscored by the multiplicity of discourses and communication technologies—visual, verbal, and aural—foregrounded in the form as well as the content of the film. If the wall of official speech, the omnipresent systems of public address, and the very strategy of the women's takeover of a television station assert the fundamental link of communication and power, the film also insists on representing the other, unofficial social discourses, their heterogeneity, and *their* constitutive effects vis-à-vis the social subject.

In this respect, I would argue, both the characters and the spectators of Borden's film are positioned in relation to social discourses and representations (of class, race, and gender) within particular "subjective limits and discursive boundaries" that are analogous, in their own historical specificity, to those which Silverman saw symbolized by the Berlin wall in *Redupers*. For the spectators, too, are limited in their vision and understanding, bound by their own social and sexual positioning, as their "discomfort" or diverse responses suggest. Borden's avowed intent to make the spectator a locus ("a repository") of different points of view and discursive configurations ("these different styles of rhetoric") suggests to me that the concept of a heterogeneity of the audience also entails a heterogeneity of, or in, the individual spectator.

If, as claimed by recent theories of textuality, the Reader or the Spectator is implied in the text as an effect of its strategy—either as the figure of a unity or coherence of meaning which is constructed by the text (the "text of pleasure"), or as the figure of the division, dissemination, incoherence inscribed in the "text of jouissance"—then the spectator of *Born in Flames* is somewhere else, resistant to the text and other from it. This film's spectator is not only *not* sutured into the "classic" text by narrative and psychological identification; nor is it bound in the time of repetition, "at the limit of any fixed subjectivity, materially inconstant, dispersed in process," as Stephen Heath aptly describes the spectator intended by avant-garde (structural-materialist) film.[26] What happens is, this film's spectator is finally not liable to capture by the text.

And yet one is engaged by the powerful erotic charge of the film; one responds to the erotic investment that its female characters have in each other, and the filmmaker in them, with something that is neither pleasure nor *jouissance,* oedipal nor pre-oedipal, as they have been defined for us; but with something that is again (as in *Jeanne Dielman*) a recognition, unmistakable and unprecedented. Again the textual space extends to the spectator, in its erotic and critical dimensions, addressing, speaking-to, making room, but not (how very unusual and remarkable) cajoling, soliciting, seducing. These films do not put me in the place of the female spectator, do not assign me a role, a self-image, a positionality in language or desire. Instead, they make a place for what I will call me, knowing that I don't know it, and give "me" space to try to know, to see, to understand. Put another way, by addressing me as *a* woman, they do not bind me or appoint me as Woman.

The "discomfort" of Borden's reviewers might be located exactly in this dis-appointment of spectator and text: the disappointment of not finding oneself, not finding oneself "interpellated" or solicited by the film, whose images and discourses project back to the viewer a space of heterogeneity, differences and fragmented coherences that just do not add up to one individual viewer or one spectator-subject, bourgeois or otherwise. There is no one-to-one match between the film's discursive heterogeneity and the discursive boundaries of any one spectator. We are both invited in and held at a distance, addressed intermittently and only insofar as we are able to occupy the position of addressee; for example, when Honey, the Phoenix Radio disc jockey, addresses to the audience the words: "Black women, be ready. White women, get ready. Red women, stay ready, for this is our time and all must realize it."[27] Which individual member of the audience, male or female, can feel singly interpellated as spectator-subject or, in other words, unequivocally addressed?

There is a famous moment in film history, something of a parallel to this one, which not coincidentally has been "discovered" by feminist film critics in a woman-made film about women, Dorothy Arzner's *Dance, Girl, Dance*: it is the moment when Judy interrupts her stage performance and, facing the vaudeville audience, steps out of her role and speaks to them as a woman to a group of people. The novelty of this direct address, feminist critics have noted, is not only that it breaks the codes of theatrical illusion and voyeuristic pleasure, but also that it demonstrates that no complicity, no shared discourse, can be established between the woman performer (positioned as image, representation, object) and the male audience (positioned as the controlling gaze); no complicity, that is, outside the codes and rules of the performance. By breaking the codes, Arzner revealed the rules and the relations of power that constitute them and are in turn sustained by them. And sure enough, the vaudeville audience in her film showed great discomfort with Judy's speech.

I am suggesting that the discomfort with Honey's speech has also to do with codes of representation (of race and class as well as gender) and the rules and power relations that sustain them—rules which also prevent the establishing of a shared discourse, and hence the "dream" of a common language. How else could viewers see in this playful, exuberant, science-fictional film a blueprint for political action which, they claim, wouldn't work anyway? ("We've all been through this before. As a man I'm not threatened by this because we know that this doesn't work. This is infantile politics, these women are being macho like men used to be macho. . . .")[28] Why else would they see the film, in Friedberg's phrase, "as a *prescription through fantasy*"? Borden's opinion is that "people have not really been upset about class and race. . . . People are really upset that the women are gay. They feel it is separatist."[29] My own opinion is that people are upset with all three, class, race, and gender—lesbianism being precisely the demonstration that the concept of gender is founded across race and class on the structure which Adrienne Rich and Monique Wittig have called, respectively, "compulsory heterosexuality" and "the heterosexual contract."[30]

The film-theoretical notion of spectatorship has been developed largely in the attempt to answer the question posed insistently by feminist theorists and well summed up in the words of Ruby Rich already cited above: "How does one formulate an understanding of a structure that insists on our absence even in the face of our presence?" In keeping with the early divergence of feminists over the politics of images, the notion of spectatorship was developed along two axes: one starting from the psychoanalytic theory of the subject and employing concepts such as primary and secondary, conscious and unconscious, imaginary and symbolic processes; the other starting from sexual difference and asking questions such as, How does the female spectator see? With what does she identify? Where/How/In what film genres is female desire represented? and so on. Arzner's infraction of the code in *Dance, Girl, Dance* was one of the first answers in this second line of questioning, which now appears to have been the most fruitful by far for women's cinema. *Born in Flames* seems to me to work out the most interesting answer to date.

For one thing, the film assumes that the female spectator may be black, white, "red," middle-class or not middle-class, and wants her to have a place within the film, some measure of identification—"identification with a position," Borden specifies. "With men [spectators] it is a whole different question," she adds, obviously without much interest in exploring it (though later suggesting that black male spectators responded to the film "because they don't see it as just about women. They see it as empowerment").[31] In sum, the spectator is addressed as female in gender and multiple or heterogeneous in race and class; which is to say, here too all points of identification are female or feminist, but rather than the "two logics" of character and filmmaker, like *Jeanne Dielman, Born in Flames* foregrounds their different discourses.

Second, as Friedberg puts it in one of her questions, the images of women in *Born in Flames* are "unaestheticized": "you never fetishize the body through masquerade. In fact the film seems consciously de-aestheticized, which is what gives it its documentary quality."[32] Nevertheless, to some, those images of women appear to be extraordinarily beautiful. If such were to be the case for most of the film's female spectators, however socially positioned, we would be facing what amounts to a film-theoretical paradox, for in film theory the female body is construed precisely as fetish or masquerade.[33] Perhaps not unexpectedly, the filmmaker's response is

amazingly consonant with Chantal Akerman's, though their films are visually quite different, and the latter's is in fact received as an "aesthetic" work.

    Borden: "The important thing is to shoot female bodies in a way that they
have never been shot before. . . . I chose women for the stance I liked. The
stance is almost like the gestalt of a person."[34]
    And Akerman (cited above): "I give space to things which were never,
almost never, shown in that way. . . . If you choose to show a woman's
gestures so precisely, it's because you love them."

The point of this cross-referencing of two films that have little else in
common beside the feminism of their makers is to remark the persistence
of certain themes and formal questions about representation and difference which I *would* call aesthetic, and which are the historical product of
feminism and the expression of feminist critical-theoretical thought.
    Like the works of the feminist filmmakers I have referred to, and many
others too numerous to mention here, *Jeanne Dielman* and *Born in Flames*
are engaged in the project of transforming vision by inventing the forms
and processes of representation of a social subject, women, that until now
has been all but unrepresentable; a project already set out (looking back,
one is tempted to say, programmatically) in the title of Yvonne Rainer's *Film
about a Woman Who . . .* (1974), which in a sense all of these films continue to
reelaborate. The gender-specific division of women in language, the distance from official culture, the urge to imagine new forms of community as
well as to create new images ("creating something else to be"), and the
consciousness of a "subjective factor" at the core of all kinds of work—
domestic, industrial, artistic, critical, or political work—are some of the
themes articulating the particular relation of subjectivity, meaning, and
experience which en-genders the social subject as female. These themes,
encapsulated in the phrase "the personal is political," have been formally
explored in women's cinema in several ways: through the disjunction of
image and voice, the reworking of narrative space, the elaboration of
strategies of address that alter the forms and balances of traditional representation. From the inscription of subjective space and duration inside the
frame (a space of repetitions, silences, and discontinuities in *Jeanne Dielman*) to the construction of other discursive social spaces (the discontinuous but intersecting spaces of the women's "networks" in *Born in
Flames*), women's cinema has undertaken a redefinition of both private and
public space that may well answer the call for "a new language of desire"
and actually have met the demand for the "destruction of visual pleasure,"

if by that one alludes to the traditional, classical and modernist, canons of
aesthetic representation.

So, once again, the contradiction of women in language and culture is
manifested in a paradox: most of the terms by which we speak of the
construction of the female social subject in cinematic representation bear in
their visual form the prefix *de-* to signal the deconstruction or the destructuring, if not destruction, of the very thing to be represented. We speak of
the deaestheticization of the female body, the desexualization of violence,
the deoedipalization of narrative, and so forth. Rethinking women's cinema
in this way, we may provisionally answer Bovenschen's question thus:
There is a certain configuration of issues and formal problems that have
been consistently articulated in what we call women's cinema. The way in
which they have been expressed and developed, both artistically and critically, seems to point less to a "feminine aesthetic" than to a feminist
deaesthetic. And if the word sounds awkward or inelegant . . .

Notes

I am very grateful to Cheryl Kader for generously sharing with me her knowledge and insight from the conception through the writing of this essay, and to Mary
Russo for her thoughtful critical suggestions.
  1. Silvia Bovenschen, "Is There a Feminine Aesthetic?" trans. Beth
Weckmueller, *New German Critique*, no. 10 (Winter 1977): 136. [Originally published
in *Aesthetik und Kommunikation* 25 (September 1976).]
  2. Laura Mulvey, "Feminism, Film, and the Avant-Garde," *Framework*, no. 10
(Spring 1979): 6. See also Christine Gledhill's account "Recent Developments in
Feminist Film Criticism," *Quarterly Review of Film Studies* 3, no. 4 (1978).
  3. Laura Mulvey, "Visual Pleasure and Narrative Cinema," *Screen* 16, no. 3
(Autumn 1975): 18.
  4. B. Ruby Rich, in "Women and Film: A Discussion of Feminist Aesthetics,"
New German Critique, no. 13 (Winter 1978): 87.
  5. J. Laplanche and J.-B. Pontalis, *The Language of Psycho-analysis*, trans. D.
Nicholson-Smith (New York: W. W. Norton, 1973), p. 206.
  6. Lea Melandri, *L'infamia originaria* (Milano: Edizioni L'Erba Voglio, 1977),
p. 27; my translation. For a more fully developed discussion of semiotic theories of
film and narrative, see Teresa de Lauretis, *Alice Doesn't: Feminism, Semiotics, Cinema*
(Bloomington: Indiana University Press, 1984).
  7. See Audre Lorde, "The Master's Tools Will Never Dismantle the Master's
House," and "An Open Letter to Mary Daly," in *This Bridge Called My Back: Writings
by Radical Women of Color*, ed. Chérrie Moraga and Gloria Anzaldúa (New York:
Kitchen Table Press, 1983), p. 96. Both essays are reprinted in Audre Lorde, *Sister
Outsider: Essays and Speeches* (Trumansburg, N.Y.: Crossing Press, 1984).
  8. "Chantal Akerman on *Jeanne Dielman*," *Camera Obscura*, no. 2 (1977): 118–19.
  9. In the same interview, Akerman said: "I didn't have any doubts about any of
the shots. I was very sure of where to put the camera and when and why. . . . I *let*
her [the character] live her life in the middle of the frame. I didn't go in too close,
but I was not *very* far away. I let her be in her space. It's not uncontrolled. But the

camera was not voyeuristic in the commercial way because you always knew where I was. . . . It was the only way to shoot that film—to avoid cutting the woman into a hundred pieces, to avoid cutting the action in a hundred places, to look carefully and to be respectful. The framing was meant to respect the space, her, and her gestures within it" (ibid., p. 119).

10. Janet Bergstrom, "*Jeanne Dielman, 23 Quai du Commerce, 1080 Bruxelles* by Chantal Akerman," *Camera Obscura*, no. 2 (1977): 117. On the rigorous formal consistency of the film, see also Mary Jo Lakeland, "The Color of Jeanne Dielman," *Camera Obscura*, nos. 3–4 (1979): 216–18.

11. Kaja Silverman, "Helke Sander and the Will to Change," *Discourse*, no. 6 (Fall 1983): 10.

12. Gertrud Koch, "Ex-changing the Gaze: Re-visioning Feminist Film Theory," *New German Critique*, no. 34 (Winter 1985): 144.

13. Sheila Rowbotham, *Woman's Consciousness, Man's World* (Harmondsworth: Penguin Books, 1973), p. 28.

14. Claire Johnston, "Women's Cinema as Counter-Cinema," in *Notes on Women's Cinema*, ed. Claire Johnston (London: SEFT, 1974), p. 31. See also Gertrud Koch, "Was ist und wozu brauchen wir eine feministische Filmkritik," *frauen und film*, no. 11 (1977).

15. Mary Ann Doane, Patricia Mellencamp, and Linda Williams, eds., *Re-vision: Essays in Feminist Film Criticism* (Frederick, Md.: University Publications of America and the American Film Institute, 1984), p. 4.

16. Ibid., p. 6. The quotation from Adrienne Rich is in her *On Lies, Secrets, and Silence* (New York: W. W. Norton, 1979), p. 35.

17. See Barbara Smith, "Toward a Black Feminist Criticism," in *All the Women Are White, All the Blacks Are Men, but Some of Us Are Brave: Black Women's Studies*, ed. Gloria T. Hull, Patricia Bell Scott, and Barbara Smith (Old Westbury, N.Y.: Feminist Press, 1982).

18. Helen Fehervary, Claudia Lenssen, and Judith Mayne, "From Hitler to Hepburn: A Discussion of Women's Film Production and Reception," *New German Critique*, nos. 24–25 (Fall/Winter 1981–82): 176.

19. Toni Morrison, *Sula* (New York: Bantam Books, 1975), p. 44.

20. Kathleen Hulser, "Les Guérillères," *Afterimage* 11, no. 6 (January 1984): 14.

21. Anne Friedberg, "An Interview with Filmmaker Lizzie Borden," *Women and Performance* 1, no. 2 (Winter 1984): 43. On the effort to understand one's relation as a feminist to racial and cultural differences, see Elly Bulkin, Minnie Bruce Pratt, and Barbara Smith, *Yours in Struggle: Three Feminist Perspectives on Anti-Semitism and Racism* (Brooklyn, N.Y.: Long Haul Press, 1984).

22. Interview in *Women and Performance*, p. 38.

23. Craig Owens, "The Discourse of Others: Feminists and Postmodernism," in *The Anti-Aesthetic: Essays in Postmodern Culture*, ed. Hal Foster (Port Townsend, Wash.: Bay Press, 1983), pp. 57–82. See also Andreas Huyssen, "Mapping the Postmodern," *New German Critique*, no. 33 (Fall 1984): 5–52, now reprinted in Huyssen, *After the Great Divide: Modernism, Mass Culture, Postmodernism* (Bloomington: Indiana University Press, 1986).

24. Borden's nonprofessional actors, as well as her characters, are very much part of the film's intended audience: "I didn't want the film caught in the white film ghetto. I did mailings. We got women's lists, black women's lists, gay lists, lists that would bring different people to the Film Forum. . ." (Interview in *Women and Performance*, p. 43).

25. Betsy Sussler, "Interview," *Bomb*, no. 7 (1983): 29.

26. Stephen Heath, *Questions of Cinema* (Bloomington: Indiana University Press, 1981), p. 167.

27. The script of *Born in Flames* is published in *Heresies*, no. 16 (1983): 12–16. Borden discusses how the script was developed in conjunction with the actors and according to their particular abilities and backgrounds in the interview in *Bomb*.

28. Interview in *Bomb*, p. 29.

29. Interview in *Women and Performance*, p. 39.

30. Adrienne Rich, "Compulsory Heterosexuality and Lesbian Existence," *Signs* 5, no. 4 (Summer 1980): 631–60; Monique Wittig, "The Straight Mind," *Feminist Issues* (Summer 1980): 110.

31. Interview in *Women and Performance*, p. 38.

32. Ibid., p. 44.

33. See Mary Ann Doane, "Film and the Masquerade: Theorising the Female Spectator," *Screen* 23, nos. 3–4 (September/October 1982): 74–87.

34. Interview in *Women and Performance*, pp. 44–45.

INDEX OF NAMES